GEORGIA'S
CRIMINAL JUSTICE SYSTEM

CAROLINA ACADEMIC PRESS

State-Specific Criminal Justice Series

North Carolina's Criminal Justice System
Second Edition
Paul E. Knepper and Mark Jones

Georgia's Criminal Justice System
Deborah Mitchell Robinson

GEORGIA'S
CRIMINAL JUSTICE SYSTEM

Deborah Mitchell Robinson

PROFESSOR OF CRIMINAL JUSTICE
VALDOSTA STATE UNIVERSITY

CAROLINA ACADEMIC PRESS
Durham, North Carolina

Library of Congress Cataloging-in-Publication Data

Robinson, Deborah Mitchell.
Georgia's criminal justice system / Deborah M. Robinson.
   p. cm. -- (State-specific criminal justice series)
Includes bibliographical references and index.
ISBN 978-1-59460-965-7 (alk. paper)
1. Criminal justice, Administration of--Georgia. I. Title.

HV9955.G4R63 2011
364.9758--dc23

2011041751

CAROLINA ACADEMIC PRESS
700 Kent Street
Durham, North Carolina 27701
Telephone (919) 489-7486
Fax (919) 493-5668
www.cap-press.com

This textbook is dedicated to James Stanley Mitchell, Ed.D. (1939–2008). His influence on me, both personally and professionally, is immeasurable and everlasting. For the love of academe and of writing that he gave to me, I will be forever grateful. I love and miss you Daddy!

CONTENTS

List of Tables   xv

Series Note   xix

Acknowledgments   xxi

Chapter 1 • Georgia's Criminal Justice System   3
    Learning Objectives   3
    Key Terms   3
  Goals of Georgia's Criminal Justice System   6
  Justice in the Criminal Justice System   7
  National Crime Rates   9
    Uniform Crime Reporting Program   9
    National Incident-Based Reporting System   9
    National Crime Victimization Survey   10
  Crime in Georgia   11
    Georgia Uniform Crime Reporting Program   11
    Georgia Family Violence Statistics   12
  Conclusion   16
    Chapter Review Questions   16
  References   16

Chapter 2 • Georgia's Constitutions   19
    Learning Objectives   19
    Key Terms   19
  Rules and Regulations of the Colony of Georgia 1776   20
  The Constitution of 1777   21
  Georgia Constitution of 1789   22
  Georgia Constitution of 1798   23
  Georgia Constitution of 1861   24
  Georgia Constitution of 1865   25
  Georgia Constitution of 1868   26
  Georgia Constitution of 1877   28

Georgia Constitution of 1945 28
Georgia Constitution of 1976 29
Georgia Constitution of 1983 30
Conclusion 32
    Chapter Review Questions 33
References 33

Chapter 3 · Crimes in Georgia 35
    Learning Objectives 35
    Key Terms 35
The General Assembly 36
Local Ordinances 38
State Statutes 39
    Chapter 1 General Provisions 40
    Chapter 2 Criminal Liability 41
    Chapter 3 Defenses to Criminal Prosecutions 42
        Minimum Age 42
        Mental Capacity 43
        Involuntary or Voluntary Intoxication 43
        Justified Conduct 43
        Use of Force in Defense of Persons 43
        Use of Force in Defense of Habitation 44
        Use of Force in Defense of Property Other than Habitation 44
        Use of Force Immunity Exception 45
        Entrapment 45
        Coercion 45
        Alibi 45
Crimes in Georgia 46
    Chapter 4 Criminal Attempt, Conspiracy, and Solicitation 46
    Chapter 5 Crimes Against the Person 46
    Chapter 6 Sexual Offenses 48
    Chapter 7 Damage to and Intrusion Upon Property 48
    Chapter 8 Offenses Involving Theft 49
    Chapter 9 Forgery and Fraudulent Practices 49
    Chapter 10 Offenses Against Public Administration 50
    Chapter 11 Offenses Against Public Order and Safety 51
    Chapter 12 Offenses Against Public Health and Morals 53
    Chapter 13 Controlled Substances 53
    Chapter 15 Street Gang Terrorism and Prevention 53
Conclusion 54

Chapter Review Questions   55
References   55
Chapter 4 · Crime Victims in Georgia   57
Learning Objectives   57
Key Terms   57
Georgia Criminal Justice Coordinating Council   58
Georgia Crime Victims' Bill of Rights   60
Definitions of Victim and Crime   61
Notification to Victims   62
O.C.G.A. § 17-17-5   63
O.C.G.A. § 17-17-5.1   63
O.C.G.A. § 17-17-7   63
O.C.G.A. § 17-17-8   63
O.C.G.A. § 17-17-12   64
O.C.G.A. § 17-17-13   64
Victims' Rights in Dealing with Defendants   64
O.C.G.A. § 17-17-8.1   65
O.C.G.A. § 17-17-9   65
O.C.G.A. § 17-17-9.1   65
O.C.G.A. § 17-17-10   65
O.C.G.A. § 17-17-11   66
O.C.G.A. § 17-17-16   66
Georgia Victims' Rights in the Juvenile Justice System   66
O.C.G.A. § 15-11-64.2   66
O.C.G.A. § 15-11-78   67
O.C.G.A. § 15-11-155   67
State Board of Pardons and Paroles Office of Victim Services   67
Victim Information Program (V.I.P.)   68
Victim Impact Statements   69
The Prosecuting Attorneys' Council of Georgia Victim-Witness
Advocacy Office   69
Distribution of Profits of Crimes   71
Georgia's Sex Offender Registry   71
History of Sex Offender Registration   72
O.C.G.A. § 42-1-12 State Sexual Offender Registry   74
Georgia Bureau of Investigation and Local Sheriffs   76
Conclusion   78
Chapter Review Questions   79
References   79

Chapter 5 · The Criminal Justice Process 81
    Learning Objectives 81
    Key Terms 81
  General Terminology 83
    Jurisdiction and Venue 83
    Limitations on Prosecutions 84
    Probable Cause 84
  Report and Investigation of the Crime 85
    Search and Seizure 85
  Arrest of the Suspect 87
    Arrest Warrant 88
    Making the Arrest 90
    Use of Force in Arrest 91
    Booking 92
  Pretrial Procedures 92
    Initial Appearance 92
    Preliminary Hearing 93
    Accusation 93
    Grand Jury Indictment 94
    Arraignment 95
    Plea Bargaining 96
    Pretrial Motions 97
  Criminal Trial 97
    Jury Selection 98
    Presentation of Evidence 98
    Jury Deliberations 100
  Sentencing and Corrections 100
    Punishments 100
    Capital Felony Convictions 101
    Corrections 102
  Conclusion 103
    Chapter Review Questions 103
  References 103

Chapter 6 · Law Enforcement in Georgia 107
    Learning Objectives 107
    Key Terms 107
  Federal Law Enforcement in Georgia 108
    Federal Law Enforcement Training Center 108
  State Law Enforcement in Georgia 109

Department of Natural Resources   109
    Environmental Protection Division   109
    Wildlife Resources Division   110
Department of Public Safety   110
    Legal Services and Special Investigations   110
    Capital Police   111
    Georgia State Patrol   111
    Executive Security Division   113
    Motor Carrier Compliance Division   113
Georgia Bureau of Investigation   113
    Investigative Division   114
    Division of Forensic Sciences   115
    Georgia Crime Information Center (GCIC)   116
    Medical Examiner's Office   116
Georgia Emergency Management Agency/Homeland Security   117
Governor's Office of Highway Safety   117
Metropolitan Atlanta Rapid Transit Authority   118
Additional State Law Enforcement Agencies   118
County Law Enforcement in Georgia   119
    Sheriff's Office   120
        Administrative Division   120
        Patrol Division   120
        Criminal Investigations   121
        Jail Operations   121
        Court Services   122
        Special Operations   122
    Emergency 911 Communications   123
    County Police Departments   123
    County Marshal Departments/Offices   124
    Campus Police   124
Municipal Law Enforcement in Georgia   125
    Administrative Division   125
    Patrol Division   126
    Investigative Division   126
    Jail Division   127
    Emergency 911 Communications   127
Community Oriented Policing   128
Accreditation   128
    National Accreditation   129

State Certification   130
Law Enforcement Support Organizations   131
    Georgia Association of Chiefs of Police   131
    Georgia Sheriff's Association   131
    Peace Officers' Annuity and Benefit Fund of Georgia   132
    Peace Officers Association of Georgia   132
Conclusion   133
    Chapter Review Questions   133
References   133

Chapter 7 · Georgia's Courts   137
    Learning Objectives   137
    Key Terms   137
Federal Courts in Georgia   138
    U.S. Court of Appeals in Georgia   138
    U.S. District Courts   139
State Court System of Georgia   140
    Supreme Court of Georgia   141
        Officers of the Court   143
        Operation of the Court   143
        State Bar of Georgia and Office of Bar Admissions   144
        Judicial Council of Georgia   144
        Judicial Qualifications Commission   145
        The Chief Justice's Commission on Professionalism   145
        Equity Commission   145
    Georgia Court of Appeals   146
    Superior Courts   147
        Council of Superior Court Judges   148
    State Courts   148
        Council of State Court Judges   148
    Probate Courts   149
        Council of Probate Court Judges   149
    Magistrate Courts   149
        Council of Magistrate Court Judges   150
    Juvenile Courts   150
        Council of Juvenile Court Judges   151
    Municipal Courts   151
        Council of Municipal Court Judges   151
    Georgia Accountability Courts   151
Prosecuting Attorneys in the State of Georgia   152

Attorney General of Georgia 152
District Attorney 153
Solicitor-General 154
Georgia's Public Defenders 154
Conclusion 155
Chapter Review Questions 155
References 156

Chapter 8 • Corrections in Georgia 159
Learning Objectives 159
Key Terms 159
Federal Bureau of Prisons 160
State of Georgia Department of Corrections 161
History of State Corrections in Georgia 161
Today's Correctional System 162
Classifications 162
Agency Divisions 164
Correctional Facilities 165
State Prisons 165
Inmates Under Death Sentence 165
Private Prisons 167
Boot Camps 167
County Prisons 169
Pre-Release Centers 169
Transitional Centers 169
Reentry Initiative and Services 170
State Board of Pardons and Paroles 172
Supervision 172
Victim Services 173
Probation Supervision 174
Probationer Profile 175
Probation Detention Centers 177
Court Services 177
Day Reporting Centers 177
Juveniles in Adult Prisons 178
Special Operations 179
GDC Tactical Squads 179
Canine (K-9) Units 179
Correctional Emergency Response Team (CERT) 179
Inter-Agency Liaison 179

Local Corrections   180
    Jail Designs   181
    Georgia Statutes   181
    Probation Supervision   182
Conclusion   183
    Chapter Review Questions   183
References   184

Chapter 9 · Georgia's Juveniles   187
    Learning Objectives   187
    Key Terms   187
History of Juvenile Justice in Georgia   188
Federal Oversight of Juvenile Justice   190
Jurisdiction of the Juvenile Court   192
    Exclusive Original Jurisdiction of Juvenile Court
        (O.C.G.A. § 15-11-28(a))   192
    Concurrent Jurisdiction with Superior Court
        (O.C.G.A. § 15-11-28(b)(1))   193
    Exclusive Jurisdiction of the Superior Court
        (O.C.G.A. § 15-11-28(b)(2)(A))   193
Juvenile Justice Terms and Definitions   193
    Child (O.C.G.A. § 15-11-2(2))   193
    Delinquent Act (O.C.G.A. § 15-11-2(6))   194
    Delinquent Child (O.C.G.A. § 15-11-2(7))   194
    Status Offender (O.C.G.A. § 15-11-2(11))   194
    Unruly Child (O.C.G.A. § 15-11-2(12))   194
    Designated Felony (O.C.G.A. § 15-11-63,
        Uniform Juvenile Court Rule 15.2)   195
The Juvenile Justice Process   196
    Intake and Custody   196
    Probable Cause/Detention Hearing   198
    Adjudicatory Hearing   199
    Dispositional Hearing and Commitment   199
    Aftercare   200
    Sealing Records   201
Officers of the Court and Court Personnel   201
    Appointment of Juvenile Court Judges   202
    Appointment of Associate Juvenile Court Judges   203
    Appointment of Juvenile Court Personnel   203
Juvenile Justice Statistics   204

Statewide Budget   204
Arrests for Uniform Crime Report (UCR) Index Crimes   204
Juveniles Served   204
Juvenile Characteristics   206
Conclusion   206
   Chapter Review Questions   207
References   208

Chapter 10 • Training and Educating Criminal Justice Personnel   211
   Learning Objectives   211
   Key Terms   211
The Georgia P.O.S.T. Council   212
P.O.S.T. Certifications   213
Basic Mandate Certification—Local   215
   Law Enforcement Certification   215
   Jail Officer Certification   217
   Communications Officer Certification   218
   Municipal Probation Officer Certification   219
Basic Mandate Certification—State   220
   Georgia Bureau of Investigation   220
   Georgia Department of Corrections   222
   Georgia Department of Natural Resources   224
   Georgia State Patrol   225
In-Service Training   227
Career Development Certification   227
   Intermediate Certification   227
   Advanced Certification   228
   Senior Deputy Sheriff Certification   229
   Supervisory Certification   230
   Management Certification   232
   Executive Certification   233
Instructor Certification   234
   General Instructor Training   234
   Department Training Officer   235
   Field Training Officer   236
   Communications Training Officer   237
Specialized Instructor Certification   237
   Defensive Tactics Instructor   238
   Driver Instructor   238
   Firearms Instructor   239

Hazardous Materials Instructor   240
Speed Detection Instructor   242
Criminal Justice Education   243
University System of Georgia   243
Technical College System of Georgia   244
Private Higher Education Institutions   245
Accreditation   246
Professional Academic Organizations   246
American Society of Criminology (ASC)   247
Academy of Criminal Justice Sciences (ACJS)   247
American Criminal Justice Association-Lambda
    Alpha Epsilon (ACJA-LAE)   247
Southern Criminal Justice Association (SCJA)   247
Criminal Justice Association of Georgia (CJAG)   248
Conclusion   248
Chapter Review Questions   248
References   249

Index   253

LIST OF TABLES

Chapter 1 · Georgia's Criminal Justice System

Table 1.1   2010 Crime Data   12
Table 1.2   30-Year Crime Rates   13
Table 1.3   Family Violence Aggressor by Sex   14
Table 1.4   Weapons Used in Family Violence   14
Table 1.5   Relationship of Offender to Victim   14
Table 1.6   Police Action Taken   15
Table 1.7   Family Violence Incidents 1996–2010   15

Chapter 8 · Corrections in Georgia

Table 8.1   Number of Inmates by Offenses   163
Table 8.2   Inmates by Age, Gender, and Race   163
Table 8.3   Age and Race of Males Under Death Sentence   167
Table 8.4   Age of Probationers by Gender   176
Table 8.5   Race of Probations by Gender   176
Table 8.6   Offenses of Probationers by Gender   176
Table 8.7   Age of Inmates at Admission   178
Table 8.8   Race of Juveniles Serving In Adult Prisons   178

Chapter 9 · Georgia's Juveniles

Table 9.1   Juvenile Arrests versus Total Arrests   205
Table 9.2   Juveniles Served in FY 2009   205
Table 9.3   Legal Status by Gender   207
Table 9.4   Legal Status by Race   207
Table 9.5   Legal Status by Age   207

SERIES NOTE

Carolina Academic Press' state-specific criminal justice series fills a gap in the field of criminal justice education. One drawback with many current introduction to criminal justice texts is that they pertain to the essentially non-existent "American" criminal justice system and ignore the local landscape. Each state has its unique legislature, executive branch, law enforcement system, court and appellate review system, state supreme court, correctional system, and juvenile justice apparatus. Since many criminal justice students embark upon careers in their home states, they are better served by being exposed to their own states' criminal justice systems. Texts in this series are designed to be used as primary texts or as supplements to more general introductory criminal justice texts.

ACKNOWLEDGMENTS

I would like to acknowledge first and foremost my kids, Brock and Charlotte. Thank you both for being so patient with me during the writing of this textbook. And to Sweetie for keeping them occupied during the summer! A big thank you to those who read the chapters and drafts, keeping me focused on the final outcome. I also want to thank Beth and Carolina Academic Press for creating a great working environment.

GEORGIA'S
CRIMINAL JUSTICE SYSTEM

CHAPTER 1

Georgia's Criminal Justice System

Learning Objectives

After reading the chapter, students will be able to:

- Explain Governor Deal's initiative to review Georgia's Criminal Justice System.
- Discuss the concept of Justice and why it is important in Georgia's Criminal Justice System.
- Explain the development of the Uniform Crime Reporting (UCR) Program, including identifying the eight crimes analyzed.
- Explain the National Incident-Based Reporting Survey and how it differs from earlier UCR program.
- Discuss the Georgia Family Violence Statistics, including the crimes analyzed.
- Discuss the latest crime data and crime rates for the State of Georgia.

Key Terms

Corrections
Courts
Family Violence Statistics
Justice
Juvenile Justice
Law Enforcement
National Crime Victimization Survey
National Incident-Based Reporting Survey
Uniform Crime Reporting (UCR) Program

Figure 1.1 Georgia's State Capitol Building

On January 10, 2011, Nathan Deal, in his inaugural speech as Georgia's 82nd Governor, made several references to Georgia's Criminal Justice System and pledged to break the culture of crime that continues to exist throughout the state. Governor Deal stated that one of the primary responsibilities of state government is to keep citizens safe. However, "the challenge is great. Presently, one out of every thirteen Georgia residents is under some form of correctional control. It costs about Three Million Dollars per day to operate our Department of Corrections. And yet, every day criminals continue to inflict violence on our citizens and an alarming number of perpetrators are juveniles" (Deal, 2011a).

Governor Deal stated that families should not live in fear and that visitors should be treated as welcomed guests and protected. "But most of all, our dedicated law enforcement officers must not be targets for criminals. Anyone who harms one of them harms us all, for they embody the Constitutional mandate that government provide us with protection and security" (Deal, 2011a). In order to break the culture of crime, all citizens must be involved and assist law enforcement efforts. "Parents must assume more responsibility for their children. Communities must marshal their collective wills; civic and religious organizations must use their influence to set the tone for expected behavior" (Deal, 2011a).

Governor Deal hinted at what is to come during his administration: "For violent and repeat offenders, we will make you pay for your crimes. For other offenders who want to change their lives, we will provide the opportunity to do so with Day Reporting Centers, Drug, DUI and Mental Health Courts and expanded probation and treatment options. As a State, we cannot afford to have so many of our citizens waste their lives because of addictions. It is draining our State Treasury and depleting our workforce" (Deal, 2011a).

Governor Deal ended by stating that "as Governor I call on local elected officials, Sheriffs and local law enforcement personnel to work with me and State law enforcement officers to break this cycle of crime that threatens the security of all law abiding citizens" (Deal, 2011a).

In keeping his commitment to the citizens of the state, Governor Deal signed legislation, HB 265, in April 2011 that amends Title 28 of the Official Code of Georgia Annotated (O.C.G.A.) to create the 2011 Special Council on Criminal Justice Reform for Georgians and the Special Joint Committee on Georgia Criminal Justice Reform. According to the provisions in the legislation, a systematic study of the state's correctional system and criminal justice structure is needed in order to enhance public safety, reduce recidivism, hold offenders more accountable, enhance probation and parole supervision, and better manage a growing prison population. Recommendations made by the Council and the Committee will be addressed in the 2012 session of the General Assembly, with legislative changes to the state's criminal justice system made if appropriate. The statute expires on July 1, 2012 (Official Code of Georgia Annotated [O.C.G.A.] § 28-13-1).

The Council consists of 13 members, four chosen by the governor, three chosen by the lieutenant governor to represent the Senate, three chosen by the House Speaker to represent the House of Representatives, and three chosen by Georgia's Supreme Court Chief Justice to represent the judiciary. The Committee consists of 18 members from the General Assembly, nine representing the House of Representatives and nine representing the Senate.

In addressing the state in May 2011 about the newly formed Council, Governor Deal stated: "with this council now in place, it is our hope to uncover new approaches to make Georgia communities safer while increasing offender accountability, improving rehabilitation efforts and lowering costs. While this effort should ultimately uncover strategies that will save taxpayer dollars, we are first and foremost attacking the human costs of a society with too much crime, too many people behind bars, too many children growing up without a much-needed parent and too many wasted lives. I look forward to hearing the findings and recommendations of this intelligent group of individuals, and I feel confident that together they will produce good legislation that the General Assembly will take up next year" (Deal, 2011b).

Goals of Georgia's Criminal Justice System

The Criminal Justice System in Georgia consists of individuals, agencies, and facilities on the state and local level, working in collaboration toward the overarching goal of providing justice. The system includes four components: law enforcement, courts, corrections, and juvenile justice. The various components of the system are not easily delineated, as there is numerous overlap in jurisdiction and services, not only for those working within the system, but also for everyone affected by the system—the citizens of Georgia.

"This justice system includes the State Legislature that creates laws and penalties, state and local police and sheriffs' departments, prosecuting attorney offices, defense attorneys, Superior Courts, jails, state probation offices, and prisons in 159 counties throughout the state. By the time a person enters a prison to serve a sentence, he or she has had contact with at least four different agencies and public officials. Many times this number is much higher. The criminal justice process, while at times unwieldy, creates checks and balances and ensures that the administration of justice is fair and equitable" (Georgia Department of Corrections [GDC], 2011).

In addition to the legally mandated duties and responsibilities of the system's various components, individual discretion (the authority to make a decision) is a major aspect of the system, one that allows it to function continuously and in accord with the goal of justice. "Throughout this process, individuals can be returned to the 'pool' of the citizenry of Georgia. Police can elect not to arrest, prosecuting attorneys can elect not to prosecute, judges can dismiss cases, jurors can find defendants not guilty. Once an individual is found guilty and is adjudicated as a felon, the judge must decide how that person is to be treated. The length of sentence imposed by the judge is a critical factor in what happens to this offender" (GDC, 2011).

Other factors affecting the goal of justice are sometimes beyond the control of the individuals working within the components of the system. "Compared to the number of reported crimes, a relatively small percentage of offenders go to prison. The outcome of an individual case depends on many factors, such as material evidence and witnesses. Resources, such as time and personnel, frequently limit how successfully a case is resolved. There are even more factors affecting the sentence associated with the case, including the past history of the offender, the availability of viable alternatives, and the public opinion surrounding the case" (GDC, 2011).

Justice in the Criminal Justice System

With *justice* identified as the overarching goal of the Criminal Justice System, it is important to define the term. However, this term is not defined in any specific legislative statute, nor does any one or more of the components of the system specifically define the term.

Lady Justice and her Scales of Justice symbolize the ideals of *justice* in the Criminal Justice System. The image of Lady Justice wearing a blindfold indicates that all individuals processed within the Criminal Justice System will be treated fairly and equally, as Lady Justice must remain impartial. The sword in her right hand represents justice in punishment by the courts, while the scales in her left hand symbolize the weight of the defense's case against that of the prosecution. The government is required to provide more evidence, lowering the scale on the prosecution's side, in order to prove guilt.

By definition, justice means "the establishment or determination of rights according to the rules of law or equity; the quality of being just, impartial or fair; and conformity to truth, fact, or reason" (Merriam-Webster, 2011). Although justice is not clearly defined, the concepts of laws, equity, impartiality, and truth can be found in the terminology used and the ideals promoted in the mission statements and in the core beliefs and values of the agencies and the individuals who comprise the Criminal Justice System in Georgia.

The Georgia Department of Public Safety identifies truth as a core belief. "Trust is our hallmark and foundation. Our word is our bond. Truthfulness is what the public expects from us and what we demand of ourselves. We are committed to the highest ethical standards and highest level of performance beyond reproach" (Georgia Department of Public Safety, 2011). The Thomas County Sheriff's Office (2011) takes pride in promoting "fair, impartial and compassionate enforcement of county ordinances and state laws. We provide equal protection for our citizens as well as visitors in our area so that we may earn the trust and confidence of the people we serve." The Georgia Court of Appeals (2011) has its motto engraved on the marble wall behind the bench: "Upon the integrity, wisdom and independence of the judiciary depend the sacred rights of free men and women." The Georgia Department of Corrections sustains the core values of loyalty, duty, respect, selfless service, honor, integrity, and personal change (GDC, 2011). The Department of Juvenile Justice similarly includes integrity in its core values, stating "we believe DJJ staff and youth are responsible for conducting themselves with integrity and fostering a just environment in which youth can experience honesty, trust and loyalty" (Georgia Department of Juvenile Justice [DJJ], 2011).

Justice can also be defined in terms of the offender and the victim within the various components of the system. Law enforcement's role is to ensure that all victim complaints are taken seriously while maintaining compassion for all crime victims, that all crimes are investigated and all evidence is obtained within legal procedures, and that all offenders are afforded due process and constitutional rights when conducting arrests and searches. The court's role is to ensure that victims are able to have their say in the presence of the court and that offenders are processed through the pre-trial and trial stages with fairness of legal procedures. Corrections' role is to provide those individuals convicted of criminal behavior with safe and secure facilities, to treat those individuals humanely and with compassion, to ensure the rights of crime victims, and to provide effective supervision of offenders in the community. Juvenile justice has the hardest role in terms of balancing the needs of the victim with the needs of the juvenile offender, who is often seen as old enough to understand the consequences of behavior, but young enough to be naive about those consequences. The holistic approach taken by the Georgia Department of Juvenile Justice includes "proven, innovative and effective programs delivered in appropriate settings" with a commitment to the victim, the offender, and the community (DJJ, 2011).

Justice is open to interpretation by the individuals involved in a given situation. Does the victim only receive justice when the offender is convicted? Does the offender receive justice with an acquittal or is justice served when convicted on circumstantial evidence? One victim may interpret justice as having the offender caught and incarcerated for many years. Another victim of the same crime may find justice in the simple act of restitution, without incarceration. For example, a victim of theft may be satisfied that justice was served when his property was returned, while another victim of theft finds justice in having the offender pay fines and engage in community service projects.

Nowhere is the concept of justice tested more than with the death penalty. Georgia is currently one of 36 states, along with the federal government, to provide a sentence of death for certain offenses. But does the death penalty provide justice? Does the victim receive justice when the offender is executed? Does the community receive justice? Again, the matter is subject to interpretation.

If the Criminal Justice System does not provide justice in a given case for a particular victim, has the system failed? If it is understood that justice for all is a virtual impossibility, can justice then ever be achieved? The Georgia Criminal Justice System wants and makes great attempts to provide justice for all citizens, a noble goal. But in determining whether the system is just, it must be understood that the answer lies with the individual and how he or she defines and interprets the term *justice*.

National Crime Rates

There are various methods used to obtain statistical data on the amount of crime and victimization that occurs in any jurisdiction in the United States.

Uniform Crime Reporting Program

The federal government, through the U.S. Department of Justice, Federal Bureau of Investigation (FBI), compiles yearly reports of crimes known to the police. In 1929, the FBI took over the collection and monthly printing of national crime statistics from the International Association of Chiefs of Police, known as the Uniform Crime Reporting (UCR) Program. The UCR program "is a voluntary city, university and college, county, state, tribal, and federal law enforcement program that provides a nationwide view of crime based on the submission of statistics by law enforcement agencies throughout the country" (Federal Bureau of Investigation [FBI], 2011a).

Originally titled *Uniform Crime Reports for the United States and its Possessions*, the first report was printed in September 1930. In 1958, the report began annual publication, with the title changing to *Crime in the United States* in 1959. Currently, the offenses are categorized in two sections: violent crime total, which includes murder and non-negligent manslaughter, forcible rape, robbery, and aggravated assault; and property crime total, which includes burglary, larceny (theft), motor vehicle theft, and arson. "Today, *Crime in the United States* is a web-only publication that has expanded to 81 tables, along with charts and graphics, based on information provided by nearly 18,000 city, university and college, county, state, tribal, and federal law enforcement agencies from all 50 states and Washington D.C., as well as from law enforcement in Puerto Rico and other outlying areas" (FBI, 2011b).

National Incident-Based Reporting System

In the late 1970s, law enforcement nationwide called for an expanded and enhanced data collection system to collect crime data, in addition to the data already collected by the UCR program. The National Incident-Based Reporting System (NIBRS) was developed by the FBI to collect data on individual crime occurrences. The data received from participating agencies include each single incident and arrest within 22 offense categories that contain 46 specific crimes. For each offense known to the police, specific types of facts about each crime are reported. In addition, 11 other offenses are identified for which only arrest data are reported (FBI, 2011c).

When compared to the summary reports on the eight crimes provided by the UCR program, the NIBRS provides much more detail on the 46 crimes and has an additional third category involving crimes against society (i.e., drug/narcotic offenses, prostitution and pornography). "The NIBRS can furnish information on nearly every major criminal justice issue facing law enforcement today, including terrorism, white collar crime, weapons offenses, missing children where criminality is involved, drug/narcotics offenses, drug involvement in all offenses, hate crimes, spousal abuse, abuse of the elderly, child abuse, domestic violence, juvenile crime/gangs, parental abduction, organized crime, pornography/child pornography, driving under the influence, and alcohol-related offenses" (FBI, 2011c).

National Crime Victimization Survey

The Bureau of Justice Statistics was established in 1979 as a component of the Office of Justice Programs in the U.S. Department of Justice, and is responsible for collecting, analyzing, publishing, and disseminating information on crime, criminal offenders, victims of crime, and the operation of criminal justice systems at all levels of government. "These data are critical to federal, state, and local policymakers in combating crime and ensuring that justice is both efficient and evenhanded" (Bureau of Justice Statistics [BJS], 2011).

One area of research for BJS is the National Crime Victimization Survey (NCVS), developed in 1973 for the purpose of obtaining information on victims of crime. "Each year, data are obtained from a nationally representative sample of 76,000 households comprising nearly 135,300 persons on the frequency, characteristics and consequences of criminal victimization in the United States. The survey enables BJS to estimate the likelihood of victimization by rape, sexual assault, robbery, assault, theft, household burglary, and motor vehicle theft for the population as a whole as well as for segments of the population such as women, the elderly, members of various racial groups, city dwellers, or other groups" (BJS, 2011).

By interviewing victims of crime, the NCVS is able to obtain information not available in the UCR or NIBRS reports, most importantly for crimes that have not been reported to the police. "The survey provides information about victims (age, sex, race, ethnicity, marital status, income, and educational level), offenders (sex, race, estimated age, and victim-offender relationship), and the crimes (time and place of occurrence, use of weapons, nature of injury, and economic consequences). Questions also cover the experiences of victims with the criminal justice system, self-protective measures used by victims, and possible substance abuse by offenders" (BJS, 2011). The major shortfall with the NCVS is that it cannot obtain information on murder (one cannot ask a person if he or she has been a victim of murder!). But used with the UCR and NIBRS reports, the NCVS reveals a more clearly defined picture of national crime.

Crime in Georgia

Crime statistics for the State of Georgia are measured in much the same way as statistics on the national level. The Georgia Bureau of Investigation (GBI) is charged with collecting, analyzing, and disseminating to the public the crime statistics and crime rates each year.

Georgia Uniform Crime Reporting Program

The GBI administers the Georgia Uniform Crime Reporting program, which is part of the FBI's nationwide UCR program. "Georgia has voluntarily participated in this program since 1975. The Georgia Crime Information Center receives monthly crime and arrest reports from more than 600 state and local law enforcement agencies" (Georgia Bureau of Investigation [GBI], 2011). The Georgia UCR uses the same eight crimes and reporting methods as the national UCR program, while also collecting data on the age, race, and sex of persons arrested for all crimes except traffic violations. In addition, "special monthly reports are also collected for incidents of homicide, arson, juveniles arrested and law enforcement officers killed or assaulted" (GBI, 2011).

The crime data from the Georgia UCR program are reported in two different ways. The first simply presents the numbers of the eight offenses known to the police. This report is titled *Statewide Report Profile of Reported Index Crimes*. The second reports the crime data as rates, provided in a report titled *Statewide Crime Rates per 100,000 Population*. Calculating the crime data as rates is important as it allows for comparisons between jurisdictions and over time, because the calculations control for population differences. The crime rate is calculated by dividing the number of reported crimes by the total population of the jurisdiction (in this case, the State of Georgia) and then multiplying by 100,000 (GBI, 2011).

The number of reported crimes and crime rates per 100,000 population for 2010 are listed in Table 1.1.

Table 1.1 2010 Crime Data

Offense	# of Reported Crimes	Crime Rates
Murder	522	5.4
Rape	2051	21.2
Robbery	12,130	125.2
Aggravated Assault	23,071	238.1
TOTAL Violent	37,774	389.9
Burglary	94,308	973.5
Larceny	218,499	2,255.4
Auto Theft	29,836	308.0
Arson	1,185	12.2
TOTAL Property	343,828	3,549.1
TOTAL CRIMES	381,602	3,939.1

(GBI, 2011)

By using the crime rates, a comparison across years can be conducted. In the past 30 years, the crime rates for Georgia have shown a steady decrease since peaking in the early 1990s, with both Murder and Burglary peaking even earlier, in 1981 and 1980, respectively. The only exception is Auto Theft, which showed a peak in 1990 but had its low in 1983.

It is interesting to note that for three of the four violent crimes (Murder, Rape, and Robbery), the crime rates for 2010 are the lowest since 1980, while Aggravated Assault reached its low in 2004. For the property crimes, three of the four (Burglary, Larceny, and Arson) all reached lows since 2000, while Auto Theft, although statistically reaching its low seven years before its peak, has shown a steady decrease through the decades of the 1990s and 2000s, to end 2010 with a rate close to the 1983 rate. The continued decline in crime rates per 100,000 population is even more significant given the fact that the total population for the State of Georgia has increased more than 75 percent from 1980 to 2010.

Table 1.2 shows the crime rates for the peak years and low years for the eight UCR crimes.

Georgia Family Violence Statistics

In addition to the crimes listed in the UCR, "in 1995, the Georgia General Assembly mandated that Georgia law enforcement agencies also collect specific information about Family Violence offenses to include the names, sex, date of birth and relationship of the parties involved; the time, place and date

Table 1.2 30-Year Crime Rates

Offense	Year of Peak	Crime Rate	Year of Low	Crime Rate
Murder	1981	15.0	2010	5.4
Rape	1990	56.4	2010	21.2
Robbery	1989	269.1	2010	125.2
Aggravated Assault	1990	433.6	2004	235.8
TOTAL Violent	1990	768.4	2010	389.9
Burglary	1980	1,616.8	2000	708.3
Larceny	1989	3,905.1	2009	2,243.6
Auto Theft	1990	641.6	1983	277.0
Arson	1991	27.1	2004	11.3
TOTAL Property	1989	6,226.5	2010	3,549.1

(GBI, 2011)

of the incident; whether children were involved or whether the act of family violence was committed in the presence of children; the type and extent of alleged abuse; the existence of substance abuse; the number and types of weapons involved; the existence of any prior court orders; the number of complaints involving persons who have filed previous complaints; the type of police action taken; and any other information that may be pertinent" (GBI, 2011).

The GBI began collecting the appropriate crime data and published the first family violence statistics in 1996, and has continued each year since. The data are compiled into four tables. Shown below are the tables representing the 65,485 occurrences of family violence in 2010.

Table 1.3 shows the family violence aggressor by sex for 11 categories of abuse type. Although males are more likely to be the aggressor in family violence, the data indicate a substantial number of females are also acting as aggressors.

Table 1.4 shows the weapons used in family violence incidents, by number of occurrences per weapon type. It is interesting to note that the most frequent weapon of choice is the hand and/or fist, with firearms and knives being the lest frequent weapons of choice.

Table 1.5 shows the relationship of the offender to the victim. This is an important aspect of family violence as the crime itself denotes an already established, intimate relationship between the offender and the victim.

Table 1.6 shows the action and type of action taken by the police. Arrest is the most prevalent action taken by the police. It is interesting to note that in just over 12 percent of the cases, no action is taken by the police.

Table 1.3 Family Violence Aggressor by Sex

Abuse Type	Male	Female
Fatal Injury	51	12
Permanently Disabled	54	11
Temporarily Disabled	252	46
Broken Bones	198	35
Gun/Knife Wounds	374	337
Superficial Wounds	21,159	7,307
Property Damage	4,080	1,448
Threats	4,865	1,278
Abusive Language	7,002	2,558
Sexual Abuse	323	30
Other Abuse	8,721	3,136
TOTAL	47,079	16,198

(GBI, 2011)

Table 1.4 Weapons Used in Family Violence

Weapon Type	Occurrences
Firearm	1,007
Cutting/Knife	4,558
Hand/Fist	35,220
Other Weapons	24,700
TOTAL	65,485

(GBI, 2011)

Table 1.5 Relationship of Offender to Victim

Relationship	Victims
Present Spouse	16,828
Former Spouse	2,719
Child	4,339
Parent	6,228
Stepparent	733
Stepchild	533
Foster Parent	40
Foster Child	103
Lives Same Household or Did	14,097
None of the Above	19,865
TOTAL	65,485

(GBI, 2011)

Table 1.6 Police Action Taken

Action Type	Action Taken
Arrested	22,173
Citation	375
Separation	10,234
Mediation	6,149
Other	18,273
None	8,281
TOTAL	65,485

(GBI, 2011)

When examining the data for family violence since 1996, when 37,018 incidents were reported, the data show several sharp increases and decreases through 2010, with the largest change being from the high of 67,989 in 2003 to 45,666 in 2004. Table 1.7 shows the total number of family violence incidents in each year of data collection.

Table 1.7 Family Violence Incidents 1996–2010

Year	# of Incidents
1996	37,018
1997	50,539
1998	54,813
1999	43,482
2000	56,981
2001	57,710
2002	61,355
2003	67,989
2004	45,666
2005	45,400
2006	54,007
2007	61,464
2008	58,420
2009	62,156
2010	65,485

(GBI, 2011)

Conclusion

The role of Georgia's Criminal Justice System is to provide justice to victims, while also providing constitutional rights to offenders and providing safety and security to the citizens and visitors of the state. Governor Deal's initiative and the General Assembly's response in providing a legislative mandate to review, analyze, and make legislative recommendations for improvements to the system demonstrates the importance of making the system as effective and efficient as possible, and recognizes that the system plays a vital role in the lives of all Georgians.

Chapter Review Questions

1. What is the purpose of Governor Deal's initiative to create a review of Georgia's Criminal Justice System?
2. Explain the term Justice in relation to Georgia's Criminal Justice System. What does Justice mean to you?
3. Compare and contrast the Uniform Crime Reporting Program and the National Incident-Based Reporting System.
4. Explain why the National Crime Victimization Survey was developed. Why is it an important component of criminal justice statistics today?
5. Explain Georgia's Family Violence Statistics and provide several examples of the offenses examined.

References

Bureau of Justice Statistics. (2010). Criminal Victimization, 2009. Retrieved from: http://bjs.ojp.usdoj.gov.

Deal, Nathan. (2011a). Inaugural Address of Governor Nathan Deal. Retrieved from: http://gov.georgia.gov.

Deal, Nathan. (2011b). Deal names appointees for Criminal Justice Reform Council. Retrieved from: http://gov.georgia.gov.

Georgia Bureau of Investigation. (2011). GBI Crime Statistics Database. Retrieved from: http://www.georgia.gov.

Georgia Court of Appeals. (2011). History. Retrieved from: http://www.ga appeals.us.

Georgia Department of Corrections (GDC). (2011). The Criminal Justice System in Georgia. Retrieved from: http://www.dcor.state.ga.us.

Georgia Department of Juvenile Justice (DJJ). (2011). The Mission. Retrieved from: http://www.djj.state.ga.us.

Georgia Department of Public Safety. (2011). Mission and Core Beliefs. Retrieved from: http://dps.georgia.gov.

Federal Bureau of Investigation. (2011a). UCR Basics. Retrieved from: http://www2.fbi.gov/ucr.

Federal Bureau of Investigation. (2011b). Message from the Director. Retrieved from: http://www2.fbi.gov/ucr.

Federal Bureau of Investigation. (2011c). NIBRS Basics. Retrieved from: http://www2.fbi.gov/ucr.

Merriam-Webster Dictionary. (2011). Justice. Retrieved from: http://www.merriam-webster.com/dictionary/justice.

O.C.G.A. 28-13-1. (2011). Legislative Findings. Official Code of Georgia Annotated.

Thomas County Sheriff's Office. (2011). Welcome from the Sheriff. Retrieved from: http://www.thomascountyboc.org/TCSO.

CHAPTER 2

GEORGIA'S CONSTITUTIONS

Learning Objectives

After reading the chapter, students will be able to:

- Explain the importance of a constitution for the State of Georgia.
- Describe the evolution of criminal justice provisions through the ten state constitutions.
- Discuss the provisions and amendments to the state constitutions that pertain to Georgia's Criminal Justice System.
- Identify and describe the state and local criminal justice agencies and personnel established by the state constitutions.

Key Terms

Bill of Rights	Governor
Constitution	Habeas Corpus
Court of Appeals	Judicial Branch
Declaration of Fundamental	Jury
Principles	Legislative Branch
Equal Protection Clause	Preamble
Executive Branch	State Board of Pardons and Paroles
General Assembly	Supreme Court

Figure 2.1 Great Seal of the State of Georgia

Great Seal of the State of Georgia features the constitution supported by three pillars representing the legislative, judicial, and executive branches. Banners wrap the pillars with Georgia's official motto of Wisdom, Justice, and Moderation.

Since the fight for Independence from Great Britain in 1776, Georgia has been governed by ten state constitutions. Each constitution has provided the government and citizens of Georgia with specific powers, rights, and privileges pertaining to the creation of laws, the responsibilities of law enforcement, and the establishment of courts, which have been expanded and amended throughout the years.

Rules and Regulations of the Colony of Georgia 1776

Regarded by some to be Georgia's first constitution, the Rules and Regulations of the Colony of Georgia (1776) focused primarily on the issues dealt with in the fight for Independence, namely the hostile actions of the British toward the American colonies. The first paragraph states: "Whereas, the unwise and iniquitous system of administration obstinately persisted in by the British Parliament and Ministry against the good people of America hath at length driven the latter to take up arms as their last resource for the preservation of their rights and liberties which God and the Constitution gave them" (Rules and Regulations, 1776).

The document, written in April, three months before the formal Declaration of Independence, shows the thinking of the day in urging the creation of some type of governmental authority "to curb the lawless and protect the peaceful" (Rules and Regulations, 1776). The Congress, "as the representatives of the people, with whom all power originates, deeply impressed with a sense of duty to their constituents, of love of their country, and inviolable attachment to the liberties of America," presented eight rules and regulations for the province (state) (Rules and Regulations, 1776). The rules provided, among other provisions, that all laws, common or statute, would remain in full force until otherwise ordered; that a Chief-Justice, two assistant judges, an Attorney-General, a Provost-Marshal, and a Clerk of the Court of Sessions be appointed by ballot of the Congress; and that the President or Commander-in-Chief would appoint magistrates.

These rules and regulations, although not a formal constitution, laid the foundation for future constitutions and the establishment of state government. Following the signing and acceptance of the Declaration of Independence in July 1776, Georgia held its first constitutional convention to draft a state constitution (New Georgia Encyclopedia, 2011).

The Constitution of 1777

Completed in February 1777, Georgia's first formal constitution was enacted without ratification by the citizens and remained in effect for 12 years. In continuing with the break with Great Britain and the fight for Independence, this constitution identified the dissolution of allegiance to the crown and the need, "where no government, sufficient to the exigencies of their affairs, hath been hitherto established, to adopt such government as may, in the opinion of the representatives of the people, best conduce to the happiness and safety of their constituents in particular and America in general. We, therefore, the representatives of the people, from whom all power originates, and for whose benefit all government is intended, by virtue of the power delegated to us, do ordain and declare, and it is hereby ordained and declared, that the following rules and regulations be adopted for the future government of this State" (Georgia Constitution of 1777).

This constitution provided 63 articles. The first eight articles established the legislature and representatives of the people. In addition, Article Four established eight counties: Burke, Camden, Chatham, Effingham, Glynn, Liberty, Richmond, and Wilkes. The office of President as established in the Rules and Regulations of 1776 was changed to Governor, while the office of a President of the Executive Council was kept. Numerous articles established the provisions for and the right to vote, and the formation of a militia. Article 36 created a superior court in each county. Subsequent articles established the rules for court jurisdiction in various criminal and civil cases. Article 40 provided for a supreme court (this is a county court, not related to what the supreme court is today), but consisted of a chief-justice and three or more justices residing in the county. Articles 40 through 44 established the role of the jury in both criminal and civil trials. Article 55 established that courthouses and jails would be erected in each county, to be paid for by the citizens of the county. Article 59 provided that excessive fines would not be levied nor excessive bail demanded, while Article 60 provided for habeas corpus, and Article 61 provided for trial by jury (Georgia Constitution of 1777).

Georgia Constitution of 1789

In 1788, Georgia became the fourth state to ratify the United States Constitution. In November 1788, a constitutional convention began with the purpose of revising the state constitution to reflect conformity with the federal constitution. The 1789 constitution is the shortest of all Georgia's constitutions (New Georgia Encyclopedia, 2011).

This constitution contained four articles, each composed of numerous sections. Article I established the legislative power for the state, placing it in two separate and distinct branches, a senate and a house of representatives, to be known as the General Assembly. The sections established membership and responsibilities of the senate and house, while Section 16 provided that "the General Assembly shall have power to make all laws and ordinances which they shall deem necessary and proper for the good of the State, which shall not be repugnant to this constitution" (Georgia Constitution of 1789).

Article II established the executive branch, whereby a governor was elected by vote of the General Assembly. Section 7 provided the governor with the power to grant reprieves for offenses against the state and to grant pardons in all cases after conviction, except for treason and murder, in which cases he would appeal to the General Assembly for a pardon (Georgia Constitution of 1789).

Article III established that a superior court would be held in each county, twice a year, to try all criminal and civil cases, except those subject to federal jurisdiction. The General Assembly determined the mode of correcting errors and appeals, including empowering judges to direct a new trial by jury within the county of original trial, with the new trial being final. The remaining sections established court jurisdiction and compensation for judges and the attorney general (Georgia Constitution of 1789).

Article IV provided for elections and included several provisions, among them trial by jury and writ of habeas corpus. In addition, it provided that amendments to the constitution be undertaken in 1794 by an assembly comprised of three electors from each county. In 1795, eight amendments (articles) were added to the constitution, all concerning elections except Article VI, which provided that Louisville would be the permanent seat of state government (moving it from Augusta) (Georgia Constitution of 1789).

Georgia Constitution of 1798

The 1798 constitution is one of three that was framed and enacted under completely peaceful conditions, and was in effect for 63 years. Again containing four articles, each was greatly expanded from the earlier constitution, with 22 additional amendments passed between 1807 and 1857.

Article I expanded the roles and responsibilities of the legislative branch, including delineation of the boundaries of the state and its counties. No person convicted of a felony in Georgia or anywhere in the United States would be eligible for any office in the state. Several amendments were devoted to specific changes to the language concerning elections of representatives and senators, along with age and citizenship requirements, voting eligibility of citizens, and meeting requirements of the General Assembly (Georgia Constitution of 1798).

Article II expanded the roles and responsibilities of the executive branch. Several amendments included provisions concerning the governor, among them the election of the governor, for the first time, by those citizens eligible to elect members of the General Assembly. This meant that the governor would now be elected by popular vote by the citizens of the state. In addition, amendments stipulated that the governor would serve two-year terms, and provided procedures for the office if the governor were to die while in office (Georgia Constitution of 1798).

Article III provided the majority of the new provisions in this constitution, which included greatly expanding the judicial power of the state. The numerous amendments to the constitution, however, led to the greatest expansion and development of the state courts. Justices of inferior courts and justices of the peace would be elected by those eligible to elect members of the General Assembly, just as with the governor. Amendment X expanded the state courts to include a supreme court for the correction of errors, consisting of three judges.

The supreme court was to have no original jurisdiction but appellate jurisdiction from superior courts. However, it was not until 1846 that the supreme court was officially established. In addition, a court of ordinary or register of probate would be vested in an ordinary for each county, to issue citations, grant temporary letters of administration, and grant marriage licenses (Georgia Constitution of 1798).

Within five years of the passage of this constitution, all state laws, criminal and civil, were revised, digested, and arranged under proper headings and disseminated as the legislature directed (Georgia Constitution of 1798).

Article IV provided an expansion of voting and individual rights. In addition, Section 11 provided that there would be no further importation of slaves into the state, from Africa or another foreign country, after October 1, 1798. However, the provision also stated that the legislature would not have the power to emancipate slaves without the consent of the owners, nor to prevent emigrants from other states bringing with them to Georgia individuals who would be defined by law as slaves. In addition, any person who maliciously dismembered or killed a slave would be punished for the same offense committed against a free white person, "except in case of insurrection by such slave, and unless such death should happen by accident in giving such slave moderate correction" (Georgia Constitution of 1798).

Georgia Constitution of 1861

With concerns over the federal government's possible outlawing of slavery, and with the balance of slave to non-slave states being disrupted by the possible admittance of California or New Mexico to the Union, the General Assembly held a state convention in 1850. The convention produced a statement of policy that warned of secession, but nothing further was done. However, with Civil War looming in the future, a second state convention held in 1861 formally adopted the Ordinance of Secession, and a meeting of the seceded states adopted the Constitution of the Confederate States of America (New Georgia Encyclopedia, 2011).

This constitution was the first in Georgia to be ratified by the citizens of the state. The major difference between this constitution and previous ones is the delineation and expansion of numerous individual rights, found in Article I, titled Declaration of Fundamental Principles. The following rights pertain to the criminal justice system:

- protection of persons and property is the duty of government;
- no citizen shall be deprived of life, liberty or property, except by due process of law, and of life or liberty, except by judgment of his peers;

- the writ of habeas corpus shall not be suspended unless in case of rebellion or invasion;
- the right of the people to appeal to courts;
- every citizen ought to obtain justice without purchase, denial or delay;
- every person charged with an offense against the laws of the state shall have privilege and benefit of counsel, be furnished with a copy of the accusation, provided with a list of witnesses against him and have compulsory process to obtain his own witnesses, be confronted with witnesses, and have a public and speedy trial by an impartial jury;
- no person shall be put twice in jeopardy of life or liberty for the same offense;
- excessive bail shall not be required, nor excessive fines imposed, nor cruel and unusual punishment inflicted;
- the powers of the court to punish for contempt limited by legislative acts;
- ex post facto laws are prohibited;
- laws should have a general operation;
- the right of the people to be secure in their persons, houses, papers and effects against unreasonable search and seizure, and no warrants shall be issued but upon probable cause, supported by oath or affirmation, particularly describing the place or places to be searched, and the persons or things to be seized; and
- martial law shall not be declared, except in cases of extreme necessity.

(Georgia Constitution of 1861).

Georgia Constitution of 1865

After the Civil War ended in 1865, Georgia's provisional governor, James Johnson, assembled a constitutional convention with the purpose of creating a state constitution that would be acceptable to the federal government (Georgia Constitution, 2011). This was the first constitution to include a preamble: "We, the people of the State of Georgia, in order to form a permanent Government, establish justice, insure domestic tranquility, and secure the blessings of liberty to ourselves and our posterity, acknowledging and invoking the guidance of Almighty God, the author of all good government, do ordain and establish this Constitution for the State of Georgia" (Georgia Constitution of 1865).

With the exception of small modifications to language and format, there are two major distinctions between this constitution and the 1861 version. The first distinction is found in Article II, Section V, which states that "it shall be the duty of the General Assembly at its next session, and thereafter as the public welfare may require, to provide by law for the government of free persons of color, or the protection and security of their persons and property, guarding them and the State against any evil that may arise from their sudden emancipation" (Georgia Constitution of 1865). This provision abolished slavery in the State of Georgia.

The second distinction is found in Article V, Section I, which is the repeal of the Ordinance of Secession. This section makes clear that the supreme law is the Constitution of the United States, the laws of the United States, and all treaties made under the authority of the United States. The next authority in law is this constitution, with the third authority being laws declared by acts of the General Assembly. All local and private laws previously passed for counties, cities, towns, corporations, and private persons that were not inconsistent with supreme law were to remain in force as statute law. In addition, "If in any statute law herein declared of force, the word 'Confederate' occurs before the word States, such law is hereby amended by substituting the word 'United' for the word 'Confederate'" (Georgia Constitution of 1865).

Although the provisions for the abolishment of slavery and the repeal of the Ordinance of Secession were placed within the constitution of 1865, ratification of the Fourteen Amendment to the U.S. Constitution was required as a specific condition for readmission to the Union. In November 1866, the General Assembly refused to ratify the amendment. As a result, the Constitution of 1865 was rejected by the federal government and the state was placed under military control (New Georgia Encyclopedia, 2011).

Georgia Constitution of 1868

Military rule was established in Georgia in 1867. From December 1867 to March 1868, a group of elected delegates assembled for a new constitutional convention. Dominated by northerners who had relocated to Georgia, the convention debated the Fourteenth Amendment, qualifications of the electorate, debts and the relief of debtors, and separation of powers (New Georgia Encyclopedia, 2011).

The 1868 constitution expanded the Declaration of Fundamental Principles to 33 sections, including expanded and new criminal justice provisions. Section 2 provided that all persons born or naturalized in the United States who resided in Georgia were citizens of the state and would have due process and equal protection of the law (the basic principles found in Section 1 of the Fourteenth Amendment). Section 4 provided a prohibition against slavery or involuntary servitude, except as punishment for crime. Section 8 expanded that no person would be put twice in jeopardy of life or liberty for the same offense with "save on his or her own motion for a new trial after conviction, or in case of mistrial" (Georgia Constitution of 1868). Section 16, which prohibited excessive bail, fines, and cruel and unusual punishment, added "nor shall any person be abused in being arrested, whilst under arrest, or in prison" (Georgia Constitution of 1868).

Section 18 provided no imprisonment for debt. Section 21 provided for proportioned penalties to the nature of the offense, while Section 22 prohibited whipping as a punishment for crime. Section 25 addressed treason against the state, providing that it "shall consist only in levying war against the State, or the United States, or adhering to the enemies thereof, giving them aid and comfort; and no person shall be convicted of treason except on the testimony of two witnesses to the same overt act, or his own confession in open court" (Georgia Constitution of 1868).

The final section of the Declaration delineates the citizenship of Georgians. "The State of Georgia shall ever remain a member of the American Union; the people thereof are a part of the American nation; every citizen thereof owes paramount allegiance to the Constitution and Government of the United States, and no law or ordinance of this State, in contravention or subversion thereof, shall ever have any binding force" (Georgia Constitution of 1868).

Article II Franchise and Elections was created with expanded provisions for determining eligibility to vote and hold office within the state, specifically identifying those convicted of crime. Section 3 provided that "no person convicted of felony or larceny before any court of this State, or of or in the United States, shall be eligible to any office or appointment of honor or trust within this State, unless he shall have been pardoned" (Georgia Constitution of 1868). In addition, Section 6 provided that "the general assembly may provide, from time to time, for the registration of all electors, but the following classes of persons shall not be permitted to register, vote, or hold office: 1st. Those who shall have been convicted of treason, embezzlement of public funds, malfeasance in office, crime punishable by law with imprisonment in the penitentiary, or bribery; 2d. Idiots or insane persons" (Georgia Constitution of 1868).

Other additions to this constitution included moving the power of pardon from the General Assembly to the governor, prohibiting the sale of intoxicating liquors on days of election, as well as articles dealing with education (the General Assembly would provide a system of general education to be forever free to all children of the state), homestead and exemption, militia, county officers, and the seat of state government (to permanently be in the City of Atlanta) (Georgia Constitution of 1868). In addition, the federal Congress, in admitting the State of Georgia to representation in Congress on June 25, 1868 (thereby admitting Georgia to the Union), provided two amendments, with a third ratified by the citizens of Georgia in 1877.

Georgia Constitution of 1877

In July 1877, 193 elected members assembled for a constitutional convention, with a new constitution completed the following month and enacted in December. Although this constitution was much more detailed, it was amended 301 times during its existence (New Georgia Encyclopedia, 2011).

The Declaration of Fundamental Principles was now called Bill of Rights, with several important provisions being added. One important provision added to this section was that "no person shall be compelled to give testimony tending in any manner to criminate himself" (Georgia Constitution of 1877). Another provision concerning the right to the courts provided that "no person shall be deprived of the right to prosecute or defend his own cause in any of the Courts of this State, in person, by attorney, or both" (Georgia Constitution of 1877). In addition, "banishment beyond the limits of the State" was added to the already acknowledged punishment of whipping not allowed in the state (Georgia Constitution of 1877).

Furthermore, five ordinances were attached to this constitution, adopted at various times during the convention in August. The first ordinance proposed to present for vote by the people during the next general election, the decision of where to place the state capital, either Atlanta or Milledgeville (which was the state capital from 1803 to 1868). Although district courts were eliminated, the fifth ordinance provided for 16 Judicial Circuits throughout the state. The General Assembly was responsible for organizing and appropriating the judges and cases, and had the power to reorganize, increase, or decrease the number of circuits (Georgia Constitution of 1877).

One interesting portion of Article II Elective Franchise, Section V, expands the forbidding of liquor sales on election days: "The General Assembly shall, by law, forbid the sale, distribution, or furnishing of intoxicating drinks within two miles of election precincts, on days of election State, county or municipal and prescribe punishment for any violation of the same" (Georgia Constitution of 1877).

Georgia Constitution of 1945

The Constitution of 1945 is legally a single amendment to the Constitution of 1877, replacing all articles and amendments. However, for practical purposes, it does represent a separate constitution because the Constitution of 1877 was replaced in its entirety (GeorgiaInfo, 2011).

At the time, this constitution was considered a streamlined version of the Constitution of 1877. The changes were aimed at form and organization, while "approximately 90 percent of the provisions, however, were taken from the Constitution of 1877" (New Georgia Encyclopedia, 2011). Despite this fact, several substantial changes and additions in regards to criminal justice were provided.

Article V Executive Department, Section I, created the State Board of Pardons and Paroles, "composed of three members, who shall be appointed by the Governor and confirmed by the Senate. The State Board of Pardons and Paroles shall have power to grant reprieves, pardons and paroles, to commute penalties, remove disabilities imposed by law, and may remit any part of a sentence for any offense against the State, after conviction except in cases of treason or impeachment, and except in cases in which the Governor refuses to suspend a sentence of death" (Georgia Constitution of 1945).

Section IV created the Game and Fish Commission, which "shall have such powers, authority, duties, and shall receive such compensation and expenses as may be delegated or provided for by the General Assembly" (Georgia Constitution of 1945). In addition, Section V created the State Board of Corrections, "composed of five members in charge of the State penal system. The Board shall have such jurisdiction, powers, duties and control of the state penal system and the inmates thereof as shall be provided by law" (Georgia Constitution of 1945).

Article VI Judiciary, Section II, increased the number of Supreme Court justices to seven, all with the title of Associate Justice, "who shall from time to time as they may deem proper, elect one of their members as Chief Justice, and one as Presiding Justice" (Georgia Constitution of 1945). Although added to the state judiciary system in 1906 by amendment to the Constitution of 1877, the Court of Appeals is clearly defined, with provisions for terms and duties. In addition, Section XVI, provided that, for the first time, "The General Assembly shall have the power to require jury service of women also, under such regulations as the General Assembly may prescribe" (Georgia Constitution of 1945).

Georgia Constitution of 1976

Attempts to revise the Constitution of 1945 occurred several times before 1976. A revision commission presented a draft in 1964 that was approved by the General Assembly, but because of legal concerns, was never submitted for ratification by the citizens. Another revision commission was created in 1969, with a constitutional draft approved by the house, but rejected by the senate in 1970 (New Georgia Encyclopedia, 2011).

George Busbee, a member of the General Assembly in 1969 when the revised constitutional draft failed, became governor in 1974. Governor Busbee's campaign platform included a call for an article-by-article revision of the state constitution, as he believed a revision of the entire document at once would be too difficult to process. He requested the Office of Legislative Counsel to prepare a "new" constitution to be put on the 1976 election ballot for ratification. However, the charge for the Office of Legislative Counsel was to reorganize the document, not to make substantive changes. The revision was ratified, thus creating the Constitution of 1976, a document different from the Constitution of 1945 in organization only (New Georgia Encyclopedia, 2011).

Georgia Constitution of 1983

Almost immediately upon the ratification of the Constitution of 1976, the General Assembly created the Select Committee on Constitutional Review to begin work in 1977 on a total revision of the state constitution. "Members included the governor as chair, the lieutenant governor, the speaker of the house, the attorney general, and representatives from both houses of the legislature and the judicial branch" (New Georgia Encyclopedia, 2011).

The Select Committee worked to draft and approve each article individually, with the General Assembly also having approval vote. The revision took five years, and the new constitution was approved by the General Assembly in 1981. The new constitution was placed on the ballot of the 1982 general election, overwhelmingly ratified by the voters, and went into effect on July 1, 1983 (New Georgia Encyclopedia, 2011).

With the full revision of all articles, this constitution is the first truly new constitution since 1877. While it maintained some of the provisions found in the Constitution of 1877, it provided entirely new provisions, many pertaining to criminal justice (New Georgia Encyclopedia, 2011).

A major inclusion in the Bill of Rights is an equal protection clause. Article I Bill of Rights, Section I, provides that "Protection to person and property is the paramount duty of government and shall be impartial and complete. No person shall be denied the equal protection of the laws" (Georgia Constitution of 1983).

Section I also expands the provisions in the right to trial by jury. "(a) The right to trial by jury shall remain inviolate, except that the court shall render judgment without the verdict of a jury in all civil cases where no issuable defense is filed and where a jury is not demanded in writing by either party. In criminal cases, the defendant shall have a public and speedy trial by an impartial jury; and the jury shall be the judges of the law and the facts. (b) A trial jury shall consist of 12 persons; but the General Assembly may prescribe any number, not less than six, to constitute a trial jury in courts of limited jurisdiction and in superior courts in misdemeanor cases. (c) The General Assembly shall provide by law for the selection and compensation of persons to serve as grand Jurors and trial jurors" (Georgia Constitution of 1983). In addition, the language regarding self-incrimination and double jeopardy was refined, without making substantive changes.

Article IV Constitutional Boards and Commissions, Section II, provides an expanded description of the powers and authority of the State Board of Pardons and Paroles. These provisions include the authority of the General Assembly, by law, to prohibit and prescribe the terms and conditions for the Board granting parole or a pardon to "(1) Any person incarcerated for a second or subsequent time for any offense for which such person could have been sentenced to life imprisonment; and (2) Any person who has received consecutive life sentences as the result of offenses occurring during the same series of acts" (Georgia Constitution of 1983). The Section also provides that "when a sentence of death is commuted to life imprisonment, the board shall not have the authority to grant a pardon to the convicted person until such person has served at least 25 years in the penitentiary; and such person shall not become eligible for parole at any time prior to serving at least 25 years in the penitentiary. When a person is convicted of armed robbery, the board shall not have the authority to consider such person for pardon or parole until such person has served at least five years in the penitentiary" (Georgia Constitution of 1983). In addition, Section VI renames the Game and Fish Commission as the Board of Natural Resources, whose duties include setting rules and regulations for air and water quality, hunting seasons and bag limits, and other issues (Department of Natural Resources, 2011).

Article V Executive Branch, Section III, delineates the duties of the Attorney General, who will "act as the legal advisor of the executive department, shall represent the state in the Supreme Court in all capital felonies and in all civil and criminal cases in any court when required by the Governor, and shall perform such other duties as shall be required by law" (Georgia Constitution of 1983).

Other major changes occurred with the judiciary. Article VI Judicial Branch, Section I, divides the judicial power of the state into seven classes of courts: magistrate, probate, juvenile, state, superior, Court of Appeals, and Supreme Court. Magistrate, probate, juvenile, and state courts are courts of limited jurisdiction.

"In addition, the General Assembly may establish or authorize the establishment of municipal courts and may authorize administrative agencies to exercise quasi-judicial powers. Municipal courts shall have jurisdiction over ordinance violations and such other jurisdiction as provided by law" (Georgia Constitution of 1983).

Section IV increases the number of justices on the Supreme Court to nine. The provisions also define exclusive appellate jurisdiction, general appellate jurisdiction, as well as jurisdiction over questions of law from other states or federal appellate courts. Section VII provides for the nonpartisan election and terms for judges in the state. "All superior court and state court judges shall be elected on a nonpartisan basis for a term of four years. All Justices of the Supreme Court and the Judges of the Court of Appeals shall be elected on a nonpartisan basis for a term of six years" (Georgia Constitution of 1983).

Section IX provides for the publishing of court rules. "Not more than 24 months after the effective date hereof and from time to time thereafter by amendment the Supreme Court shall with the advice and consent of the council of the affected class or classes of trial courts, by order adopt and publish uniform court rules and record-keeping rules which shall provide for the speedy, efficient, and inexpensive resolution of disputes and prosecutions. Each council shall be comprised of all of the judges of the courts of that class" (Georgia Constitution of 1983). Section X reclassifies justice of the peace courts, small claims courts, existing magistrate courts, and the County Court of Echols County as a magistrate court, while the County Court of Baldwin County and the County Court of Putnam County are reclassified as state courts. Municipal courts in existence will remain, and the City Court of Atlanta will retain its name (Georgia Constitution of 1983).

As with the previous nine constitutions, the Constitution of 1983 has been amended, most recently on November 8, 1998 with regard to general election ballots.

Conclusion

The United States Constitution, ratified in 1789, provides for a system of federalism as one of its most important elements. "Federalism is a type of political system that gives certain powers to the national government, others to the states, and some to both levels of government" (Fleischmann and Pierannunzi, n.d.). Georgia, like all other states in America, has created a constitution, although ratified and amended throughout its history, as a guide for state government. Constitutions allow the state government to create provisions for laws, business, education, and various other interactions the citizens of the state will have with government as well as with other citizens.

The Georgia Constitution has established the foundation for criminal justice in the state, while the General Assembly works to establish law and the judiciary works to establish precedent. As time and circumstance dictate, the Georgia Constitution will continue to serve as a guide, one that is capable of change when needed.

Chapter Review Questions

1. Explain the role of the constitution for the State of Georgia.
2. Identify the criminal justice agencies and personnel specifically established by the constitutions.
3. Discuss the Declaration of Fundamental Principles (later the Bill of Rights) and provide examples of the rights provided in both.
4. Explain the role of the General Assembly in Georgia's Criminal Justice System.
5. Explain the term Equal Protection Clause and what it means in the Criminal Justice System.

References

Fleischmann, A. and Pierannunzi, C. (n.d.). Georgia's Constitution and Government, 6th ed. Retrieved from: http://a-s.clayton.edu/trachtenberg/Fleischmann%206th%20Edition.pdf.

Georgia Constitution of 1777. Retrieved from: http://georgiainfo.galileo.usg.edu.

Georgia Constitution of 1789. Retrieved from: http://georgiainfo.galileo.usg.edu.

Georgia Constitution of 1798. Retrieved from: http://georgiainfo.galileo.usg.edu.

Georgia Constitution of 1861. Retrieved from: http://georgiainfo.galileo.usg.edu.

Georgia Constitution of 1865. Retrieved from: http://georgiainfo.galileo.usg.edu.

Georgia Constitution of 1868. Retrieved from: http://georgiainfo.galileo.usg.edu.

Georgia Constitution of 1877. Retrieved from: http://georgiainfo.galileo.usg.edu.

Georgia Constitution of 1945. Retrieved from: http://georgiainfo.galileo.usg.edu.

Georgia Constitution of 1976. Retrieved from: http://georgiainfo.galileo.usg.edu.

Georgia Constitution of 1983. Retrieved from: http://georgiainfo.galileo.usg.edu.

Georgia Department of Natural Resources (DNR). (2011). Georgia DNR Board. Retrieved from: http://www.gadnr.org.

GeorgiaInfo. (2011). Note to the Georgia Constitution of 1945. Retrieved from: http://georgiainfo.galileo.usg.edu.

New Georgia Encyclopedia. (2011). Georgia Constitution. Retrieved from: http://www.georgiaencyclopedia.org.

Rules and Regulations of the Colony of Georgia 1776. Retrieved from: http://georgiainfo.galileo.usg.edu.

CHAPTER 3

CRIMES IN GEORGIA

Learning Objectives

After reading the chapter, students will be able to:

- Identify and explain the Official Code of Georgia Annotated.
- Explain how state statutes and local ordinances are enacted.
- Identify the chapters in Title 16 and define key terms related to crime.
- Define the term **crime** and discuss statutes related to criminal liability.
- Identify various defenses to criminal prosecution.
- Explain the justifications for use of force in defense of persons and property.
- Explain the terms criminal attempt, conspiracy, and solicitation.
- Define the crimes against the person, including punishments.
- Define the crimes against property, including punishments.
- Define the crimes of theft and robbery, including punishments.
- Define the crimes of forgery and fraud, including punishments.
- Define crimes against the government, against public order and safety, and against public health and morals, including punishments.
- Explain street gang terrorism and prevention.

Key Terms

Conviction	Official Code of Georgia Annotated
Crime	Peace Officer
Crimes Against the Person	Prosecution
Crimes Against Property	Public Administration
Criminal Attempt	Public Health and Morals
Criminal Liability	Public Order and Safety
Defenses to Criminal Prosecution	Robbery
Felony	Sexual Offenses
Forcible Felony	State Statutes
Forcible Misdemeanor	Street Gangs
Justified Conduct	Theft

Local Ordinances   Title 16
Misdemeanor   Use of Force without Consent
Misdemeanor of High
   and Aggravated Nature

As with the federal Constitution, treason is the only crime specifically listed in the Georgia Constitution of 1983. All other behaviors and actions identified as crimes in Georgia are defined by legislatures on the state, county, and municipal levels. Georgia state statutes, created by the General Assembly, are defined in the Official Code of Georgia. These statutes are easily identified with the legal notation of O.C.G.A. (Official Code of Georgia Annotated). Legislation created on the county or municipal level is termed ordinance, but provides the same force of law as state statutes.

The General Assembly

"A form of representative government has existed in Georgia since January 1751" (New Georgia Encyclopedia, 2011a). Georgia's state legislature, known as the General Assembly, has been in constant operation since 1777, when Georgia was one of the original 13 colonies that revoked its status as a colony of Great Britain. The General Assembly consists of two chambers: Senate and House of Representatives. The Senate has 56 members with the lieutenant governor serving as chief officer, while the House of Representatives has 180 members with the Speaker of the House (elected by the entire membership) presiding. In addition, all members of the General Assembly are elected in even numbered years, to serve two-year terms, and there is no limit to the number of terms a legislator can serve (New Georgia Encyclopedia, 2011a).

The General Assembly is responsible for creating and enacting state statutes. There are 16 steps involved in passing a law in the General Assembly.

1) A legislator in either chamber, who sees a need for a new law or a revision to an existing law, will decide to introduce a bill.

2) The legislator will go to the Office of Legislative Council to meet with an attorney, who will advise the legislator on any legal issues involved and will assist with drafting the bill.

3) Once the bill is drafted, the legislator will file the bill with the Clerk of the House or the Secretary of the Senate, depending on his or her chamber.

4) On the legislative day after the bill is filed, the bill will be formally introduced in chamber. The bill's title will be read during the period of 1st readings.

5) Immediately after the completion of the 1st reading, the presiding officer will assign the bill to a standing committee.

6) In the House, on the next legislative day, the Clerk will read the bill's title (2nd reading) in chamber, although the actual bill is already in committee. In the Senate, the 2nd reading occurs after the bill is reported favorably by the committee.

7) The bill is considered by the committee. The legislator who authored the bill and other legislators may testify before the committee. If the bill is controversial, the committee may hold public hearings on the bill.

8) If the bill is reported favorably by the committee, it is returned to the Clerk or Secretary.

9) The Clerk or Secretary will prepare a General Calendar of bills that have been favorably reported by the committee. For the first ten days of session in the House, and 15 days in the Senate, the presiding officer will call up bills from the calendar for floor action.

10) Starting on the tenth day of session in the House, and 15th day in the Senate, the Rules Committee will meet and from the bills on the General Calendar will prepare a Rules Calendar for the next day's floor consideration.

11) For the last 30 days of session in the House, and 25 days in the Senate, the presiding officer calls up bills from the Rules Calendar for floor consideration.

12) Once the presiding officer calls up the bill from the Rules Calendar, the Clerk or Secretary will read the bill's title (3rd reading) and the bill is now ready for floor debate, amendments, and vote.

13) After debate, the main question is called and the members vote. If the bill is approved by the majority of total membership of the chamber, it is sent to the other chamber.

14) If the other chamber passes the bill, it is returned to the chamber where it was introduced. If changes are accepted it continues forward. If the first chamber rejects the changes and the second chamber insists, a conference committee may be appointed. If the committee report is accepted by both chambers, the bill continues forward.

15) The bill is enrolled and sent to the governor, if requested. Otherwise, all enrolled bills are sent to the governor following adjournment *sine die* (the final adjournment of a legislative session for the year).

16) The governor may sign the bill or it will become law automatically without his signature. The governor may veto the bill, which will require a two-thirds override vote of the members of each chamber for the bill to become law. The law becomes effective the following July 1, unless a specific effective date is provided in the law (GeorgiaInfo, 2011).

Local Ordinances

There are currently 535 cities and towns in Georgia, each with a charter of municipal incorporation approved by the General Assembly. However, "because municipalities are creatures of the state legislature, their boundaries, their structure, and even their existence can be altered or abolished by the state" (New Georgia Encyclopedia, 2011b). Each municipality is governed by a municipal charter, a written document that provides the authority for the municipality to exist and function. The charter is the city's fundamental law, similar in respect to a national or state constitution. The majority of cities have an elected or appointed head, who serves as a mayor or manager, and a group of legislators that make up the city council (New Georgia Encyclopedia, 2011b).

The Georgia Constitution of 1983 specified a limit of 159 counties in the state. "According to anecdotal history, Georgia established enough counties so that a farmer traveling by mule-drawn buggy could go to the county seat, take care of business, and return to his farm in the same day" (New Georgia Encyclopedia, 2011c). Politically, having smaller counties serves the majority of Georgians who live in rural areas, with many towns being the county seat for the courthouse and jail, as well as political and trade activities. Having many smaller counties allows for more representation of the citizens in state government, as each county has at least one representative in the General Assembly (New Georgia Encyclopedia, 2011c).

The Georgia Constitution originally created four elected county officers: sheriff, tax commissioner, clerk of the superior court, and judge of the probate court. In 1868, the state created the county commissioner to handle general operations of the county. Today, every county has a commissioner, with most also having a board of commissioners or county commission, with powers "to adopt ordinances, resolutions, or regulations relating to county property, county affairs, and the operation of local government" (New Georgia Encyclopedia, 2011c).

Ordinances are created and enacted by county commissions and city councils, and differ from statutes in that the jurisdiction of the law is limited to small geographic areas of counties and cities. Both of these groups are considered legislatures and the ordinances enacted have the full force of law.

Cities and counties are authorized to enact ordinances that promote peace and order within the jurisdiction, and which do not circumvent or supersede the state constitution. Local ordinances regulate such things as the placement of mobile homes, the maintenance of vicious dogs, the distribution of permits for a parade, and the licensing of taxicabs and wrecker service. For example, in regulating alcohol sales, the city ordinance for outdoor advertising in Kingsland provides that "no outdoor advertising with respect to the promotion of the sale of alcoholic beverages, malt beverages or wine shall be permitted on the exterior of any wholesale or retail outlet or elsewhere in the City of Kingsland, Georgia, except as may be authorized by the laws of the state and regulations implemented by an agency having jurisdiction thereof" (Sec. 3-35, 2011). In another ordinance regulating alcohol sales, the City of Suwanee, in Sec. 6-67 (2011), provides that "no person may sell or offer to sell any alcoholic beverage within 300 feet of a church or within 600 feet of any school building. A retail package dealer selling distilled spirits, e.g., package store, shall not offer to sell any alcoholic beverage within 200 feet of any residence in addition to the distance requirements set forth in this section for churches and schools."

In the State of Georgia, local municipal law enforcement agencies enforce city ordinances as well as any state statutes that are violated within the jurisdiction of the city. County law enforcement agencies enforce county ordinances as well as any state statutes that are violated within the jurisdiction of the county. County law enforcement agencies are also authorized to enforce city ordinances, but the practice is rare. Unless there is a need for mutual aid, county law enforcement agencies generally enforce laws in the unincorporated areas of the county. State law enforcement officers have authority to enforce any state statute or local ordinance anywhere in the state, but will generally leave local ordinances to the respective jurisdictions.

State Statutes

State statutes are published in several different forms, but each statute is individually identified by a three number code. The first number in the code refers to the title, the second number refers to the chapter, and the third number refers to the article, for example: O.C.G.A. § 16-6-1.

Most of the crimes for the state are presented in Title 16 Crimes and Offenses, while other titles may contain criminal statutes that pertain to a specific situation or individual. For example, motor vehicle offenses are provided in Title

40, while statutes dealing with domestic relations are provided in Title 19 and statutes defining criminal procedures are provided in Title 17.

Title 16 contains 17 chapters. The first three chapters provide general definitions, as well as information on what constitutes criminal liability and the criminal defenses acceptable to criminal prosecution. The remaining chapters provide the statutes for the following offenses:

- Chapter 4 Criminal Attempt, Conspiracy, and Solicitation
- Chapter 5 Crimes Against the Person
- Chapter 6 Sexual Offenses
- Chapter 7 Damage to and Intrusion upon Property
- Chapter 8 Offenses Involving Theft
- Chapter 9 Forgery and Fraudulent Practices
- Chapter 10 Offenses Against Public Administration
- Chapter 11 Offenses Against Public Order and Safety
- Chapter 12 Offenses Against Public Health and Morals
- Chapter 13 Controlled Substances
- Chapter 14 Racketeer Influenced and Corrupt Organizations
- Chapter 15 Street Gang Terrorism and Prevention
- Chapter 16 Forfeiture of Property Used in Burglary or Armed Robbery
- Chapter 17 Unlawful Loans

Chapter 1 General Provisions

The first chapter of Title 16 provides basic definitions that are used throughout the remainder of the title. Definitions found in O.C.G.A. § 16-1-3 include:

- **Conviction** means a final judgment of conviction entered by a verdict or finding of guilt of a crime or a plea of guilty.
- **Felony** is a crime punishable by death, imprisonment for life, or imprisonment for more than 12 months.
- **Forcible Felony** means the commission of any felony that involves the use of threat of physical force or violence against any person.
- **Forcible Misdemeanor** means the commission of any misdemeanor that involves the use of or the threat of physical force or violence against any person.
- **Misdemeanor or Misdemeanor of a High and Aggravated Nature** includes all crimes not classified as felony.
- **Peace Officer** refers to any person who, by virtue of office or public employment, is vested by law with a duty to maintain public order or to

make arrests for offenses, whether that duty extends to all crimes or is limited to specific offenses.

- **Property** refers to anything of value, including but not limited to, real estate, tangible and intangible personal property, contract rights, services, choses in action, and other interests in or claims to wealth, admission or transportation tickets, captured or domestic animals, food and drink, and electric or other power.
- **Prosecution** refers to all legal proceedings in which an accused person's liability for the crime is determined, beginning with the accusation or indictment, and ending with the final disposition upon appeal.
- **Without Authority** means without having a legal right or privilege or without having the permission of the person legally entitled to withhold the right.
- **Without Consent** means a person whose concurrence is required has not, with knowledge of essential facts, voluntarily yielded to the proposal of the accused or another.

O.C.G.A. § 16-1-4 provides a definition of what constitutes a crime: "No conduct constitutes a crime unless it is described as a crime in this title or in another statute of this state. However, this Code section does not affect the power of a court to punish for contempt or to employ any sanction authorized by law for the enforcement of an order, civil judgment, or decree."

O.C.G.A. § 16-1-5 provides that "Every person is presumed innocent until proved guilty. No person shall be convicted of a crime unless each element of such crime is proved beyond a reasonable doubt."

Chapter 2 Criminal Liability

This chapter defines the term **crime**: "(a) A 'crime' is a violation of a statute of this state in which there is a joint operation of an act or omission to act and intention or criminal negligence. (b) Criminal negligence is an act or failure to act which demonstrates a willful, wanton, or reckless disregard for the safety of others who might reasonably be expected to be injured thereby" (O.C.G.A. § 16-2-1).

In keeping with the concept of innocent until proven guilty, O.C.G.A. § 16-2-6 explains the consideration of criminal intent: "A person will not be presumed to act with criminal intention but the trier of facts may find such intention upon consideration of the words, conduct, demeanor, motive, and all other circumstances connected with the act for which the accused is prosecuted."

Motive and purpose in committing a crime are important concepts, as "a person shall not be found guilty of any crime committed by misfortune or accident where it satisfactorily appears there was no criminal scheme or undertaking, intention, or criminal negligence" (O.C.G.A. § 16-2-2).

Statutes are also provided that pertain to the presumption of sound mind and discretion. The state presumes that everyone acts willfully and that the natural and probable consequences of any act are intended (O.C.G.A. § 16-2-3/4/5).

Every person who is connected to the commission of a crime is considered a "party to commission of a crime" (O.C.G.A. § 16-2-20). All persons who are considered a party to a crime may be charged with and convicted of the commission of the crime if: 1) the person directly commits the crime; 2) the person intentionally causes another to commit the crime under such circumstances that the other person is not guilty of the crime either in fact or because of legal incapacity; 3) the person intentionally aids or abets in the commission of the crime; or 4) the person intentionally advises, encourages, hires, counsels, or procures another to commit the crime (O.C.G.A. § 16-2-20).

In addition, any party to a crime may be indicted, tried, convicted, and punished for the commission of the crime, even if the party did not directly commit the crime, and even if the person who directly committed the crime was not prosecuted or convicted, or was acquitted (O.C.G.A. § 16-2-21).

Chapter 3 Defenses to Criminal Prosecutions

The State of Georgia recognizes numerous defenses to criminal prosecutions by providing definitions of the defenses and outlining the requirements for the acceptance of these defenses in statutes. An important concept with regards to a viable defense is "reasonable." The state does not specifically define this term, but leaves it up to the court or jury to determine if the defendant acted in a "reasonable" manner. However, the standard of "reasonable person" as defined in several U.S. Supreme Court cases is generally interpreted as what the average person would have done in the same situation as the defendant.

Minimum Age

In Georgia, a person cannot be held liable and found guilty of a crime unless he or she has reached the age of 13 at the time of the act, omission, or negligence constituting the crime (O.C.G.A. § 16-3-1).

Mental Capacity

There are several statutes dealing with the mental capacity of the accused at the time of the crime. The statutes provide the basis upon which to use the defense of insanity, providing that the accused was not able to distinguish between right and wrong in relation to the commission or omission of the criminal act, or the accused acted in a delusional compulsion because of a mental disease, injury, or congenital deficiency (O.C.G.A. §16-3-2/3).

Involuntary or Voluntary Intoxication

Under O.C.G.A. §16-3-4, a person will not be found guilty of a crime when, at the time of the crime, omission, or negligence, the person did not have sufficient mental capacity to distinguish between right from wrong because of involuntary intoxication. "Involuntary intoxication means intoxication caused by: 1) consumption of a substance through excusable ignorance; or 2) the coercion, fraud, artifice or contrivance of another person" (O.C.G.A. §16-3-4). However, the statute provides that voluntary intoxication will not be accepted as an excuse for any criminal act or omission.

Justified Conduct

The state provides for a person's conduct to be justified and excused, and a defense to a prosecution under certain circumstances: 1) when the use of force is justified in defending oneself or another, defending habitation or property other than habitation, or for entrapment, or coercion; 2) when the conduct is in reasonable fulfillment of duties as a government officer; 3) when the conduct is the reasonable discipline of a minor by parents; 4) when the conduct is reasonable and performed in making a lawful arrest; 5) when the conduct is justified for any other reason under the laws of the state; or 6) in other instances of reason and justice enumerated in this article (O.C.G.A. §16-3-20).

Use of Force in Defense of Persons

O.C.G.A. §16-3-21 provides specific details surrounding the use of force in the defense of self or others. According to this statute, a person is permitted to threaten use or to use force against another when he reasonably believes that the threat or use of force is necessary to defend himself or another against the imminent use of unlawful force. However, in regard to the use of deadly force, a person is justified in using force intended or likely to cause death or great bodily harm only if there is a reasonable belief that such force is necessary to prevent the death or great bodily injury to himself or another, or to prevent the commission of a forcible felony.

The statute also outlines that the use of force is not justified if the person using force initially provokes the use of force against himself; is attempting to commit, committing, or fleeing after the commission or attempted commission of a felony; or was the aggressor or engaged in combat by agreement, unless he effectively communicates his intent to withdraw from the encounter. In addition, if a defendant raises this defense to a prosecution for murder, the defendant may introduce, as evidence, prior victimization of family violence or child abuse, and relevant expert testimony of the prior victimization (O.C.G.A. § 16-3-21).

Use of Force in Defense of Habitation

Habitation is defined as "any dwelling, motor vehicle, or place of business" (O.C.G.A. § 16-3-24.1). According to O.C.G.A. § 16-3-23, a person is justified in threatening or using force against another when he or she reasonably believes such threat or force is necessary to prevent or terminate an unlawful entry into or attack upon a habitation. The use of force intended or likely to cause death or great bodily harm is justified only if: 1) the entry is made or attempted in a tumultuous manner and he or she reasonably believes the purpose of the entry is assaulting or offering personal violence to any person within the dwelling and the force is necessary to prevent the personal violence; 2) the force is used against another who is not a member of the family or household and who unlawfully and forcibly entered and the person using force knew or had reason to believe the entry was unlawful and forcible; or 3) the person using force reasonably believes the purpose of the entry or attempted entry is to commit a felony within the dwelling and the force is necessary to prevent the commission of the felony.

Use of Force in Defense of Property Other than Habitation

Personal property is defined as "personal property other than a motor vehicle" (O.C.G.A. § 16-3-24.1). A person is justified in threatening or using force against another when he reasonably believes such threat or force is necessary to prevent or terminate another's trespass on or criminal interference with real property other than habitation or personal property when the property is: 1) lawfully in his possession; 2) lawfully in the possession of a member of his immediate family; or 3) belonging to another whose property he has a legal duty to protect (O.C.G.A. § 16-3-24).

The statute also provides that the use of force intended to cause death or great bodily harm to prevent trespass on or criminal interference with real property other than habitation or personal property is not justified unless the person using the force reasonably believes such force is necessary to prevent the commission of a forcible felony (O.C.G.A. §16-3-24).

Use of Force Immunity Exception

The state recognizes the use of threats or deadly force to protect habitation and personal property, but grants immunity from criminal prosecution only to those persons who have a lawful right to carry or possess a deadly weapon (O.C.G.A. §16-3-24.2).

Entrapment

Entrapment is defined in the U.S. Supreme Court case of *Jacobson v. U.S.* (503 U.S. 540 [1992]) to consist of two parts: the actions of government agents and the predisposition of the defendant to commit the crime. Generally, the defense must show that government agents designed the crime and induced the defendant to commit a crime that he would not have committed without the government's inducement.

In O.C.G.A. §16-3-25, the state provides that a person is not guilty of a crime by entrapment if his conduct is induced or solicited by a government agent, officer, or employee for the purpose of obtaining evidence to be used in prosecuting the person for a crime. "Entrapment exists where the idea and intention of the commission of the crime originated with a government officer or employee, or with an agent of either, and he, by undue persuasion, incitement, or deceitful means, induced the accused to commit the act which the accused would not have committed except for the conduct of such officer" (O.C.G.A. §16-3-25).

Coercion

In O.C.G.A. §16-3-26, the state recognizes the role that coercion can play in the commission of a crime and provides that a person will not be found guilty of a crime, except murder, if the supposed crime is performed under such coercion that the person reasonably believes performing the crime is the only way to prevent his imminent death or great bodily injury.

Alibi

A defendant may provide an alibi for any criminal prosecution that shows the impossibility of his presence at the scene of the crime at the time of its commission. "The range of the evidence in respect to time and place must be such as reasonably to exclude the possibility of presence" (O.C.G.A. § 16-3-40).

Crimes in Georgia

Throughout Title 16, crimes are separated into Chapters. Each chapter contains the statutes for crimes that are similar in nature. The following includes definitions and discussions of the most prevalent crimes committed in Georgia.

Chapter 4 Criminal Attempt, Conspiracy, and Solicitation

The State of Georgia recognizes that the commission of a crime does not have to completed. The state provides several statutes that criminalize steps taken toward the commission of a crime, even if the crime was not completed.

O.C.G.A. § 16-4-1 provides that any person commits the offense of criminal attempt when he has intent to commit a specific crime and he takes any action that constitutes a substantial step toward the commission of the crime. Criminal solicitation is charged when a person solicits, requests, commands, importunes, or otherwise attempts to cause another person to engage in conduct that would constitute a felony (O.C.G.A. § 16-4-7). Conspiracy to commit a crime is charged when a person, together with one or more persons, conspires to commit a crime and at least one person performs an overt act toward the commission of the crime (O.C.G.A. § 16-4-8).

Domestic terrorism is also included in this chapter, and is defined as any violation or attempt to violate any laws of this state or the United States which: 1) is intended or reasonably likely to injure or kill ten individuals or more; 2) is intended to intimidate the civilian population of this state, political subdivisions, or the United States; 3) is intended to alter, change, or coerce, by intimidation or coercion, the policy of the government of this state or political subdivisions; or 4) is intended the affect the conduct of the government or political subdivisions by use of destructive devices, assassination, or kidnapping (O.C.G.A. § 16-4-10).

Chapter 5 Crimes Against the Person

This chapter delineates both felony and misdemeanor crimes that are committed against a person. Article 1 involves Homicide, which provides statutes for murder, voluntary manslaughter, involuntary manslaughter, and assisting or offering to assist in the commission of a suicide. Murder is punished by life in prison or death, while voluntary manslaughter receives one to 20 years in prison, involuntary manslaughter receives one to ten years in prison, and assisting suicide receives one to ten years (O.C.G.A. § 16-5-1/2/3/5).

Article 2 involves Assault and Battery, and provides statutes for simple assault, aggravated assault, simple battery, battery, and aggravated battery. The "simple" crimes are misdemeanors. When committed against a person 65 years of age or older, in a public transit vehicle or station, or against a current or former family member, then the crime becomes a misdemeanor of high and aggravated nature. Battery moves from misdemeanor to felony upon the third or subsequent conviction, while the "aggravated" crimes are felonies (O.C.G.A. § 16-5-20/21/23/23.1/24).

Article 3 involves Kidnapping, False Imprisonment, Hijacking an Aircraft, Hijacking of Motor Vehicle, and Interference with Custody. Because of the possibility of severe injury or death to the victims, kidnapping and hijacking an aircraft are both eligible for a sentence of death or life in prison. Hijacking a motor vehicle is distinctive in that the offense cannot be merged with any other offense and the punishment may not be deferred, suspended, or probated. Interference with custody becomes a felony on the third and subsequent conviction (O.C.G.A. § 16-5-40/41/44/44.1/45).

Article 4 involves Reckless Conduct on the part of the offender. The statutes criminalize sexual behaviors by an individual who is HIV positive without disclosure to his or her sexual partners, with a punishment of five to 20 years. Hazing of students in any school, college, or university within the state carries a punishment as a misdemeanor of a high and aggravated nature (O.C.G.A. § 16-5-60/61).

Article 5 involves Cruelty to Children, which includes tattooing of children, body piercing of children, reckless abandonment of a child, and the manufacturing of methamphetamine in the presence of a child. For this section, a child is considered to be under the age of 18. The cruelty to children statute includes subjecting a child to excessive physical or mental pain or depriving the child of necessary sustenance to jeopardize the child's health or well-being. The statute also provides that cruelty to children can involve allowing a child to witness the commission of a forcible felony, battery, or family violence battery. Cruelty to children, reckless abandonment, and methamphetamine manufacturing are punished as felonies, while tattooing and body piercing are punished as misdemeanors (O.C.G.A. § 16-5-70/71/71.1/72/73).

Article 6 involves Feticide, which is the killing of an unborn child by any injury to the mother, which would be murder if the act resulted in the death of the mother. The punishment is life in prison (O.C.G.A. §16-5-80). Article 7 involves Stalking, which includes stalking that is punished as a misdemeanor and aggravated stalking (a felony), as well as provisions for obtaining restraining orders and felony punishments for violations of family violence orders (O.C.G.A. §16-5-90/91/94/95).

Chapter 6 Sexual Offenses

This chapter delineates both misdemeanor and felony crimes that contain a sexual component. The crimes are varied in nature, and include sexual activities between consenting partners. Children under the age of 16 are not able to consent to any type of sexual activity. The statutes are: rape; sodomy and aggravated sodomy; statutory rape; child molestation and aggravated child molestation; enticing a child for indecent purposes; sexual assault; bestiality; necrophilia; public indecency; prostitution; keeping a place of prostitution; pimping; pandering and pandering by compulsion; solicitation of sodomy; masturbation for hire; unlawful practice of massage; fornication; adultery; bigamy and marrying a bigamist; incest; sexual battery; unlawful publication of name or identity (to protect the victim of rape); and loitering and related activities (O.C.G.A. §16-6).

Chapter 7 Damage to and Intrusion Upon Property

This chapter involves crimes against property. Article 1 Burglary includes entering a house, building, vehicle, railroad car, watercraft, aircraft, or other such structure with intent to commit a felony or theft, with a punishment of one to 20 years, and increasing punishments for subsequent convictions (O.C.G.A. §16-7-1).

Article 2 involves Criminal Trespass and Damage to Property, which includes both misdemeanors and felonies. The crimes of criminal trespass (including defacing any military monument, memorial or grave), interference with government property, damaging mailboxes and mail, damaging wildfire equipment, and littering are punished as misdemeanors. The crimes of possession of tools for the commission of a crime, criminal damage to property (first and second degrees), vandalism to a place of worship, tampering with the operation of an electronic monitoring device, and dumping in prohibited areas are punished as felonies (O.C.G.A. §16-7-20 through 16-7-29 and O.C.G.A. §16-7-43/52).

Article 3 involves Arson, which is separated into three degrees (with first degree receiving one to 20 years in prison, second degree receiving one to ten years in prison, and third degree receiving one to five years in prison) (O.C.G.A. §16-7-60/61/62). Article 4 involves Bombs, Explosives, and Chemical and Biological Weapons. The statutes identify destructive devices, hoax devices, obstruction of safety officials, and terrorism, all of which are felonies except hoax devices (unless used to obtain property or interfere with the business of another, which raises the offense to a felony) (O.C.G.A. § 16-7-80 through 16-7-97).

Chapter 8 Offenses Involving Theft

The chapter is divided into four articles. Article 1 defines Theft and includes: theft by taking; theft by deception; theft by conversion; theft of services; theft of lost or mislaid property; theft by receiving stolen property; theft by receiving stolen property in another state; theft by bringing stolen property into the state; theft of trade secret; theft by shoplifting; illegal use of payments received for real property improvements; theft by extortion; fraudulent retail sales receipts or Universal Product Code labels; entering a motor vehicle with intent to commit a felony or theft; livestock theft; and removing or abandoning of shopping carts. The majority of theft statutes are defined as misdemeanors, with the property value of the stolen item(s) determining the increase to felony (O.C.G.A. § 16-8-1 through 16-8-21).

Article 2 involves Robbery, which is defined as taking the property of another from the person or immediate presence of the person by use of force or intimidation, by putting the person in fear of immediate serious bodily injury, or by sudden snatching. The punishment for robbery is one to 20 years, but if the victim is 65 year of age or older, then the minimum sentence is five years (O.C.G.A. § 16-8-40). Armed robbery, with the presence of an offensive weapon, carries a punishment of ten years to a sentence of death (O.C.G.A. § 16-8-41). Unlike theft, robbery is always a felony and the level of punishment does not depend on the value of items taken.

Article 3 involves the reproduction and sale of recorded material (including sounds or visual images on a phonograph record, disc, wire, tape, videotape, or film), without consent of the owner, a felony, and film piracy, a felony on second and subsequent convictions (O.C.G.A. § 16-6-60/62). Article 4 involves motor vehicle chop shops (the dismantling of stolen vehicles and selling the parts), and includes the seizure of property used or possessed in a chop shop operation. All are felonies punished by one to ten years in prison (O.C.G.A. § 16-8-80 through 16-8-86).

Chapter 9 Forgery and Fraudulent Practices

This chapter contains eight articles whose statutes involve misdemeanors and felonies for the following crimes related to forgery and fraud: forgery; false identification; counterfeit insurance; fraud by judiciary against the elderly; deposit account fraud; financial transaction card theft, forgery, and fraud; fraudulently obtaining goods, services, and discount transportation tickets; deceptive business practices; false statements by telephone solicitors; fraudulently obtaining public housing benefits; pretense of being a representative of a peace officer or fire service organization; foreclosure fraud; unauthorized removal of identifying items from animals; computer crimes; selling or transferring motor vehicles that do not meet federal standards; faulty airbag installation; and financial identify fraud. The difference between misdemeanor and felony relies on the extent of the forgery or fraud on the victim, and repeat or subsequent convictions for the same offense (e.g., false identification constitutes a felony on the second and subsequent convictions) (O.C.G.A. § 16-9).

Chapter 10 Offenses Against Public Administration

This chapter relates to offenses committed by and against government officials. Article 1 involves Abuse of Governmental Office. Felony offenses include the violation of terms of oath of office, bribery, acceptance or solicitation of anything of value in return for influence of legislative action or the action of any other officer or employee, and making or giving false official certificates or writings. Misdemeanors include making false acknowledgments, certificates, or statements of appearance or oath, and holding office while being employed in more than one branch of government (O.C.G.A. § 16-10-1 through 16-10-9).

Article 2 involves Obstruction of Public Administration, which means obstructing public officials in their official duties and responsibilities. Felony offenses include falsifying statements; impersonating an officer; obstructing or hindering law enforcement officers, firefighters, or emergency medical technicians; concealing a person's death; attempting to murder or threatening a witness in an official proceeding; and taking a law enforcement officer's weapon. Misdemeanor offenses include obstructing an emergency telephone call; giving false identify information to a law enforcement officer; giving or causing a false report of a crime; transmitting a false report of a fire; transmitting a false public alarm; requesting ambulance service when it is not needed; and refusing to move at the request of a peace officer or firefighter (O.C.G.A. § 16-10-20 through 16-10-33).

Article 3 involves Escape and offenses related to confinement. Felony offenses include escape (specifically, escape after being convicted of a felony or charged with a felony but in lawful confinement, or escape while armed with a dangerous weapon); hindering the apprehension or punishment of a criminal; bail jumping if charged with or convicted of a felony; helping or permitting a person in custody to escape; mutiny by a person in lawful custody of a penal institution (assails, opposes, or resists an officer of the law of such penal institution with intent to cause serious bodily injury); and violence while in confinement. Misdemeanor offenses include escape by anyone not charged as a felony and bail jumping if charged with or convicted of a misdemeanor (O.C.G.A. § 16-10-50 through 16-10-56).

Article 4 involves Perjury and False Swearing. Perjury is defined as making a false statement while under oath in a judicial proceeding, while false swearing is making a false statement while under oath in any other official proceeding. Both constitute a felony (O.C.G.A. § 16-10-70/71). Article 5 involves other offenses related to the judiciary. Felony offenses include embracery (influencing the vote of a juror), threatening or bribing a witness, tampering with evidence in a felony case, impersonating another person in legal proceedings, and threatening or injuring jurors or court officers. Misdemeanor offenses include tampering with evidence in a misdemeanor case and destroying, altering, or falsifying medical records (O.C.G.A. § 16-10-90 through 16-10-98).

Chapter 11 Offenses Against Public Order and Safety

This chapter involves those offenses that directly affect the safety and security of citizens of the state and local jurisdictions. Article 1 defines the crimes of treason, insurrection, advocating the overthrow of the government, and sedition. All of these crimes are felonies, with a treason conviction being eligible for the death penalty.

Article 2 provides a range of misdemeanor and misdemeanor of high and aggravated nature offenses against public order. The offenses include: riot; inciting to riot; unlawful assembly; affray; disruption of a lawful meeting; disruption of a legislative meeting or activities within the state capital area; failing to leave a public school or university campus or facility when directed; loitering or prowling; terrorist threats via computer or computer network; concealing identity by wearing a mask, hood, or other device; using obscene or abusive language or engaging in indecent or disorderly conduct; making harassing telephone calls; criminal defamation; public intoxication; refusing to relinquish a telephone party line in an emergency; obstructing streets or other public passages; and keeping and maintaining a disorderly house (O.C.G.A. § 16-11-30 through 16-11-44).

The only identified felonies in Article 2 are terroristic threat and terroristic act. A terroristic threat occurs when a person threatens to commit any crime of violence, to release any hazardous substance, to burn or damage property with the intent to terrorize another, or to cause the evacuation of a building, place of assembly, or public transportation with reckless disregard for causing terror or inconvenience. A terroristic act is defined as using a burning or flaming cross or symbol to terrorize another's household, throwing an object at a conveyance (vehicle), releasing any hazardous substance to terrorize another, or causing the evacuation of a building, place of assembly, or public transportation with reckless disregard for causing terror or inconvenience. A conviction for terroristic threat is punished by one to five years in prison, while a conviction for terroristic act is punished by one to ten years in prison. However, if a victim of the terroristic act suffers a serious physical injury as a direct result of the act, the offender shall be punished by five to 40 years in prison (O.C.G.A. § 16-11-37).

Article 3 involves the Invasions of Privacy. All of the statutes are classified as felony, with punishment from one to five years in prison. The offenses include: peeping tom, eavesdropping and clandestine surveillance, and possessing or selling eavesdropping devices. Other statutes provide guidelines for the use of eavesdropping, wiretapping, and surveillance devices by law enforcement officers, and the emergency authorization for the surveillance and interception of communications (O.C.G.A. § 16-11-60 through 16-11-69).

Article 4, Dangerous Instrumentalities and Practices, contains six parts, each extensively providing definitions, guidelines, and punishments for both felony and misdemeanor offenses involving firearms and other dangerous weapons. These include selling and furnishing weapons to minors; licensing restrictions for hunting and possession of firearms; possession of dangerous weapons such as sawed-off shotguns and machine guns; carrying and possessing concealed weapons; and unlawful training with and making of dangerous weapons. Article 4 also describes the enhanced penalties for possession of dangerous weapons during crimes and the Brady Bill regulations (O.C.G.A. § 16-11-100 through 16-11-184).

Several examples of specific statutes in Article 4 are as follows. O.C.G.A. § 16-11-105 makes it illegal to willfully or wantonly discharge a firearm on Sunday, unless the person is in defense of persons or property, is a law enforcement officer, is on an approved firing range, or is legally hunting. This offense is punished as a misdemeanor. O.C.G.A. § 16-11-107 makes it a felony to intentionally destroy or cause serious or debilitating physical injury to a police dog or police horse, with a punishment of one to five years in prison. O.C.G.A. § 16-11-127.1 makes it illegal to carry or possess a firearm within 1,000 feet of any real property of an elementary, secondary, or postsecondary school or campus (school safety zone), unless the person is licensed to carry a weapon and is only dropping off or picking up children, or the weapon is in a locked container within a vehicle on school property. Punishments include a sentence of two to ten years in prison, with an enhanced punishment of five to ten years in prison if the weapon is defined as dangerous or is a machine gun. O.C.G.A. § 16-11-160, in addition to making it illegal to possess dangerous weapons, provides that it is unlawful to wear a bulletproof vest during the commission or attempted commission of any crime which carries a punishment of life imprisonment, any felony involving controlled substances or marijuana, or trafficking in cocaine, illegal drugs, marijuana, or methamphetamine. Punishment is five years in prison to run consecutively to any other sentence.

Chapter 12 Offenses Against Public Health and Morals

This chapter contains seven articles. Felony and misdemeanor statutes identify and define behaviors related to various activities that are seen as detrimental to public welfare and in need of regulation. The statutes include provisions concerning cruelty to animals; unlawful tattooing; contributing to the delinquency, unruliness, or deprivation of a minor; smoking tobacco in public places; gambling and bingo; distribution of obscene material; sexually explicit conduct by minors; Computer Pornography and Child Exploitation Prevention Act of 1999; furnishing harmful materials to minors; unlawful acts in public transportation; transportation passenger safety; abortion; human body trafficking; and distributing to or possession of cigarettes and tobacco by minors (O.C.G.A. § 16-12-1 through 16-12-176).

Chapter 13 Controlled Substances

This chapter identifies and defines a controlled substance as being a drug, substance, or immediate precursor in Schedules I through V. The State of Georgia follows the definitions established by the Code of Federal Regulations (Title 21 C.F.R. Section 1308) when presenting the drugs identified in the various schedules. The statutes delineate the illegal manufacturing, distribution, trafficking, and sale of the identified drugs and drug-related objects, and describe the enhanced punishments of seizure and forfeiture of property. Also defined in the chapter are all of the more than 1,000 drugs listed as "dangerous" by the General Assembly, including those that are, by federal law, available by prescription only (O.C.G.A. § 16-13).

Chapter 15 Street Gang Terrorism and Prevention

This chapter is relatively new when compared to others in Title 16, having been enacted and revised in the last 30 years. The purpose of the chapter is to identify what it means to be involved in a criminal street gang and to provide punishments for the criminal activities of street gangs and their members. The chapter also defines a pattern of criminal gang activity as the commission, attempted commission, or conspiracy, solicitation, coercion, or intimidation of another to commit at least two of the following offenses, provided at least one occurred after July 1, 1998 and the last within three years: 1) racketeering activity; 2) stalking; 3) rape, aggravated sodomy, statutory rape, or aggravated sexual battery; 4) escape or other offenses related to confinement; 5) dangerous instrumentalities or practices; 6) security of state or county correctional facilities; or 7) aiding or encouraging a child to escape from custody (O.C.G.A. § 16-15-3).

Another purpose for the creation of the Street Gang Terrorism and Prevention Act and subsequent statute is to provide enhanced punishments for those engaged in street gangs. Any person found guilty of violating any provision of these statutes (which includes being employed by or associated with a street gang, deriving proceeds from street gang activity, encouraging or soliciting participation of others in the street gang, threatening injury or damage to the person or property of anyone who assists another to withdraw from the street gang, or threatening injury or damage to the person or property of another who withdraws from the street gang), shall be punished, in addition to any other penalty imposed by law, from one to ten years in prison. Any person who is convicted of occupying a position of organizer, supervisory position, or any other position of management in a criminal street gang, in addition to any other penalty imposed by law, shall be punished by imprisonment for an additional ten years. Furthermore, any crime committed in this code section is considered a separate offense (O.C.G.A. § 16-15-4).

Other specific crimes not listed here may be found within other portions of the above chapters, within the remaining chapters of Title 16, or within other titles provided in the Official Code of Georgia.

Conclusion

The State of Georgia is very active in its enactment of legislation that promotes safety and security among its citizens. The Georgia Constitution of 1983 defines treason, the only specific crime listed in the document. This leaves the remainder of the identifying, defining, and enacting of criminal laws to the General Assembly and local legislatures. State statutes and local ordinances are written and published in various formats and available for everyone to read and review, which is why ignorance of the law is in most cases not an acceptable defense to a criminal prosecution in Georgia and elsewhere in the country. Legislation is also in constant motion, periodically and sometimes yearly being reviewed, updated, and amended, as circumstances in the state and local communities dictate.

Chapter Review Questions

1. Explain how state statutes and local ordinances are created in the State of Georgia.
2. Discuss the defenses to criminal prosecution.
3. Describe the justifications for the use of force in defense of persons and property.
4. Define the term crime, including definitions for felony and misdemeanor.
5. Explain the types of crimes identified as against the person and the types of crimes identified as against property.

References

City of Kingsland, GA. (2011). Sec. 3-36 Outdoor Advertising.

City of Suwanee, GA. (2011). Sec. 6-67 Distance Requirements.

GeorgiaInfo. (2011). Passing a Law in the Georgia General Assembly. Retrieved from: http://georgiainfo.galileo.usg.edu.

New Georgia Encyclopedia. (2011a). Georgia General Assembly. Retrieved from: http://www.georgiaencyclopedia.org.

New Georgia Encyclopedia. (2011b). Georgia's City Governments. Retrieved from: http://www.georgiaencyclopedia.org.

New Georgia Encyclopedia. (2011c). Georgia's County Governments. Retrieved from: http://www.georgiaencyclopedia.org.

O.C.G.A. § 16-1. (2011). General Provisions. Official Code of Georgia Annotated.

O.C.G.A. § 16-2. (2011). Criminal Liability. Official Code of Georgia Annotated.

O.C.G.A. § 16-3. (2011). Defenses to Criminal Liability. Official Code of Georgia Annotated.

O.C.G.A. § 16-4. (2011). Criminal Attempt, Conspiracy and Solicitation. Official Code of Georgia Annotated.

O.C.G.A. § 16-5. (2011). Crimes Against the Person. Official Code of Georgia Annotated.

O.C.G.A. § 16-6. (2011). Sexual Offenses. Official Code of Georgia Annotated.

O.C.G.A. § 16-7. (2011). Damage to and Intrusion Upon Property. Official Code of Georgia Annotated.

O.C.G.A. § 16-8. (2011). Offenses Involving Theft. Official Code of Georgia Annotated.

O.C.G.A. § 16-9. (2011). Forgery and Fraudulent Practices. Official Code of Georgia Annotated.

O.C.G.A. § 16-10. (2011). Offenses Against Public Administration. Official Code of Georgia Annotated.

O.C.G.A. § 16-11. (2011). Offenses Against Public Order and Safety. Official Code of Georgia Annotated.

O.C.G.A. § 16-12. (2011). Offenses Against Public Health and Morals. Official Code of Georgia Annotated.

O.C.G.A. § 16-13. (2011). Controlled Substances. Official Code of Georgia Annotated.

O.C.G.A. § 16-14. (2011). Racketeer Influenced Corrupt Organizations. Official Code of Georgia Annotated.

O.C.G.A. § 16-15. (2011). Street Gang and Terrorism Prevention. Official Code of Georgia Annotated.

O.C.G.A. § 16-16. (2011). Forfeiture of Property Used in Burglary or Armed Robbery. Official Code of Georgia Annotated.

O.C.G.A. § 16-17. (2011). Unlawful Loans. Official Code of Georgia Annotated.

CHAPTER 4

CRIME VICTIMS IN GEORGIA

Learning Objectives

After reading the chapter, students will be able to:

- Explain the purpose for the Criminal Justice Coordinating Council.
- Discuss the provisions of the Georgia Crime Victims' Bill of Rights.
- Define the term victim and identify what acts constitute a crime under the Crime Victims' Bill of Rights.
- Explain victims' rights in the Juvenile Justice System.
- Identify the provisions of the Victim Information Program (VIP) and the Victim Impact Statements (VIS).
- Discuss the services provided by the Victim-Witness Advocacy Office.
- Explain the Georgia Sex Offender Registry, including history and legislation.
- Explain the role of the Georgia Bureau of Investigation (GBI) and local sheriffs with the Sex Offender Registry.

Key Terms

Crime
Crime Victims' Bill of Rights
Crime Victims Compensation
   Program
Criminal Justice Coordinating
   Council
Georgia Bureau of Investigation
Juvenile Justice System
Office of Victim Services

Sex Offender Registry
State Board of Pardons
   and Paroles
Victim
Victim Impact Statement
Victim Information Program
Victim Notification
Victim-Witness Advocacy Office

Crime victims in Georgia are no different than victims in any other juris-diction in the United States. All victims have suffered a decrease in well-being, physically, emotionally, and/or psychologically, and are in need of assistance. In Georgia, the General Assembly, as well as numerous community and state organizations, have recognized these needs and have created legislation, edu-cation, training, and service initiatives to assist victims of all types of crime in healing and restoring their lives.

Georgia Criminal Justice Coordinating Council

The Criminal Justice Coordinating Council (CJCC) was established by the Georgia General Assembly in 1981 (and assigned to the Georgia Bureau of In-vestigation for administrative purposes) "as the agency responsible for ongo-ing planning, policy development and coordination of the diverse criminal justice stakeholders." The Council is comprised of "a 24-member board charged with coordinating, researching and policy making regarding the justice sys-tem in Georgia" (Criminal Justice Coordinating Council [CJCC], 2011). The legislative intent for the Council is found in O.C.G.A. §35-6A-1, which stip-ulates that "the General Assembly finds that the high incidence of crime in Georgia is detrimental to the general welfare of the state and its citizens and that criminal justice efforts must be better coordinated, intensified, and made more effective in all components of the system and at all levels of government."

As defined in O.C.G.A. §35-6A-7, the functions of the Council include preparing, publishing, and disseminating fundamental criminal justice infor-mation; serving as a statewide clearinghouse for criminal justice information and research; maintaining a research program to identify criminal justice is-sues and effective solutions; coordinating with criminal justice agencies to de-velop legislative proposals; serving in an advisory capacity to the governor; coordinating high visibility criminal justice research projects; convening statewide criminal justice conferences; coordinating criminal justice agencies to improve the state's response to crime and its effects; administering grants; and devel-oping rules that govern approval of victim assistance programs. O.C.G.A. §35-6A-8 stipulates that the authority of the Council is limited in that it cannot perform any function assigned to the governor, attorney general, or local or state prosecuting or investigatory agencies.

One major aspect of the Council is the administration of the Georgia Crime Victims Compensation Program (CVCP). The CVCP was created to assist vic-tims and families "through the emotional and physical aftermath of a crime by easing the monetary impact placed upon them by providing financial benefits for expenses such as medical bills, loss of earnings, funeral expenses, mental health counseling, and crime scene clean-up" (CJCC, 2011). The requirements to be eligible for compensation from the CVCP are:

- you are physically injured as a result of a violent crime;
- you personally witnessed or were threatened with a violent crime;
- you were hurt helping a victim of a violent crime;
- you are the parent or guardian of a person killed or injured as a result of a crime;
- you are a dependent of a homicide victim who relied on the victim for support;
- you did not provoke or consent to the events that led up to the crime;
- the victim/witness must have reported the crime to the proper authorities within 72 hours of the crime, unless good cause is shown; and
- the victim/witness must file an application within one year of the crime unless good cause is shown (CJCC, 2011).

Although the CVCP provides monetary compensation, it is not an entitlement program and is considered a payer of last resort (benefits not covered by a third-party payer). Applicants will be screened to determine if all eligibility requirements are met. The maximum amount of compensation is $25,000 per victim. The maximum amount per category is: $15,000 for medical/dental expenses, $3,000 for counseling expenses, $3,000 for funeral expenses, $10,000 for economic support, and $1,500 for crime scene clean-up. In 2009, 316 crime victims processed claims to the CVCP, receiving awards totaling $965,177 (CJCC, 2011).

In addition to monetary compensation, under O.C.G.A. § 17-5-72, victims of sexual assault are entitled to a free forensic medical examination. The CVCP is billed for all expenses related to the forensic medical examination, including lab work, emergency room fees, physician fees, nurse fees, and all clinical fees associated with the examination (CJCC, 2011).

The Victim Services Division of the Council was created to be an advocate for victims, providing information and education on victim services and programs, on victim's legal rights, and on the criminal justice system as a whole. The primary function of the Division is to provide financial assistance to eligible victims who have applied to the CVCP for assistance. In addition, the Division administers the DUI Memorial Fund, the Victims Unclaimed Restitution Program, and the Advocate Service Program (CJCC, 2011).

The Council also provides victims with information on local and state victim organizations, many identified with specific crimes so victims may have a direct link to individuals and organizations who can provide immediate assistance. These include the Georgia Coalition Against Domestic Violence, Children's Advocacy Centers of Georgia, Georgia Network to End Sexual Assault, Parents of Murdered Children, Mothers Against Drunk Driving, and many more (CJCC, 2011).

The Council is active, on behalf of the state, in securing and disseminating federal grants for funding programs and services for crime victims. The Council serves as the state administering agency for numerous federal grant programs, with the obligation to ensure funds are adequately and appropriately disseminated and all requirements for the grant are met. In 2009, the CVCP applied for and was awarded $1,015,976 from the Recovery Act Victims of Crime Act/Victim Compensation Formula Grant Funds. The purpose of these funds is to assist the state with providing financial assistance to victims of crime. Through the Grant Programs of the Recovery Act of 2009, the Council administered the Edward Byrne Memorial Justice Assistance Grant, which provided $36.2 million; the STOP Violence Against Women Act (VAWA), which provided $3.97 million; and the Victims of Crime Act Victim Assistance (VOCA), which provided $1.1 million (CJCC, 2011).

Georgia Crime Victims' Bill of Rights

The General Assembly enacted the Crime Victims' Bill of Rights in 1995, presented in Title 17, Chapter 17 of the Official Code of Georgia Annotated (O.C.G.A.). According to O.C.G.A. § 17-17-1, "the General Assembly hereby finds and declares it to be the policy of this state that victims of crimes should be accorded certain basic rights just as the accused are accorded certain basic rights. These rights include:

(1) The right to reasonable, accurate, and timely notice of any scheduled court proceedings or any changes to such proceedings;

(2) The right to reasonable, accurate, and timely notice of the arrest, release, or escape of the accused;

(3) The right not to be excluded from any scheduled court proceedings, except as provided in this chapter or as otherwise required by law;

(4) The right to be heard at any scheduled court proceedings involving the release, plea, or sentencing of the accused;

(5) The right to file a written objection in any parole proceedings involving the accused;

(6) The right to confer with the prosecuting attorney in any criminal prosecution related to the victim;

(7) The right to restitution as provided by law;

(8) The right to proceedings free from unreasonable delay; and

(9) The right to be treated fairly and with dignity by all criminal justice agencies involved in the case."

Definitions of Victim and Crime

The Crime Victims' Bill of Rights also defines key terms. For example, a victim, as defined in O.C.G.A. §17-17-3, is:

"(A) A person against whom a crime has been perpetrated or has al-legedly been perpetrated; or

(B) In the event of the death of the crime victim, the following relations if the relation is not either in custody for an offense or the defendant:
   (i) The spouse;
   (ii) An adult child if division (i) does not apply;
   (iii) A parent if divisions (i) and (ii) do not apply;
   (iv) A sibling if divisions (i) through (iii) do not apply; or
   (v) A grandparent if divisions (i) through (iv) do not apply; or

(C) A parent, guardian, or custodian of a crime victim who is a minor or a legally incapacitated person except if such parent, guardian, or custodian is in custody for an offense or is the defendant."

For purposes of the Crime Victims' Bill of Rights, a crime is defined as any of the following acts or related components of the acts as they appear in Georgia statutes O.C.G.A. §16-5, §16-6, §16-7-1, §16-7-3, §16-7-4, §16-8-1, §16-8-2, §16-9, §16-12-3.3, §30-5-8, §40-6-393, §40-6-393.1, and §40-6-394:

- murder, voluntary manslaughter, involuntary manslaughter, feticide
- simple assault, aggravated assault, simple battery, battery, aggravated battery, female genital mutilation, assault or battery on an unborn child, sexual battery, aggravated sexual battery
- kidnapping, false imprisonment, highjacking an aircraft or motor vehicle, interference with custody, trafficking of persons for labor or sexual servitude
- reckless conduct, hazing
- cruelty to children, reckless abandonment

- stalking, aggravated stalking, restraining orders
- cruelty to person 65 years of age or older
- rape, aggravated sodomy, statutory rape
- child molestation, aggravated child molestation, enticing a child for indecent purposes
- bestiality, necrophilia, public indecency
- prostitution, pimping, pandering, solicitation
- fornication, adultery, bigamy, incest
- burglary, arson, bombs, explosives, chemical or biological weapons
- theft, robbery
- forgery, deposit account fraud, illegal use of financial transaction cards, fraud, removal of identification from property, computer crimes, spam email, Internet and email fraud, identify fraud, computer security
- sale or distribution of harmful material to minors
- abuse, neglect, or exploitation of a disabled adult or elder person
- homicide or feticide by vehicle, serious injury by vehicle (O.C.G.A. § 17-17-3).

Notification to Victims

Notification is defined as a written notice or a documented effort to contact the victim by telephone or other means. Prompt notification is further defined as providing the victim with information as soon as practically possible. This allows the victim a meaningful opportunity to exercise his or her rights (O.C.G.A. § 17-17-3). In addition, law enforcement officers and court personnel throughout the state are required to provide victims, at the point of initial contact, with the following information, written in plain language: the possibility of pretrial release of the accused, the victim's rights (Crime Victims' Bill of Rights), the victim's role in the various stages of the criminal justice process, the means by which additional information can be obtained, the availability of victim compensation, and the availability of community-based victim service programs (O.C.G.A. § 17-17-6).

Several specific sections of the Georgia Crime Victims' Bill of Rights pertain to notification to victims of certain procedures occurring and/or of information pertaining to the offender. O.C.G.A. § 17-17-14 makes the victim who desires notification responsible for providing a current address and telephone number to the investigating law enforcement agency, the prosecuting attorney, the custodial authority, and the State Board of Pardons and Paroles. The victim's information provided for the purpose of notification is confidential and not subject to disclosure under public records.

O.C.G.A. §17-17-5

This statute ensures notification to the victim of the accused's arrest, the accused's release from custody, any judicial proceeding at which the release of the accused will be considered, an escape by the accused, and whether the accused violates conditions of an electronic release and monitoring program. In addition, notification is subject to the victim providing a current address and phone number to the appropriate criminal justice agency or custodial authority.

O.C.G.A. §17-17-5.1

This statute provides that if the accused is committed to the Department of Behavioral Health and Developmental Disabilities, the department must provide the victim with a written notice at least ten days before the release or discharge of the accused. In addition, immediate written notification must be sent to the victim after an escape or subsequent readmission of the accused. The notification is subject to the written request of the victim to be so notified.

O.C.G.A. §17-17-7

This statute provides that the investigating law enforcement agency will provide prompt notification to the victim of the accused's arrest. The prosecuting attorney, whenever possible, will notify the victim prior to any proceeding in which the release of the accused is considered, and will offer the victim the opportunity to express his or her opinion on the release of the accused pending judicial proceedings. In addition, whenever possible, the custodial authority shall provide prompt notification by telephone to the victim of the release of the accused from custody. The victim also has the right to file a complaint with the prosecuting attorney regarding the release of the accused if the victim or the victim's immediate family has received threats of physical violence or intimidation by the accused.

O.C.G.A. §17-17-8

This statute requires that the prosecuting attorney, upon initial contact with the victim, give prompt notification to the victim of the procedural steps in processing a criminal case, the rights and procedures of victims in the case, suggested procedures if the victim is subjected to threats or intimidation, the names and telephone numbers of contact persons in the prosecutor's office and the custodial authority, and the names and telephone numbers of contact persons in the investigating agency. If the victim provides the prosecuting attorney with a written request, prompt advance notification will be given for any scheduled court proceedings. If the victim is going to seek restitution, the victim must provide the prosecuting attorney with his or her own contact information and contact information for a secondary person. The prosecuting attorney will forward all information to the Department of Corrections, Department of Juvenile Justice, or the State Board of Pardons and Paroles, as applicable, if an order of restitution is entered.

O.C.G.A. § 17-17-12

This statute requires that the prosecuting attorney, upon the written request of the victim, provide notification to the victim of the following:

- if the accused has filed a motion for a new trial, an appeal of conviction, or an extraordinary motion for a new trial;
- if the accused has been released on bail or other recognizance pending the disposition of the motion or appeal;
- the time and place of any appellate court proceedings related to the motion or appeal; and
- the result of the motion or appeal.

In addition, the Attorney General, in cases in which the accused is convicted and sentenced to death, shall notify the victim (upon written request) of the following:

- the filing and disposition of appeals, including a writ of habeas corpus, and the time and place of proceedings; and
- the status of all pending appeals and other litigation every six months until the case is resolved.

O.C.G.A. § 17-17-13

This statute requires the State Board of Pardons and Paroles to provide the victim with 20 days' advance notification whenever it considers a final decision to grant parole or other manner of executive clemency action to release a defendant for a period exceeding 60 days. The Board must also allow the victim with an opportunity to file a written objection. The victim must express to the Board a desire for such notification and provide a current address and telephone number.

Victims' Rights in Dealing with Defendants

The Georgia Crime Victims' Bill of Rights also includes several statutes that pertain to the interaction of the victim with the defendant and/or defense attorney.

O.C.G.A. § 17-17-8.1

This statute regulates the procedures for a victim to be interviewed by the defense. The victim does has the right to refuse to be interviewed by the accused or the accused's attorney or agent. It is the responsibility of the prosecuting attorney to advise the victim of this right to refusal. If, however, the victim agrees to be interviewed, the victim may set the conditions for the interview as he or she desires. "Conditions may include, but shall not be limited to, the time, date, and location of the interview, what other persons may be present during the interview, any security arrangements for the interview, and whether or not the interview may be recorded." The victim also has the right to terminate the interview at any time and the right to refuse to answer any question during the interview. In addition, the accused, the accused's attorney or agent cannot contact the victim in an unreasonable manner, and if the victim has indicated a desire not to be contacted, no contact shall be made.

O.C.G.A. § 17-17-9

This statute affords the victim the right to be present at all criminal proceedings in which the accused has the right to be present. "A victim or member of the immediate family of a victim shall not be excluded from any portion of any hearing, trial, or proceeding pertaining to the offense based solely on the fact that such person is subpoenaed to testify" unless the court finds there is a substantial probability that the victim's presence will impair the conduct of a fair trial. In addition, the victim has the right to be placed in a room separate from the accused, the family of the accused, and the witnesses for the accused.

O.C.G.A. § 17-17-9.1

This statute provides that all communications between a victim and victim assistance personnel appointed by a prosecuting attorney, including notes, memoranda or other records, shall be considered attorney work and privilege information, and not subject to disclosure.

O.C.G.A. § 17-17-10

This statute affords the court the ability to require all court personnel, including the defense counsel, not to disclose the victim's current address, telephone number, or place of employment to the defendant.

O.C.G.A. § 17-17-11

This statute requires the prosecuting attorney to offer the victim the opportunity to express his or her opinion on the disposition of an accused's case. This includes providing an opinion regarding plea or sentencing negotiations and participation in pretrial or post-conviction diversion programs.

O.C.G.A. § 17-17-16

This statute provides temporary restraining and protective orders for victims or witnesses who have provided an affidavit or verified complaint showing reasonable grounds that harassment in a criminal case exists. The temporary restraining order, which may be issued without written or oral notice to the adverse party, expires ten days after the date of issuance, unless extended by the court. If the temporary restraining order is issued without notice, a motion for a protective order will be heard. If the court determines, based on the preponderance of the evidence, that harassment of an identified victim or witness in a criminal case exists, a protective order will be issued for a maximum period of three years. Within 90 days of the expiration of a protective order, the prosecuting attorney may apply for a new protective order.

Georgia Victims' Rights in the Juvenile Justice System

An individual who has been a victim of a crime or delinquent act committed by a juvenile has certain rights regarding participation in hearings, disposition, and other processes of the Juvenile Justice System, all of which are provided through state statutes.

O.C.G.A. § 15-11-64.2

This statute deals with victim impact statements presented in delinquency proceedings. The Juvenile Court must notify any victims that they may submit a victim impact form in any delinquency proceeding if the alleged delinquent act would constitute a felony if committed by an adult and caused physical, psychological or economic injury, or would constitute a misdemeanor if committed by an adult and caused serious physical injury or death. "Prior to the imposition of a dispositional order for an allegedly delinquent child, the juvenile court shall permit the victim to address the juvenile court. It shall be the duty of the juvenile court to advise the victim of the right to address the court prior to the entry of a dispositional order for a delinquent child. The victim shall have the discretion to exercise the right to be present and be heard at the dispositional hearing."

O.C.G.A. § 15-11-78

This statute allows the victim to be present in any court hearing from which the public has been excluded.

O.C.G.A. § 15-11-155

This statute allows the victim to be present in any disposition hearing for the purpose of approving the mental competency plan for a juvenile. The victim shall be provided with at least ten days' prior notice of the disposition hearing and any subsequent hearing to review the juvenile's condition. The victim is also allowed the opportunity to be heard at the hearing and to present a victim impact form to the court at any such hearing.

State Board of Pardons and Paroles Office of Victim Services

The Georgia State Board of Pardons and Paroles dedicates numerous resources and services to the victims of crime, their survivors, and the community. "The Parole Board continues to give the highest priority and greatest compassion to those citizens who are most affected by crime" (State Board of Pardons and Paroles [PAP], 2011). In 2005, the Parole Board joined with the Georgia Department of Corrections to combine their victim services into the Corrections and Parole Board Office of Victim Services. "This afforded both agencies the opportunity to accommodate victims, and provide victims with the highest possible level of customer service" (PAP, 2011).

One function of the Board is to gather comprehensive information on the impact of offender actions on victims and the community. The Office of Victim Services continuously works with victims to provide for their parole system rights: "to give the Board views about the crime and the offender, to find out what the Board is doing on the case, and upon request, to be notified of any planned parole" (PAP, 2011).

According to O.C.G.A. § 17-17-13, as part of the Crime Victims' Bill of Rights, "The State Board of Pardons and Paroles shall give 20 days' advance notification to a victim whenever it considers making a final decision to grant parole or any other manner of executive clemency action to release a defendant for a period exceeding 60 days; and the board shall provide the victim with an opportunity to file a written objection to such action." Victims wishing to receive such notification must provide the State Board of Pardons and Paroles with a current address and phone number. If no such request is made, the Board, under this statute is not required to provide notification.

In working with victims of crime, the Board provides several services designed to allow for maximum participation in the parole process and to keep victims informed about their cases.

Victim Information Program (V.I.P.)

The Victim Information Program, or V.I.P., is an automated 24-hour information system designed to provide victims of crime and/or their families with immediate access to information regarding their cases and to provide notification calls to registered victims. To register with V.I.P., victims or family members must return a completed Crime Victim Notification Request Form and/or a Victim Impact Statement to the Office of Victim Services. Victims will receive a four digit PIN that will be used to acknowledge the notification was received.

Each inmate in the Georgia Department of Corrections is assigned a six digit case/EF number as well as a GDC ID number. Using these numbers, victims may receive updates on the following information:

- current incarceration location;
- parole status/eligibility;
- maximum or scheduled release date; and/or
- indication that the offender is not currently in custody.

Once a victim has registered, automatic computer generated notification calls will be placed when any of the following occurs:

- inmate is released from prison after completing the court-ordered term of incarceration;
- release from prison after completing the confinement portion of the sentence to begin a court-ordered probation period; and/or
- upon being granted a parole release.

Notification calls continue throughout a 24-hour period or until the notification PIN is entered during a call.

Victim Impact Statements

Victim Impact Statements are provided to crime victims as a way to voice their opinions regarding parole eligibility and as a way to express the impact that the crime has had on the victim and his or her family. The information is maintained in the Parole Board's case file for the inmate and becomes a permanent and strictly confidential part of the file. In addition, by completing the Impact Statement, the victim "automatically receive[s] early notification of any parole consideration," which gives the victim the opportunity to express his or her opinion about the inmate's possible parole (PAP, 2011).

The form may be completed and submitted online on the State Board of Pardons and Paroles website. The victim can also receive the form from a local law enforcement office, a local court, a state correctional facility, or from any State Board of Pardons and Paroles office.

The Prosecuting Attorneys' Council of Georgia Victim-Witness Advocacy Office

With the passage of the Georgia Crime Victims' Bill of Rights in 1995, prosecutors' offices are legislatively mandated to provide services to victims of crime, regardless of victimization type. "Through the district attorney offices in each of the 49 Georgia judicial circuits and the solicitor-general offices in 27 of the 159 counties, victim-witness personnel are mandated and available to guide these individuals through what can be a confusing, complicated judicial process. Victim-witness personnel assist with obtaining appropriate restitution and compensation through the Criminal Justice Coordinating Council" (Prosecuting Attorneys' Council of Georgia [PACGA], 2011).

Each judicial circuit and county has unique needs, services, and resources. The victim-witness personnel can make referrals for professional as well as community resources, and provide notification for a variety of court proceedings. The Victim-Witness Advocacy Office provides training, education, consultation, networking, and professional development to advocacy personnel. The Office also makes the needs and concerns of crime victims known to the community, elected officials, agencies and public policy makers. In addition, "the Prosecuting Attorneys' Council coordinates and trains a Georgia Crisis Response Team consisting of advocates, chaplains, community leaders standing ready to respond and assist other agencies in the event of mass trauma and disaster" (PACGA, 2011).

Services provided by the Victim-Witness Advocacy Office are numerous and depend on the needs and available resources of individual jurisdictions. Some of the services provided include:

- Stabilizing Lives through coordination of referrals, assistance with application forms, assistance with bill collectors and employers, crime scene clean-up services, and assistance with property return.
- Meeting Emotional/Physical Needs through advocate availability 24 hours per day, assisting with death notification, preparation of victim impact statements, follow-up services in hospitals or funeral homes, personnel available during interviews and at court appearances, and emotional support to victims and families.
- Meeting Safety and Security Needs through assistance with safety planning, coordinating communication with professionals, taking necessary action to expedite the case for victim protection, assisting with Temporary Protective Orders, assisting with notification requests to local corrections, and providing a comfortable waiting area apart from the defendant's family and friends.
- Assistance with the Criminal Justice System through explaining the stages of the process and legal terminology, advocating restitution at time of sentencing, coordinating transportation, serving as liaison between victim and investigators, providing courtroom orientation and pre-trial preparation of testifying, escorting victims to court, providing ongoing communication throughout the trial, attending hearings in the absence of the victim, and assisting with making contact with the State Board of Pardons and Paroles and the Department of Corrections to request notification.
- Education/Collaboration through service on community activist committees, board, and task forces; acting as liaison to the local prosecutor's office and judicial system; representing the Office on victims service boards; serving on Victim Impact Panels; providing training to the community, law enforcement, and other professionals on victim assistance; and providing ongoing information and literature to educate victims about the Victim Assistance Programs.
- Prosecutorial Assistance through assisting investigators and prosecutors in obtaining necessary reports, assisting in completing referral forms and forensic interviews, attending forensic interviews and multidisciplinary team meetings, and assisting with documentation in domestic and family violence cases (PACGA, 2011).

Distribution of Profits of Crimes

Another aspect of victimization is the ability of offenders to gain profit from their criminal behavior, at the expense of their victims. The State of Georgia has attempted to rectify this situation by providing the victim with the monetary profits that would otherwise be given to the offender. O.C.G.A. § 17-14-31 provides that any individual or company contracting with any person accused or convicted of a crime in the state to reenact the crime through a movie, book, magazine article, tape recording, phonograph record, radio or television presentation, or live entertainment, shall provide a copy of the contract and all monies to the Board of Corrections. "The board shall deposit such moneys in an escrow account for the benefit of and payable to any victim or the legal representative of any victim of crimes committed by the accused or convicted person" (O.C.G.A. § 17-14-31). Payments will be made if the accused is convicted within five years of the date of establishment of the escrow account and the victim brings a civil action and recovers a money judgment for damages.

Georgia's Sex Offender Registry

Georgia, like all of the 50 states and the federal government, is keenly aware of the issues related to sex offenses and sex offenders. And like the other governmental entities, Georgia has enacted legislation to protect its citizens from being victims of sex crimes.

For all adult victims of rape or aggravated sodomy, O.C.G.A. § 17-18-1 requires law enforcement or court officers, or any employee of the Departments of Human Services, Community Health, Public Health, or Behavioral Health and Developmental Disabilities, to provide a written statement to the victims. The written statement is expressed in O.C.G.A. § 17-18-2: "If you are the victim of rape or forcible sodomy, you have certain rights under the law. Rape or forcible sodomy by a stranger or a person known to you, including rape or forcible sodomy by a person married to you, is a crime. You can ask the government's lawyer to prosecute a person who has committed a crime. The government pays the cost of prosecuting for crimes. If you are the victim of rape or forcible sodomy, you should contact a local police department or other law enforcement agency immediately. A police officer will come to take a report and collect evidence. You should keep any clothing you were wearing at the time of the crime as well as any other evidence such as bed sheets. Officers will take you to the hospital for a medical examination. You should not shower or douche before the examination. The law requires that the Georgia Crime Victims Emergency Fund pay for the medical examination to the extent of the cost for the collection of evidence of the crime."

In addition, victims have the right to refuse the government's request to take a polygraph examination. O.C.G.A. §17-5-73 provides that "no prosecuting attorney, investigating law enforcement agency, or government official shall ask or require any victim of a sexual assault to submit to a polygraph examination or any other truth-telling device as a condition precedent to investigating such alleged crime. The refusal of a victim to submit to a polygraph examination or any other truth-telling device shall not prevent an investigation or prosecution of any sexual assault."

History of Sex Offender Registration

In 1947, the State of California became the first state in the country to enact legislation that required a sex offender to register with the state. Because other states did not enact similar legislation until the 1990s, "California today has the largest number of registered sex offenders of any state" (California Department of Justice, 2009).

It was not until 1994 that the federal government became involved with the issue of sex offender registration. The Jacob Wetterling Crimes Against Children and Sexually Violent Offender Registration Act (the Wetterling Act) was enacted as part of the Federal Violent Crime Control and Law Enforcement Act of 1994. Named in honor of Jacob Wetterling, who was abducted in 1989 and has remained missing, the purpose of the Wetterling Act is to require states to implement a sex offender and crimes against children registry, and to track sex offenders for ten years after release or for life if convicted of a violent sex crime (Office of Sex Offender Sentencing, Monitoring, Apprehending, Registering, and Tracking [SMART], 2011).

However, it was not until the passage of Megan's Law that community notification of sex offenders was mandated. Megan's Law is named in honor of Megan Kanka, a seven-year-old girl who was brutally raped and murdered by a twice convicted sex offender living across the street from her. The law, enacted by Congress on May 17, 1996 as an amendment to the Wetterling Act:

- provides public dissemination of information from states' sex offender registries;
- provides that information collected under state registration programs is disclosed for purposes permitted by state law; and

- requires state and local law enforcement agencies to release relevant information, necessary to protect the public, about individuals registered under state programs established by the Wetterling Act (SMART, 2011).

Also in 1996, the federal government made a second amendment to the Wetterling Act with the passage of the Pam Lychner Sexual Offender Tracking and Identification Act of 1996. Named in honor of Pam Lychner, a former flight attendant who was brutally assaulted by a twice convicted sex offender posing as a home buyer, the addition of the Pam Lychner Act created a national sex offender registry, to be monitored by the Federal Bureau of Investigation. The Pam Lychner Act:

- mandates certain sex offenders to register with the FBI;
- requires the FBI to periodically verify addresses of sex offenders;
- allows the dissemination of information collected by the FBI necessary to protect the public to federal, state, and local law enforcement officials; and
- sets provisions for notification to the FBI and state agencies when certain sex offenders move to another state (SMART, 2011).

In 1998, Congress made another amendment to the Wetterling Act, enacted as part of the Appropriations Act of 1998. This amendment increased registration requirements for sexually violent offenders, required the registration of federal and military offenders, required the registration of nonresident workers and students, and required state participation in the National Sex Offender Registry (Bureau of Justice Assistance, 2011).

In 2000, as part of the Victims of Trafficking and Violence Protection Act, Congress passed the Campus Sex Crimes Prevention Act. The purpose of this statute is to:

- require any person obligated to register on a state's sex offender registry to notify the institution of higher education as to the status of registration;
- require that information collected by the institution of higher education be promptly reported to local law enforcement and entered into state records; and
- amend the Higher Education Act of 1965 to require institutions, in addition to disclosing the campus security policy and crime statistics, to provide notice of how information related to registered sex offenders can be obtained (SMART, 2011).

The latest federal legislation concerning sex offenders is the Adam Walsh Child Protection and Safety Act of 2006. The legislation was named in honor of Adam Walsh, a six-year-old boy who was abducted from a mall and whose severed head was found two weeks later. The legislation includes:

- the creation of a new baseline standard for state registration and notification systems, creating a three-tier system for classifying offenders based on their risk to the community;
- an expansion of the number of sex offenses to be included in the registry; and
- the creation of the Office of Sex Offender Sentencing, Monitoring, Apprehending, Registering, and Tracking (SMART) within the Department of Justice's Office of Justice Programs to administer the standards for registration and notification, to administer grant programs authorized by the Act, and to coordinate related training and technical assistance (SMART, 2011).

O.C.G.A. §42-1-12 State Sexual Offender Registry

The Georgia Sex Offender Registry is created in O.C.G.A. §42-1-12. The statute, covering 15 pages of text, provides numerous definitions and delineates the responsibilities of the sex offender, law enforcement and investigating agencies, custodial agencies, and probation/parole supervising agencies.

The various provisions of the Registry provide both government entities and the sex offender with information on how to register, what information is needed in the registry, who will monitor and maintain the registry, and other requirements related to the sex offender's residence and employment.

The Sexual Offender Registration Review Board is composed of three professionals who are knowledgeable in the field of behavior and treatment of sex offenders. One member is a representative of a victims' rights advocacy group or agency, and the other two members are active or retired state certified peace officers. The commissioner of the Department of Behavioral Health and Developmental Disabilities appoints the members to serve four-year terms. The purpose of the Board is to complete a risk assessment classification for all sex offenders placed on the Registry (O.C.G.A. §42-1-13).

The Level I risk assessment classification means the sex offender poses a low risk for recidivism and committing future sex offenses. The Level II risk assessment classification means the sex offender poses an intermediate risk for recidivism and committing future sex offenses. The classification of Sexually Dangerous Predator means the sex offender was designated a sexually violent predator between July 1, 1996 and June 30, 2006, or is at risk to commit future dangerous sex offenses. All sexually dangerous predators are required to wear an electronic monitoring system that has the capability to locate and record the offender's location through a global positioning satellite system, the capacity to report or record the offender's presence near a crime scene or prohibited area or departure from specific geographic locations, and an alarm that is automatically activated and broadcasts the offender's location if the monitor is tampered with or removed (O.C.G.A. §42-1-14).

Sex offenders on the Registry must provide required registration information:

- name, social security number, age, race, sex, date of birth, height, weight, hair and eye color, fingerprints, and photograph;
- address, including descriptions and license/permit numbers of motor homes/trailers, mobile homes, or vessels;
- date, place, and address of employment;
- place and address of vocation;
- vehicle make, model, color, and license tag number;
- name and address of higher education institution (if enrolled); and
- list of crime or crimes for which the offender is registering and date released from prison or placed on probation or supervised release.

In addition, if any of the above information changes, it is the responsibility of the sex offender to provide, within 72 hours, the new information to the sheriff of the county of residence. If the change is for residence, the sex offender must notify the sheriff of the county of current residence within 72 hours prior to the move and notify the sheriff of the county of future residence within 72 hours prior to moving. If the sex offender is moving out of Georgia, he or she must provide the sheriff of the county of current residence with the new address and must also register with a designated law enforcement agency in the new state within 72 hours after establishing residence (O.C.G.A. §42-1-12).

Registered sex offenders are restricted in terms of residence and employment as delineated in O.C.G.A. §42-1-15. As of July 1, 2008, registered sex offenders cannot reside within 1,000 feet of any child care facility, church, school, or area where minors congregate, if the commission of the offense occurred on or after July 1, 2008. The distance is measured from the outer boundary of the residence to the outer boundary of the restricted property.

In terms of employment, as of July 1, 2008, no registered sex offender or sexually dangerous predator may be employed by or volunteer at any child care facility, church, school, or any business or entity located within 1,000 feet of a child care facility, church, school, or area where minors congregate, if the commission of the offense occurred on or after July 1, 2008. Also, registered sex offenders are prohibited from loitering at any child care facility, school, or area where minors congregate.

If a registered sex offender resides or is employed at a location prior to the establishment of a child care facility, church, or school within 1,000 feet of such residence or employment, or if the offender established property ownership before July 1, 2008, the offender will not be deemed in violation of the statute. If the offender believes he or she should be exempt from the residence and/or employment restrictions, the offender must provide sufficient proof of the exemption to the sheriff of the county of registration. Any offender who knowingly violates any of the provisions in O.C.G.A. §42-1-15 will be guilty of a felony and imprisoned from ten to 30 years.

One more restriction on registered sex offenders concerns photographing minors. A minor is defined as any individual under the age of 18. According to O.C.G.A. §42-1-18, no individual shall intentionally photograph a minor without the consent of the parent or guardian. In this statute, photograph is defined as any picture, film or digital photography, motion picture film, videotape, or similar visual representation or image.

Georgia Bureau of Investigation and Local Sheriffs

The Georgia Bureau of Investigation (GBI) is responsible for maintaining the state sex offender registry. Because sex offender registration information is required under federal mandate to be disseminated to all citizens, the GBI provides an Internet link on its website to the registry information. Individuals are able to access, within a matter of seconds, a listing of all registered sex offenders in the state. The information is searchable using one of three different databases—the sex offender search page, the predator search page, and the absconder search page. Once on one of the pages, the searcher may enter an individual offender's name and/or address, may search by city or zip code, gender, currently incarcerated, or by county of interest. A map identifying the number of registered sex offenders in each county is also available (Georgia Bureau of Investigation, 2011).

When the selection criteria are chosen, the searcher will obtain a list of offenders, with their names, addresses, and photos. Clicking on the name or photo will provide the searcher with the required registration information for the offender, as well as conviction date, registration date, residence verification date, and conviction state.

In addition to the daily monitoring and updating of the Registry, the GBI is also responsible, under O.C.G.A. §42-1-12, for:

- transmitting all information to the Federal Bureau of Investigation within 24 hours of entering the data;

- establishing operating policies and procedures for record ownership, verification, quality, modification, and cancellation; and
- performing mail out and verification duties, including identifying offenders due for verification each month, providing photos to the sheriff's office to assist with verification, mailing a verification form to the offender ten days prior to the offender's birthday, notifying appropriate law enforcement agency if an offender moves out of state, and maintaining records required by statute.

The sheriff's office in each county, under O.C.G.A. §42-1-12, is responsible for the following:

- preparing and maintaining a list of all registered sex offenders residing in the county, and making that list available for inspection at the sheriff's office, any county administrative building, the main administrative building for any municipal corporation, in the office of the clerk of superior court, and on the sheriff's website;
- electronically submitting and updating all information within two business days to the GBI;
- updating the public notices within two business days;
- informing the public of the presence of registered sex offenders in the community;
- updating changes to offender required registration information within 72 hours;
- notifying the GBI within 72 hours of changes to offender required registration information;
- retaining the verification form for the offender's address;
- enforcing the criminal provisions of the statute;
- cooperating and communicating with other sheriff's offices in the state and country to maintain current data on the offender's location;
- determining the appropriate reporting time of day for offenders;
- placing electronic monitoring devices on sexually dangerous predators;
- providing current information to campus police within the jurisdiction; and
- collecting the annual $250 registration fee and transmitting collections to the state for deposit in the general fund.

On at least an annual basis, the Department of Education will obtain a complete list of registered sex offenders from the GBI and provide the list to all schools in the state. In addition, on at least an annual basis, the Department of Early Care and Learning will provide to all child care programs, child care learning centers, day-care, group day-care, and family day-care programs, and the Department of Human Services will provide to all long-term care facilities for children current information on accessing and retrieving a list of the names and addresses of all registered sex offenders from the GBI's website (O.C.G.A. §42-1-12).

The GBI and sheriff's offices maintaining sex offender registration information may release other information collected if it is deemed relevant and necessary to protect the public. The exception is that the identify of a victim of an offense that requires registration shall not be released (O.C.G.A. §42-1-12).

In addition to maintaining the Registry, the GBI has partnered with Prevent Child Abuse (PCA) Georgia "to provide Georgia's adults with the most comprehensive information possible to help protect children from sexual harm" (Prevent Child Abuse [PCA] Georgia, 2011). The PCA Georgia was founded in 1984 as an independent, statewide, non-profit agency, and "is the state's only non-profit agency that focuses exclusively on the **prevention** of all forms of child abuse and neglect" (GBI, 2011). The PCA Georgia currently provides an online information and resource page titled *Stop It Now! Georgia*. The purpose of the website is to provide information about preventing the sexual abuse of children, while encouraging all adults to take responsibility for preventing child sexual abuse before another child is harmed. "Research and experience show that **child sexual abuse is not inevitable. It's preventable.** We know that children are most likely to be abused by someone they know, love, and trust. The vast majority of those who may sexually abuse children will not be listed in the Registry. The GBI maintains the registry information with the understanding that it is only one small piece of a complicated puzzle" (PCA Georgia, 2011). The website contains numerous web links to various organizations and services throughout the state, and also provides specific information on Internet safety, online behavior, and resources for the reporting of Internet crime.

Conclusion

As noted previously, victims of crime in Georgia are similar in many aspects to victims in other states and around the world. The State of Georgia, with its many legislative statutes, its state and local organizations and their numerous service initiatives, has created a system whereby victims are treated with respect, compassion and as a vital part of the Criminal Justice System.

Chapter Review Questions

1. What are the major provisions of the Georgia Crime Victims' Bill of Rights?
2. Explain the rights of victims in the Juvenile Justice System.
3. Describe the history of sex offender registries. How does the Georgia Sex Offender Registry work?
4. What are the services provided by the Victim-Witness Advocacy Office?
5. Do you believe the sex offender registry is effective?

References

Bureau of Justice Assistance. (2011). Overview and History of the Jacob Wetterling Act. Retrieved from: http://www.ojp.usdoj.gov.

California Department of Justice. (2009). Sex Offender Registration and Exclusion Information. Retrieved from: http://www.meganslaw.ca.gov.

Criminal Justice Coordinating Council. (2011). Retrieved from: http://cjcc.ga.gov.

Georgia Bureau of Investigation. (2011). Georgia Sex Offender Registry. Retrieved from: http://gbi.georgia.gov.

O.C.G.A. § 15-11-64.2. (2011). Official Code of Georgia Annotated.

O.C.G.A. § 11-11-78. (2011). Official Code of Georgia Annotated.

O.C.G.A. § 15-11-155. (2011). Official Code of Georgia Annotated.

O.C.G.A. § 16-5. (2011). Official Code of Georgia Annotated.

O.C.G.A. § 16-6. (2011). Official Code of Georgia Annotated.

O.C.G.A. § 16-7-1. (2011). Official Code of Georgia Annotated.

O.C.G.A. § 16-7-3. (2011). Official Code of Georgia Annotated.

O.C.G.A. § 16-7-4. (2011). Official Code of Georgia Annotated.

O.C.G.A. § 16-8-1. (2011). Official Code of Georgia Annotated.

O.C.G.A. § 16-8-2. (2011). Official Code of Georgia Annotated.

O.C.G.A. § 16-9. (2011). Official Code of Georgia Annotated.

O.C.G.A. § 16-12-3.3. (2011). Official Code of Georgia Annotated.

O.C.G.A. § 17-5-72. (2011). Official Code of Georgia Annotated.

O.C.G.A. § 17-5-73. (2011). Official Code of Georgia Annotated.

O.C.G.A. § 17-17-1. (2011). Official Code of Georgia Annotated.

O.C.G.A. § 17-17-3. (2011). Official Code of Georgia Annotated.

O.C.G.A. § 17-17-5. (2011). Official Code of Georgia Annotated.

O.C.G.A. § 17-17-5.1. (2011). Official Code of Georgia Annotated.

O.C.G.A. §17-17-6. (2011). Official Code of Georgia Annotated.

O.C.G.A. §17-17-7. (2011). Official Code of Georgia Annotated.

O.C.G.A. §17-17-8. (2011). Official Code of Georgia Annotated.

O.C.G.A. §17-17-8.1. (2011). Official Code of Georgia Annotated.

O.C.G.A. §17-17-9. (2011). Official Code of Georgia Annotated.

O.C.G.A. §17-17-9.1. (2011). Official Code of Georgia Annotated.

O.C.G.A. §17-17-10. (2011). Official Code of Georgia Annotated.

O.C.G.A. §17-17-11. (2011). Official Code of Georgia Annotated.

O.C.G.A. §17-17-12. (2011). Official Code of Georgia Annotated.

O.C.G.A. §17-17-13. (2011). Official Code of Georgia Annotated.

O.C.G.A. §17-17-14. (2011). Official Code of Georgia Annotated.

O.C.G.A. §17-17-16. (2011). Official Code of Georgia Annotated.

O.C.G.A. §17-18-1. (2011). Official Code of Georgia Annotated.

O.C.G.A. §17-17-2. (2011). Official Code of Georgia Annotated.

O.C.G.A. §30-5-8. (2011). Official Code of Georgia Annotated.

O.C.G.A. §35-6A-1. (2011). Official Code of Georgia Annotated.

O.C.G.A. §35-6A-7. (2011). Official Code of Georgia Annotated.

O.C.G.A. §35-6A-8. (2011). Official Code of Georgia Annotated.

O.C.G.A. §35-8-10. (2011). Official Code of Georgia Annotated.

O.C.G.A. §40-6-393. (2011). Official Code of Georgia Annotated.

O.C.G.A. §40-6-393.1. (2011). Official Code of Georgia Annotated.

O.C.G.A. §40-6-394. (2011). Official Code of Georgia Annotated.

O.C.G.A. §42-1-12. (2011). Official Code of Georgia Annotated.

O.C.G.A. §42-1-13. (2011). Official Code of Georgia Annotated.

O.C.G.A. §42-1-14. (2011). Official Code of Georgia Annotated.

O.C.G.A. §42-1-15. (2011). Official Code of Georgia Annotated.

O.C.G.A. §42-1-18. (2011). Official Code of Georgia Annotated.

Office of Sex Offender Sentencing, Monitoring, Apprehending, Registering, and Tracking [SMART]. (2011). Federal Sex Offender Legislation. Retrieved from: http://www.ojp.usdoj.gov.

Prevent Child Abuse (PCA) Georgia. (2011). Welcome. Retrieved from: http://www.preventchildabusega.org/html/pcaga.

Prosecuting Attorneys' Council of Georgia [PACGA]. (2011). Victim Witness Advocacy. Retrieved from: http://www.pacga.org.

State Board of Pardons and Paroles. (2011). Victim Services. Retrieved from: http://www.pap.state.ga.us.

CHAPTER 5

THE CRIMINAL JUSTICE PROCESS

Learning Objectives

After reading the chapter, students will be able to:

- Explain the steps in the Criminal Justice Process.
- Explain the arrest process, including the arrest warrant, use of force, and booking.
- Explain search and seizure, including probable cause.
- Describe the pretrial process, including hearings and motions.
- Describe the trial process, including jury selection, presentation of evidence, jury deliberation, and sentencing.
- Explain the role of corrections.

Key Terms

Accusation	Jury Selection
Affidavit	Limitations on Prosecution
Arraignment	*Miranda v. Arizona*
Arrest	Plea Bargaining
Arrest Warrant	Preliminary Hearing
Booking	Presentation of Evidence
Capital Felony	Pretrial Motions
Corrections	Probable Cause
Grand Jury Indictment	Search and Seizure
Initial Appearance	Sentencing and Punishment
Jurisdiction and Venue	Title 17
Jury Deliberation	Use of Force

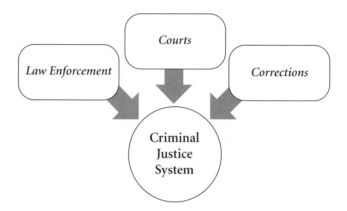

The criminal justice process in Georgia is similar to that of other states across the country. The statutes governing the process, and covering all criminal procedures, are found in O.C.G.A. Title 17. The steps taken to process an individual suspected of committing a crime through the Criminal Justice System generally occur in a specific order: report of the crime, investigation of the crime, arrest, booking, initial hearing, preliminary hearing, grand jury indictment or accusation, arraignment, trial, sentencing, and finally, corrections.

The process begins with initial contact with law enforcement (report of a crime). Once initial contact is made, the law enforcement officer will conduct an investigation to determine if a crime has been committed. If the investigation reveals that the individual in question is a viable suspect, the suspect is then arrested. Once placed under arrest, the suspect is booked into a detention facility. The next steps involve the prosecuting attorney and the court in the jurisdiction in which the crime occurred. The suspect is taken before the court for the initial hearing, where the court determines if there is probable cause to charge the suspect with the crime. If there is probable cause, the suspect is either given bail or detained until the preliminary hearing, where a formal plea is entered. Based on the information presented at the hearing, the prosecuting attorney will file an accusation or will convene a grand jury for the purpose of determining if an indictment is warranted. With the accusation or indictment presented, the suspect will again appear in court during arraignment. If the suspect pleads not guilty, the case will proceed to trial. If the suspected offender is adjudicated guilty at trial, a sentence will be imposed. Based upon the facts of the case, the judge will provide a sentence that is suitable to the crime and in compliance with the law, providing state supervision through corrections.

General Terminology

Throughout the criminal justice process, general terminology is used, regardless of whether the process occurs on the local level for violations of county or municipal ordinances, or on the state level for violations of state statutes.

Jurisdiction and Venue

Which law enforcement agency will investigate, which court will conduct the trial, and which corrections institution will house the convicted are all determined by legal jurisdiction. Jurisdiction is defined as "the lawful exercise of authority; the area within authority may be exercised" (Reid, 2007).

For law enforcement, jurisdiction is defined as "the geographical area within which a particular police force has authority" (Reid, 2007). Jurisdiction is also an issue with the court system, as each court has one of several types of jurisdiction. "Courts may have original jurisdiction to hear the case; if more than one court has authority to hear the case, the jurisdiction is concurrent. Appellate jurisdiction refers to the power of a court to hear the case on appeal. Exclusive jurisdiction means that only one court may hear the case" (Reid, 2007).

Jurisdiction in Georgia for the state to exercise authority "over crime and persons charged with the commission of crime" is defined in O.C.G.A. §17-2-1. According to this statute, "a person shall be subject to prosecution in this state for a crime which he commits, while either within or outside the state, by his own conduct or that of another for which he is legally accountable, if: (1) The crime is committed either wholly or partly within the state; (2) The conduct outside the state constitutes an attempt to commit a crime within the state; or (3) The conduct within the state constitutes an attempt to commit in another jurisdiction a crime under the laws of both this state and the other jurisdiction" (O.C.G.A. §17-2-1). In addition, a crime legally occurs partly within the state if conduct that is an element of the crime or the result of the crime occurs within the state. "In homicide, the 'result' is either the act which causes death or the death itself; and, if the body of a homicide victim is found within this state, the death is presumed to have occurred within the state" (O.C.G.A. §17-2-1).

O.C.G.A. §17-2-2 provides guidelines for venue, which is defined as the "location of the trial" (Reid, 2007). Where the crime was committed will determine the location of the trial. For example, if the crime was committed on the boundary line or water boundary of two counties, the crime will be considered as having been committed in either county. If the crime occurred while in transit within the state, the crime will be considered has having been committed within any county where the transit occurred.

Law enforcement officers in Georgia exist on the federal, state, and local levels. Federal law enforcement officers are provided with statewide jurisdiction to enforce federal laws. State law enforcement officers are provided with statewide jurisdiction to enforce state laws. Local law enforcement officers on the county and municipal levels have jurisdiction to enforce local ordinances, but also have the authority to enforce state laws that occur within their jurisdictions.

Limitations on Prosecutions

Under O.C.G.A. § 17-3-1, the state has time limitations for beginning a prosecution for specific crimes, while other crimes have no time limits. For the crime of murder, a prosecution may begin at any time. If deoxyribonucleic acid (DNA) evidence is used to establish the identity of the offender, a prosecution for the following crimes may begin at any time: armed robbery, kidnapping, rape, aggravated child molestation, aggravated sodomy, and aggravated sexual battery.

For other crimes punishable by death or life in prison, a prosecution must begin within seven years after the crime occurred, while the prosecution for the crime of forcible rape must begin within 15 years after the crime occurred. Prosecutions for all other felonies must begin within four years after the crime occurred, while felonies against a victim who was under the age of 18 at the time of the crime must begin within seven years after the crime occurred.

All prosecutions for misdemeanor crimes must begin within two years after the crime occurred.

In addition, O.C.G.A. § 17-3-2.1 provides enhanced limitations for specific crimes committed against minors, victims under the age of 16. If the victim is under the age of 16 when the following crimes occurred, the applicable period within which a prosecution must begin will not start until the victim reaches 16 years of age or the crime is reported to a law enforcement or government agency: cruelty to children, rape, sodomy and aggravated sodomy, statutory rape, child molestation and aggravated child molestation, enticing a child for indecent purposes, or incest. O.C.G.A. § 17-3-2.2 provides that for victims 65 years of age or older, the prosecution must not begin more than 15 years after the crime occurred, except if law provides for a longer or unlimited period.

Probable Cause

Probable cause is the standard needed to arrest, search, seize, and prosecute an individual through the Criminal Justice System. The most significant reference to probable cause is found in the 4th Amendment to the U.S. Constitution: "and no Warrants shall issue, but upon probable cause." The concept of probable cause was concisely defined by the U.S. Supreme Court in *Brinegar v. U.S.* (338 U.S. 160 [1949]): "Probable cause exists where the facts and circumstances within the officers' knowledge, and of which they have reasonably trustworthy information, are sufficient in themselves to warrant a belief by a man of reasonable caution that a crime is being committed."

In general terms, probable cause needed for a lawful arrest is defined as the facts and circumstances that would lead to the reasonable belief that the suspect has committed a crime. For a lawful search and seizure, probable cause is defined as the facts and circumstances that would lead to the reasonable belief that the items to be seized are located in the place to be searched (Reid, 2007). With or without a warrant, probable cause in arrest and search and seizure cases will be determined by the court, either at the time of application for a warrant or at trial.

Report and Investigation of the Crime

The criminal justice process in all states and the federal government begins with the acknowledgment that a crime has been committed. Crimes typically come to the attention of state and local law enforcement through a call to an emergency dispatch center or through occurrence in the presence of a law enforcement officer. Once a crime has been reported to or seen by a law enforcement officer, the criminal justice process is put into motion. The law enforcement contribution to the process will continue with the investigation of the crime and the arrest of the suspect.

The investigation of a crime may be conducted at the point of initial contact between law enforcement and the victim, or it may take several hours, days, or weeks. If a crime has been alleged and the suspect is not immediately apprehended (for example, in a theft or burglary case), the initial law enforcement officer may turn the case over to the agency's detectives or investigators to complete the investigation.

Within the investigation, officers and detectives may use one of numerous investigative techniques. These range from interviewing the victim and witnesses, running background checks and obtaining personal information from crime databases, obtaining fingerprints and DNA evidence, and other specialized techniques.

Search and Seizure

In conducting investigations of criminal behavior, detectives will often seek to search the private property and personal effects of the victim, the suspect, and/or the witnesses. The ability of law enforcement officers to search and/or seize personal property is guided by the 4th Amendment of the U.S. Constitution: "The right of the people to be secure in their persons, houses, papers, and effects, against unreasonable searches and seizures, shall not be violated, and no Warrants shall issue, but upon probable cause, supported by Oath or affirmation, and particularly describing the place to be searched, and the persons or things to be seized."

Law enforcement officers must obtain search warrants from a judicial officer who has jurisdiction over the case. O.C.G.A. § 17-5-20 stipulates that "a search warrant shall not be issued upon the application of a private citizen or for his aid in the enforcement of personal, civil, or property rights."

The law enforcement officer must provide a written complaint, under oath or affirmation, "which states facts sufficient to show probable cause that a crime is being committed or has been committed and which particularly describes the place or person, or both, to be searched and things to be seized" (O.C.G.A. § 17-5-21). Based upon the written complaint, the judicial officer may issue a search warrant for:

- any instruments, articles or things, including private papers, which are designed, intended for use or which have been used in the commission of a crime;
- any person who has been kidnapped in violation of the laws of this state, ho has been kidnapped in another jurisdiction and is now concealed within this state, or any human fetus or corpse;
- stolen or embezzled property;
- any item, substance, object, thing, or matter which is unlawful to possess; or
- any item, substance, object, thing, or matter, other than private papers, which is tangible evidence of the commission of a crime for which probable cause is shown (O.C.G.A. § 17-5-21).

Search warrants are limited in time and may expire. According to O.C.G.A. § 17-5-25, "the search warrant shall be executed within ten days from the time of issuance." If the warrant is not executed in this time, it becomes void and is returned to the court. However, search warrants may be executed at any reasonable time (O.C.G.A. § 17-5-26).

Law enforcement officers may use force when executing a search warrant, with force being defined as necessary and reasonable "to effect an entry into any building or property or part thereof" (O.C.G.A. § 17-5-27). However, the officer must provide verbal notice or attempt in good faith to give verbal notice of his authority and purpose to execute the search warrant. If the officer is refused admittance, if persons within the building or property refuse to acknowledge and answer the verbal notice or the presence of persons is unknown, or the building or property is unoccupied, force is considered necessary and reasonable (O.C.G.A. § 17-5-27).

Items and things seized during the execution of the search warrant must be inventoried and a written list of all items seized must be provided to the owner of the property (O.C.G.A. § 17-5-29). Law enforcement officers executing a search warrant may also detain and search any person in the place being searched to protect from attack or to prevent the disposal or concealment of items or things described in the search warrant (O.C.G.A. § 17-5-28).

During any investigation of a criminal suspect, where probable cause exists that the suspect committed a crime, the investigating peace officer is authorized to verify the suspect's immigration status when the suspect is unable to provide a valid Georgia driver's license or identification card, a valid driver's license from another state, or any other information sufficient to allow the officer to independently verify the identity of the suspect. In attempting to identify a suspect's immigration status, the investigating officer may use any authorized federal identification database, fingerprint readers or similar devices, or may contact an appropriate federal agency (O.C.G.A. § 17-5-100).

Arrest of the Suspect

Arrest is defined as "the act of taking an individual into custody in order to make a criminal charge against that person" (Reid, 2007). Law enforcement officers are permitted to make arrests, on the basis of probable cause, with or without first obtaining an arrest warrant. An arrest warrant is "a court-issued writ authorizing an officer to arrest a suspect" (Reid, 2007).

Arrest of the suspect may occur at the initial contact with law enforcement, particularly when the officer has witnessed the crime, conducted without first obtaining an arrest warrant. In other instances, a suspect is identified at some point after the crime has occurred and an arrest warrant is obtained.

Law enforcement officers in Georgia may make a lawful arrest with or without a warrant. O.C.G.A. § 17-4-20 provides that an arrest may be made in the following conditions:

- if the offense is committed in the officer's presence or within the officer's immediate knowledge;
- if the offender is endeavoring to escape;
- if the officer has probable cause to believe an act of family violence has occurred;

- if the officer has probable cause to believe an offense involving physical abuse against a vulnerable adult has occurred; or
- for other causes if there is a likely failure of justice in waiting for a judicial officer to issue a warrant.

In addition, Georgia law provides private citizens with the authority to make an arrest of an offender "if the offense is committed in his presence or within his immediate knowledge. If the offense is a felony and the offender is escaping or attempting to escape, a private person may arrest him upon reasonable and probable grounds of suspicion" (O.C.G.A. § 17-4-60).

Arrest Warrant

Although the majority of arrests are made without an arrest warrant, obtaining an arrest warrant provides the officer and the court with an already determined probable cause for the arrest, and provides the officer serving the warrant with protection against criminal and civil claims of unlawful arrest. Law enforcement officers are not authorized to process an arrest warrant. They must complete an affidavit, which is then submitted to the court having jurisdiction and venue over the case. According to O.C.G.A. § 17-4-40, "Any judge of a superior, city, state, or magistrate court or any municipal officer clothed by law with the powers of a magistrate may issue a warrant for the arrest of any offender against the penal laws, based on probable cause either on the judge's or officer's own knowledge or on the information of others given to the judge or officer under oath."

The affidavit for an arrest warrant is guided by O.C.G.A. § 17-4-45, which provides that the affidavit is sufficient when substantially complying with the following form:

Georgia, _____ County.

Personally came (name of affiant), who on oath says that, to the best of his knowledge and belief, (name of person against whom the warrant is sought) did, on the _____ day of _____, ____, in the county aforesaid, commit the offense of (insert here all information describing offense as required by Code Section 17-4-41) and this affiant makes this affidavit that a warrant may issue for his arrest.

_____
(Signature of the affiant)

Sworn to and subscribed before me, this _____ day of _____, ____.

_____
Judicial Officer

Once the affidavit is submitted to the court, the judge will determine, based on all of the evidence presented by the law enforcement officer, whether or not probable cause exists to support the issuance of an arrest warrant. If the arrest warrant is approved, the form for the arrest warrant is guided by O.C.G.A. § 17-4-46, which provides that the warrant is sufficient when substantially complying with the following form:

Georgia, _____ County.

To any sheriff, deputy sheriff, coroner, constable, or marshal of said state—Greetings:
(Name of the affiant) makes oath before me that on the _____ day of _____, in the year ____, in the county aforesaid, (name of person against whom the warrant is sought) did commit the offense of (insert here all information describing offense as required by Code Section 17-4-41). You are therefore commanded to arrest (name of person against whom the warrant is sought) and bring him before me, or some other judicial officer of this state, to be dealt with as the law directs. You will also levy on a sufficiency of the property of (name of person against whom the warrant is sought) to pay the costs in the event of his final conviction. Herein fail not.

_____
Judicial Officer

As noted in the affidavit and actual arrest warrant, O.C.G.A. § 17-4-41 requires that certain information about the specific law allegedly violated be inserted. According to this statute, the following information must be included: time, date, and place of offense; against whom the offense occurred; a statement describing the offense; and the county in which the offense occurred. In addition, if the offense is theft, additional information about the name and description of the property, including value, alleged to have been stolen, and the name of the owner of the property is to be included (O.C.G.A. § 17-4-41).

Unlike search warrants, arrest warrants do not expire. In addition, individuals who are not certified peace or law enforcement officers may make an application for an arrest warrant. If this is done, the judge will schedule a warrant application hearing, to determine if probable cause exists to issue the warrant. At this hearing, evidence may be presented by both sides, including the presentation and cross-examination of witnesses. The judge will determine if there is sufficient evidence of probable cause and will either issue the arrest warrant or deny the application. In addition, O.C.G.A. §17-4-40 provides that the judge may immediately issue an arrest warrant based on the application by a person other than a peace or law enforcement officer if:

- an immediate or continuing threat exists to the safety of the affiant or third party;
- the person whose arrest is sought will attempt to evade or obstruct justice if notice is given;
- the person whose arrest is sought is incarcerated or in the custody of a federal, state, or local law enforcement agency;
- the person whose arrest is sought is a fugitive from justice;
- the offense for which the application for the warrant is made is deposit account fraud; or
- the offense for which the application for the warrant is made consists of an act of family violence.

Making the Arrest

Under O.C.G.A. §17-4-1, a valid arrest does not require the touching of the person being placed under arrest. "If the person voluntarily submits to being considered under arrest or yields on condition of being allowed his freedom of locomotion, under the discretion of the officer, the arrest is complete" (O.C.G.A. §17-4-1).

Georgia law also provides law enforcement officers, upon making a lawful arrest, with the authority to "reasonably search the person arrested and the area within the person's immediate presence for the purpose of: (1) Protecting the officer from attack; (2) Preventing the person from escaping; (3) Discovering or seizing the fruits of the crime for which the person has been arrested; or (4) Discovering or seizing any instruments, articles, or things which are being used or which may have been used in the commission of the crime for which the person has been arrested" (O.C.G.A. §17-5-1). Any evidence found during the search pursuant to a lawful arrest may be seized and used as evidence at trial.

The Supreme Court has required that all individuals being subjected to a custodial interrogation (being asked incriminating questions while being in custody and not allowed to leave) are entitled to be informed of certain constitutional rights. These rights are commonly known as Miranda Rights, named after the case of *Miranda v. Arizona* (384 U.S. 436 [1966]) in which the Supreme Court expressly identified what information about rights individuals subjected to a custodial interrogation must receive. Although not required until a suspect in custody is being interrogated, most law enforcement agencies require officers to provide the Miranda Rights to all individuals at the point of arrest. As prescribed by the Supreme Court, officers must advise suspects "prior to any questioning that he has the right to remain silent, that anything he says can be used against him in a court of law, that he has the right to the presence of an attorney, and that, if he cannot afford an attorney one will be appointed for him prior to any questioning if he so desires" (*Miranda v. Arizona*, 1966).

Use of Force in Arrest

Georgia code O.C.G.A. § 17-4-20 allows law enforcement officers to use deadly force to apprehend a suspected felon **only** when:

- the officer reasonably believes that suspect possesses a deadly weapon or any object, device or instrument that is likely to or actually does result in serious bodily injury;
- the officer reasonably believes the suspect poses an immediate threat of physical violence to the officer or others; or
- there is probable cause to believe the suspect has committed a crime involving the infliction or threatened infliction of serious physical harm.

However, law enforcement officers may use any reasonable nondeadly force as necessary to apprehend and arrest a suspected felon or misdemeanant. In addition, "nothing in this Code section shall be construed so as to restrict the use of deadly force by employees of state and county correctional institutions, jails, and other places of lawful confinement or by peace officers of any agency in the State of Georgia when reasonably necessary to prevent escapes or apprehend escapees from such institutions" (O.C.G.A. § 17-4-20).

One interesting aspect of the arrest procedures in Georgia is the ability of law enforcement officers to summon a posse. The original statute enacted in 1863, now stated as O.C.G.A. § 17-4-24, provides that "every law enforcement officer is bound to execute the penal warrants given to him to execute. He may summon to his assistance, either in writing or orally, any of the citizens of the neighborhood or county to assist in the execution of such warrants. The acts of the citizens formed as a posse by such officer shall be subject to the same protection and consequences as official acts."

Under O.C.G.A. § 17-4-3, law enforcement officers have the authority, when attempting to make an arrest under a warrant charging a crime, to break open the door of any house where the offender is concealed.

Booking

Booking is the "official recording of the name, photograph, and fingerprints of a suspect, along with the offense charged and the name of the officer who made the arrest" (Reid, 2007). In Georgia, under O.C.G.A. § 17-4-27, sheriffs, police chiefs, and other heads of law enforcement agencies have the duty to obtain the name, address, and age of each person arrested by officers under their supervision, and to maintain appropriate records of this information, which are open for public inspection.

Pretrial Procedures

Pretrial procedures include all aspects of the criminal justice process that occur between the time of arrest and the criminal trial. As with the requirement of providing suspects in custody with certain legal and constitutional rights, the suspect will also be provided, at every point in the process, with information on his or her legal and constitutional rights, and with the opportunity to maintain innocence or plead guilty to the charges.

Once an arrest warrant has been served, the person arrested must be brought before a judicial officer within 72 hours after arrest (O.C.G.A. § 17-4-26). For arrests without a warrant, the person arrested must be brought before a judicial officer within 48 hours, as defined in O.C.G.A. § 17-4-62.

Initial Appearance

"The purpose of the initial appearance is to make sure that the person accused of a crime is aware of the charges and is given due process" (Carl Vinson Institute of Government, 2001). The initial appearance will take place in the magistrate court having jurisdiction. At this time, the judge will ascertain whether or not the accused has an attorney, and whether or not the accused is indigent (meaning unable to afford an attorney). This is important as the state must provide all indigent persons with assistance of an attorney in all crucial stages of the criminal justice process, as required by the Supreme Court cases of *Gideon v. Wainwright* (372 U.S. 335 [1963]) and *Argersinger v. Hamlin* (407 U.S. 25 [1972]).

In addition, the judge at initial appearance will set the bail, which is money posted with the court to allow the accused to avoid spending time in jail awaiting trial. The money posted is used as a guarantee that the accused will appear in court for all required appearances, including trial. The judge will typically determine bail after hearing from the prosecuting attorney and the defense attorney regarding the opportunity for bail and the bail amount. "In Georgia, a suspect is usually allowed to get out of jail by posting bail unless he or she is accused of a capital crime" (Carl Vinson Institute of Government, 2001).

Preliminary Hearing

The preliminary hearing, known as the commitment hearing, is typically held in magistrate court as a court of inquiry. The purpose of the hearing is not to determine guilt, but "simply to determine whether there is sufficient reason to suspect the guilt of the accused and to require him to appear and answer before the court competent to try him. Whenever such probable cause exists, it is the duty of the court to commit" (O.C.G.A. § 17-7-23).

During the hearing, both the prosecuting attorney and defense attorney will present evidence. The prosecution will attempt to show the probable cause that the accused committed the crime(s) as charged and the case should proceed to trial, while the defense will attempt to show a lack of probable cause and why the defendant should be released without further proceedings. If the court deems that probable cause is established and the case involves a misdemeanor, an accusation will be prepared, the case will be forwarded to the appropriate court, and a trial date will be set. If probable cause is established and the case involves a felony, the prosecuting attorney will present an indictment for grand jury approval (Carl Vinson Institute of Government, 2001).

Accusation

An accusation is a formal charging document, prepared by the prosecuting attorney, used to bring the accused to trial. It functions in the same manner as the grand jury indictment, but it has not been reviewed or approved by any judicial body. Accusations are typically provided for misdemeanor cases; however, certain cases may be brought to court on a citation or summons without an accusation. Charges involving the operation and licensing of motor vehicles may be tried upon the uniform traffic citation and complaint, while charges involving game, fish, or boating may be tried upon a summons. Charges of possession of one ounce or less of marijuana or under age possession of alcohol heard in probate court may be tried by summons or citation (O.C.G.A. § 17-7-71/72).

An accusation must provide certain information, and will be considered sufficient for all cases if it substantially complies with the following form:

> IN THE _____ COURT OF _____ COUNTY
> STATE OF GEORGIA
>
> On behalf of the people of the State of Georgia, the undersigned, as prosecuting attorney for the county and state aforesaid, does hereby charge and accuse (name of accused) with the offense of ; for that the said (name of accused) (state with sufficient certainty the offense and the time and place it occurred) contrary to the laws of this state, the good order, peace, and dignity thereof.
>
> /s/
> (District attorney)
> (Solicitor-general)

If there is more than one charge, each additional charge shall state:

> The undersigned, as prosecuting attorney, does further charge and accuse the said (name of accused) with the offense of (the offense as before); for that the said (name of accused) (state with sufficient certainty the offense and the time and place it occurred), contrary to the laws of this state, the good order, peace, and dignity thereof (O.C.G.A. § 17-7-71).

The prosecuting attorney also has the authority to amend the accusation, (prior to the trial), to add an allegation, or to change the existing allegation. The amendment must be provided to the defendant. If the defendant submits a motion for continuance, the court shall grant the motion, which is reasonably necessitated by the amendment (O.C.G.A. § 17-7-71).

Grand Jury Indictment

Grand juries in Georgia consist of no less than 16 nor more than 23 persons. In addition, three alternate grand jurors may be sworn and serve in cases where any grand juror is unable to fulfill the responsibilities and duties (O.C.G.A. § 15-12-61). Grand juries function to determine if there is probable cause to reasonably believe that the suspect has committed the crime as charged.

The grand jury proceeding is different from the other pretrial procedures. The prosecutor will present an indictment, containing the allegations and summary of the evidence against the accused. The prosecutor will be the only one presenting evidence. Because the grand jury is an investigatory body and not a trier of facts, it is not bound by the rules of evidence required at trial. The deliberations are secret and the defendant does not have a right to be present or to present evidence (Reid, 2007).

If the grand jury determines there is sufficient probable cause to believe the accused has committed the crime(s) as charged, it will return a true bill of indictment, meaning the prosecutor's indictment has been approved and the accused is formally indicted on the charge(s). If the grand jury determines there is not enough probable cause, it will issue a no bill of indictment (Carl Vinson Institute of Government, 2001).

In addition to the duties of the indictment, grand juries in Georgia are also responsible for performing the following duties:

- inspect the condition and operations of the county jail at least once in each calendar year;
- inspect and examine the offices and operations of the clerk of superior court, the judge of probation court, and county treasurer or county depository at least once every three calendar years; and
- inspect and examine the offices of the district attorney at least once every three calendar years if the office is within the county (O.C.G.A. § 15-12-71).

Whenever deemed necessary by eight or more of its members, the grand jury may "appoint a committee of its members to inspect or investigate any county office or county public building or any public authority of the county or the office of any county officer, any court or court official of the county, the county board of education, or the county school superintendent or any of the records, accounts, property, or operations of any of the foregoing" (O.C.G.A § 15-12-71).

Arraignment

Once the accusation or indictment has been officially filed with the court, the accused will be brought to court for the arraignment. "Upon the arraignment of a person accused of committing a crime, the indictment or accusation shall be read to him and he shall be required to answer whether he is guilty or not guilty of the offense charged" (O.C.G.A. § 17-7-93).

The State of Georgia accepts three types of pleas. The guilty plea, offered by the accused at arraignment, will have the same force of law as if the accused had been found guilty by the verdict of a jury. At this point, the judge will determine if the accused is freely offering the plea before it is accepted by the court (O.C.G.A. § 17-7-93).

The not guilty plea offered at arraignment means that the accused is not accepting responsibility for the crimes as charged and will be held to answer for the charges at a criminal trial. At any time in the criminal justice process before judgment is pronounced, the accused may withdraw a guilty plea and offer a plea of not guilty (O.C.G.A. § 17-7-93).

The nolo contendere plea offered at arraignment means that the accused is not admitting responsibility for the crimes as charged but is willing to accept the full punishment as provided by law. The nolo contendere plea may be offered in all criminal cases, except capital felony, in any court in the state. However, the nolo contendere plea must have the consent and approval of the judge of the court. An advantage for the accused in offering the nolo contendere plea is that it cannot be used in any other court or proceedings as an admission of guilt or used for the purpose of civil disqualification to hold public office, vote, or serve on a jury (O.C.G.A. § 17-7-95).

Plea Bargaining

During any stage in the criminal justice process, a defendant may enter into a plea bargain with the prosecuting attorney. The purpose of the plea bargain is for the defendant to avoid going to trial while accepting guilt to some specific charge, typically a lesser charge than would be presented at trial.

Plea negotiations are typically carried out with the knowledge of the presiding trial judge. Even if the prosecution and defense enter into a plea agreement, the judge "is not legally bound by the agreement reached by the prosecutor and the defense attorney," and may have reason to believe the defendant is claiming guilt because of fear of the trial (Carl Vinson Institute of Government, 2001).

Although the majority of criminal cases are disposed of through plea bargains, there remains a constant controversy over the benefit and detriment of plea bargaining. "On the one hand, many people believe that our court system could not survive without plea bargaining. They argue that if it were forced to try everyone accused of a crime, the court system would collapse because of too many cases and enormous costs of so many trials. Other people oppose plea bargaining because it seems to put the responsibility of determining guilt on the prosecutor instead of on the judge and jury. They argue that plea bargaining works against a person's right to a trial by a jury of one's peers. They claim that plea bargaining enables guilty parties to get off with sentences that are too light" (Carl Vinson Institute of Government, 2001).

Pretrial Motions

All pretrial motions must be filed within ten days after the date of the arraignment, unless the court has extended the filing date (O.C.G.A. §17-7-110). There are various motions that can be presented to the court, presented by either the prosecution or the defense.

The motion to dismiss the case, typically submitted by the defense, asks the court to dismiss the case with no further proceedings. This motion is based on the presumption that there is insufficient evidence for the charges. The motion to suppress evidence petitions the court to not allow the introduction of certain evidence during the trial, thus not allowing the jury the opportunity to hear or see the evidence. This motion is based on an allegation that the evidence was obtained in violation of the defendant's rights. Either side may submit a motion for continuance, requesting additional time to prepare for the trial. The motion for change of venue asks the court to change the location of the trial. This motion is based on the presumption that the defendant will not be able to receive a fair trial or an impartial jury will be impossible to obtain in the current court of jurisdiction.

The discovery motion is typically filed by both the prosecution and the defense. The discovery process allows both sides to obtain and review the evidence that will be presented by the opposing side. The discovery process in Georgia is governed by O.C.G.A. §17-16, which provides that the prosecuting attorney must provide to the defendant, no later than ten days prior to trial, the opportunity to inspect, copy, and photograph: statements made by the defendant; the defendant's Georgia Crime Information Center (GCIC) criminal history; paper, documents, or other items; buildings or places in the control of the prosecuting attorney; any forensic evidence and testing results; and any physical or mental examinations presented by an expert witness. The same code provides that the defendant, within ten days of timely compliance by the prosecuting attorney, but no later than five days prior to trial, must provide the prosecuting attorney with the same opportunity to inspect, copy, and photograph the same evidence held by the defendant.

Criminal Trial

If the suspect has pled not guilty to the formal criminal charges, the next step in the process is the criminal trial. In this stage of the criminal justice process, certain steps are taken in a specific order.

Jury Selection

In the State of Georgia, the jury pool (venire) is selected from driver license and voter registration lists. The Council of Superior Court Clerks of Georgia compiles a statewide master jury list and provides the county master jury list to each county board of jury commissioners. For each court, the clerk will create a random list of persons from the county master jury list to comprise the venire (O.C.G.A. § 15-12-40.1). For each trial, potential jurors are sent a summons to appear at the designated court at a designated time.

During a process known as voir dire, both prosecuting and defense attorneys will question potential jurors and will decide to either keep or dismiss the juror. For misdemeanor cases, 12 jurors are impaneled, from which six jurors will be selected to constitute the jury (O.C.G.A. § 15-12-125). In felony cases, 30 jurors will be impaneled (42 jurors for death penalty cases), from which 12 jurors will be selected to constitute the jury (O.C.G.A. § 15-12-160.1).

In felony cases, each side may use the peremptory challenge for nine of the jurors impaneled, with 15 peremptory challenges being allowed in death penalty cases (O.C.G.A. § 15-12-165). In addition, each side may make the following objections to any juror, for which the juror shall be set aside for cause:

- the juror is not a citizen, resident of the county;
- the juror is under the age of 18;
- the juror is incompetent to serve because of mental illness, mental retardation, or intoxication;
- the juror is near in kin to the prosecutor, accused, or victim as to disqualify the juror;
- the juror has been convicted of a felony in federal or any court in the United States and the juror's civil rights have not been restored; or
- the juror is unable to communicate in English (O.C.G.A. § 15-12-163).

Presentation of Evidence

The prosecution will open the trial with an opening statement. Upon the end of the prosecution's statement, the defense may choose to provide an opening statement or may choose to wait to provide the opening statement until after the prosecution has rested its case.

The next step is the presentation of evidence. The prosecution will begin with the presentation of its evidence, which may include victim and/or witness oral or written testimony, demonstrative evidence (real to the senses—weapon, clothing, etc.), documentary evidence (written documents), character evidence (personality traits), or any scientific evidence (fingerprints, DNA, etc.) it deems necessary for its case. The defense has the opportunity to cross-examine and to challenge the inclusion of any evidence presented by the prosecution during the trial. The prosecution will then rest its case.

The defense will next have the opportunity to present its case. Because the burden of proof to prove a defendant guilty of a crime is on the prosecution, the defense does not have to present a case or challenge any of the prosecution's evidence. However, in most criminal trials, the defense presents its case, which includes providing witness testimony, physical and other evidence, and, in some cases, defendant testimony. As the defense was allowed with the prosecution's case, the prosecution may cross-examine and challenge any evidence presented by the defense.

During the presentation of the case by either side, the judge has the authority to regulate the admission of any evidence and to regulate the manner in which evidence is presented. If evidence is "vulgar and obscene or relates to the improper acts of the sexes, and tends to debauch the morals of the young, the presiding judge shall have the right in his discretion and on his own motion, or on motion of a party or his attorney, to hear and try the case after clearing the courtroom of all or any portion of the audience" (O.C.G.A. § 17-8-53). If the person testifying in relation to any sex offense is under 16 years of age, the judge "shall clear the courtroom of all persons except parties to the cause and their immediate families or guardians, attorneys and their secretaries, officers of the court, jurors, newspaper reporters or broadcasters, and court reporters" (O.C.G.A. § 17-8-54).

The judge also has authority to regulate the testimony of certain victims ten years of age or younger. If the child is a victim of cruelty to children, rape, sodomy or aggravated sodomy, child molestation or aggravated child molestation, or sexual assault, the child may be afforded the opportunity to present testimony outside the courtroom. The testimony is then shown in court through two-way closed circuit television. The judge may order this type of testimony if the testimony is taken during the criminal trial and if the judge determines the testimony by the child within the courtroom will result in the child suffering serious emotional distress that would keep the child from reasonably communicating. However, the child victim and defendant may, for identification purposes, be in the courtroom at the same time (O.C.G.A. § 17-8-55).

After both sides have presented their cases, the prosecution begins closing arguments, and once completed, the defense may present its closing arguments. Because the burden of proof rests with the prosecution, the prosecution may return with a final statement to the jury. In misdemeanor cases, each side is allowed one-half hour to present all closing arguments (O.C.G.A. § 17-

8-72). In felony cases, each side is allowed one hour to present all closing arguments (O.C.G.A. § 17-8-73).

Jury Deliberations

Once the trial has ended, the judge will provide instructions to the jury regarding the charges and any other pertinent information for the jury to deliberate the case. In the United States, the presumption of innocence is an important principle, as "it means that the prosecution has the responsibility of proving every element required for conviction and that the defendant does not have to prove innocence" (Reid, 2007). The standard of proof in any criminal case is beyond a reasonable doubt. This means that when jurors review all of the evidence, "they are convinced, satisfied to a moral certainty, that guilt has been established by the facts" (Reid, 2007). In Georgia, O.C.G.A. § 16-1-5 provides that "every person is presumed innocent until proved guilty. No person shall be convicted of a crime unless each element of such crime is proved beyond a reasonable doubt."

"The jury shall be the judges of the law and the facts in the trial of all criminal cases and shall give a general verdict of 'guilty' or 'not guilty'" (O.C.G.A. § 17-9-2). Once the jury has deliberated, the members may or may not reach a verdict. If there is a verdict of not guilty, the judge will move to dismiss the case and the defendant is free to leave. If the verdict is guilty, the judge will impose sentence.

Sentencing and Corrections

The State of Georgia provides punishments for those convicted of committing crimes in accordance with the provision against cruel and unusual punishment mandated by the 8th Amendment to the U.S. Constitution.

Punishments

Provided by O.C.G.A. § 17-10-2, except in cases where the death penalty or life without parole may be imposed, after a guilty verdict, the judge will conduct a presentence hearing for the sole purpose of determining punishment. For misdemeanor offenses, the punishment will include a fine not to exceed $1,000 or confinement in a county jail or county correctional facility for a maximum term of 12 months, or both (O.C.G.A. § 17-10-3). For convictions of misdemeanors of a high and aggravated nature, the fine increases to a maximum of $5,000 (O.C.G.A. § 17-10-4).

Several crimes are identified as serious violent felonies, which carry enhanced punishments. For the crimes of murder or felony murder, armed robbery, kidnapping, rape, aggravated child molestation, aggravated sodomy, or aggravated sexual battery, the punishment involves a minimum mandatory sentence of ten years, with no portion being suspended, stayed, probated, deferred, or withheld, nor reduced by any form of pardon, parole, or commutation of the sentence. In addition, a first conviction for a serious violent felony, where the offender has been sentenced to life in prison, requires the offender to serve a minimum of 14 years in prison, with no reduction for earned time, early/work release, or other sentence-reducing measures (O.C.G.A. § 17-10-6.1).

For an offender who is convicted of a felony and has a previous conviction for a felony in this or any other state with a sentence of confinement, the sentence will be for the longest period prescribed by the punishment for the current offense. An offender who is convicted of a serious violent felony and has a previous conviction for a serious violent felony, and who is not sentenced to death for the current offense, will be sentenced to life without parole. An offender who has been convicted of a felony, other than a capital felony, and who has previously been convicted of three felonies in this or any other state, will be sentenced to the maximum time for the current offense, with no eligibility for parole until the maximum sentence has been served (O.C.G.A. § 17-10-7).

If it is determined that the offender intentionally selected the victim(s) as the object of the offense based on prejudice or bias (known as hate crime), the judge may sentence the offender to enhanced penalties:

- if the conviction is for a misdemeanor, the normal punishment will be increased by 50 percent up to the maximum authorized by law;
- if the conviction is for a misdemeanor of high and aggravated nature, the normal punishment will be increased by 50 percent up to the maximum authorized by law; and
- if the conviction is for a felony, the normal punishment will be increased up to five years, not to exceed the maximum authorized by law (O.C.G.A. § 17-10-17).

Capital Felony Convictions

"In all capital cases, other than those of homicide, when the verdict is 'guilty,' with a recommendation for mercy, it shall be legal and shall mean imprisonment for life. When the verdict is 'guilty,' without a recommendation for mercy, it shall be legal and shall mean that the convicted person shall be sentenced to death" (O.C.G.A. § 17-9-3). If the offender was not 17 years of age at the time of the crime, the punishment shall not be death but imprisonment for life.

For the crimes of treason and aircraft hijacking, the death penalty may be imposed for any case. For the crimes of murder, rape, armed robbery, or kidnapping, the judge shall include in the instructions to the jury any of the following mitigating or aggravating circumstances for its consideration:

- the offender has a prior record of conviction for a capital felony;
- the offense was committed while the offender was committing another capital felony or aggravated battery, or murder was committed while committing burglary or arson in the first degree;
- the offender created a great risk of death to more than one person in a public place by means of a weapon normally hazardous to the lives of more than one person;
- the offender committed murder for the purpose of receiving money or anything of monetary value;
- the murder of a current or former judicial officer, current or former district attorney, or solicitor-general was committed during or because of the exercise of his or her official duties;
- the offender caused or directed another to commit murder or the offender committed murder as an agent or employee of another;
- the offense was outrageously or wantonly vile, horrible, or inhumane, involving torture, depravity of mind, or aggravated battery to the victim;
- the murder was committed against a peace officer, corrections employee, or firefighter engaged in official duties;
- the murder was committed by a person in, or who escaped from, the lawful custody of a peace officer or place of lawful confinement; or
- the murder was committed for the purpose of avoiding, interfering with, or preventing a lawful arrest or custody of himself or another (O.C.G.A. § 17-10-30).

Currently the State of Georgia uses lethal injection as the method of execution, carried out by the Department of Corrections. "Lethal injection is the continuous intravenous injection of a substance or substances sufficient to cause death into the body of the person sentenced to death until such person is dead" (O.C.G.A. § 17-10-38).

Corrections

There are numerous correctional options provided to those convicted of crime. Misdemeanor offenders will be incarcerated in a local jail, while felony offenders will be incarcerated in a state prison. But corrections involves more than just confinement.

The various sentencing and punishment options available in the state include fines, probation, community service, electronic monitoring (telephone lines/GPS tracking), house arrest, restitution, forfeitures (RICO Act), work release, court fees, curfews, drug and alcohol testing and treatment, and anger management courses. All of these, and any other sanctions deemed appropriate by the court, can be given separately or combined, based on the needs of the offender, the victim, and the state.

Conclusion

The criminal justice process in the State of Georgia is complex, yet similar in form and function to those in other states across the country. The process consists of various stages, each designed to provide the accused or defendant with ample opportunity to be informed of his or her constitutional and individual rights, the assistance of legal council, the opportunity to present evidence in favor of his or her innocence, and the opportunity to participate in all stages of the criminal justice process.

Most stages of the process are governed by either federal constitutional amendments, federal case law, Georgia case law, and/or Georgia statutes. The State of Georgia, in prosecuting those accused of committing crime, takes great care in providing an unbiased and legally sound process for all involved.

Chapter Review Questions

1. Describe the provisions of use of force during an arrest.
2. Explain the limitations of search and seizure.
3. Describe the various pretrial procedures.
4. Explain the steps in the trial, including jury selection, presentation of evidence, and jury deliberation.
5. Discuss the various punishments available for misdemeanors, felonies, and capital felonies.

References

4th Amendment. (1791). United States Constitution.
8th Amendment. (1971). United States Constitution.

Argersinger v. Hamlin, 407 U.S. 25 (1972)

Brinegar v. U.S., 338 U.S. 160 (1949)

Carl Vinson Institute of Government. (2001). *An Introduction to Law in Georgia, 3rd Edition*. Athens, GA: University of Georgia.

Gideon v. Wainwright, 372 U.S. 335 (1963)

Miranda v. Arizona, 384 U.S. 436 (1966)

O.C.G.A. § 15-12-40.1. (2011). Official Code of Georgia Annotated.

O.C.G.A. § 15-12-61. (2011). Official Code of Georgia Annotated.

O.C.G.A. § 15-12-71. (2011). Official Code of Georgia Annotated.

O.C.G.A. § 15-12-125. (2011). Official Code of Georgia Annotated.

O.C.G.A. § 15-12-160.1. (2011). Official Code of Georgia Annotated.

O.C.G.A. § 15-12-163. (2011). Official Code of Georgia Annotated.

O.C.G.A. § 15-12-165. (2011). Official Code of Georgia Annotated.

O.C.G.A. § 17-2-1. (2011). Official Code of Georgia Annotated.

O.C.G.A. § 17-2-2. (2011). Official Code of Georgia Annotated.

O.C.G.A. § 17-3-1. (2011). Official Code of Georgia Annotated.

O.C.G.A. § 17-3-2.1. (2011). Official Code of Georgia Annotated.

O.C.G.A. § 17-3-2.2. (2011). Official Code of Georgia Annotated.

O.C.G.A. § 17-4-1. (2011). Official Code of Georgia Annotated.

O.C.G.A. § 17-4-3. (2011). Official Code of Georgia Annotated.

O.C.G.A. § 17-4-20. (2011). Official Code of Georgia Annotated.

O.C.G.A. § 17-4-24. (2011). Official Code of Georgia Annotated.

O.C.G.A. § 17-4-26. (2011). Official Code of Georgia Annotated.

O.C.G.A. § 17-4-27. (2011). Official Code of Georgia Annotated.

O.C.G.A. § 17-4-40. (2011). Official Code of Georgia Annotated.

O.C.G.A. § 17-4-41. (2011). Official Code of Georgia Annotated.

O.C.G.A. § 17-4-45. (2011). Official Code of Georgia Annotated.

O.C.G.A. § 17-4-46. (2011). Official Code of Georgia Annotated.

O.C.G.A. § 17-4-60. (2011). Official Code of Georgia Annotated.

O.C.G.A. § 17-4-62. (2011). Official Code of Georgia Annotated.

O.C.G.A. § 17-5-1. (2011). Official Code of Georgia Annotated.

O.C.G.A. § 17-5-20. (2011). Official Code of Georgia Annotated.

O.C.G.A. § 17-5-21. (2011). Official Code of Georgia Annotated.

O.C.G.A. § 17-5-25. (2011). Official Code of Georgia Annotated.

O.C.G.A. § 17-5-26. (2011). Official Code of Georgia Annotated.

O.C.G.A. § 17-5-27. (2011). Official Code of Georgia Annotated.

O.C.G.A. § 17-5-28. (2011). Official Code of Georgia Annotated.

O.C.G.A. § 17-5-29. (2011). Official Code of Georgia Annotated.

O.C.G.A. § 17-5-100. (2011). Official Code of Georgia Annotated.

O.C.G.A. § 17-7-23. (2011). Official Code of Georgia Annotated.

O.C.G.A. § 17-7-71. (2011). Official Code of Georgia Annotated.

O.C.G.A. § 17-7-72. (2011). Official Code of Georgia Annotated.
O.C.G.A. § 17-7-93. (2011). Official Code of Georgia Annotated.
O.C.G.A. § 17-7-195. (2011). Official Code of Georgia Annotated.
O.C.G.A. § 17-7-110. (2011). Official Code of Georgia Annotated.
O.C.G.A. § 17-8-53. (2011). Official Code of Georgia Annotated.
O.C.G.A. § 17-8-54. (2011). Official Code of Georgia Annotated.
O.C.G.A. § 17-8-55. (2011). Official Code of Georgia Annotated.
O.C.G.A. § 17-8-72. (2011). Official Code of Georgia Annotated.
O.C.G.A. § 17-8-73. (2011). Official Code of Georgia Annotated.
O.C.G.A. § 17-9-2. (2011). Official Code of Georgia Annotated.
O.C.G.A. § 17-9-3. (2011). Official Code of Georgia Annotated.
O.C.G.A. § 17-10-2. (2011). Official Code of Georgia Annotated.
O.C.G.A. § 17-10-3. (2011). Official Code of Georgia Annotated.
O.C.G.A. § 17-10-4. (2011). Official Code of Georgia Annotated.
O.C.G.A. § 17-10-6.1. (2011). Official Code of Georgia Annotated.
O.C.G.A. § 17-10-7. (2011). Official Code of Georgia Annotated.
O.C.G.A. § 17-10-17. (2011). Official Code of Georgia Annotated.
O.C.G.A. § 17-10-30. (2011). Official Code of Georgia Annotated.
O.C.G.A. § 17-10-38. (2011). Official Code of Georgia Annotated.
O.C.G.A. § 17-16. (2011). Official Code of Georgia Annotated.
Reid, Sue Titus. (2007). *Criminal Justice, 8th Ed*. Cincinnati, OH: Atomic Dog Publishing.

CHAPTER 6

LAW ENFORCEMENT IN GEORGIA

Learning Objectives

After reading the chapter, students will be able to:

- Identify federal law enforcement training and presence in the state.
- Discuss the various law enforcement agencies on the state level.
- Discuss the various units within county and municipal law enforcement agencies.
- Explain the Georgia Crime Information Center and how the information collected by the Center is used by law enforcement.
- Describe the Community Oriented Policing concept.
- Explain national accreditation and state certification and why it is important to law enforcement.
- Identify state and local law enforcement support organizations.

Key Terms

Accreditation	Georgia Association of Chiefs
Campus Police	of Police
Community Oriented Policing	Georgia Sheriff's Association
County Marshals	Municipal Law Enforcement
County Police	Police Chief
E911	Sheriff
Federal Law Enforcement	
Training Center	

Law enforcement in the State of Georgia has a rich history, predating America's Independence. Law enforcement exists on the federal, state, and local levels, and includes academies and training facilities, education, and employment in a wide array of law enforcement positions. As of June 2011, there are 1,092 local and state agencies employing 59,012 certified peace officers in the state.

Law enforcement in Georgia has also seen its share of officers pay the ultimate sacrifice in the line of duty. Federal law enforcement has had 32 officers killed in the line of duty, dating back to 1794 when U.S. Marshal Robert Forsyth became the first Marshal and only the third law enforcement officer killed in the line of duty in the United States. On the state level, 58 officers have been killed in the line of duty, almost half coming from the Georgia State Patrol (26), and 16 from the Department of Corrections. On the local level, 558 officers have been killed in the line of duty, 207 at the county level and 351 at the municipal level. "When a police officer is killed, it's not an agency that loses an officer, it's an entire nation" (Officer Down Memorial Page, 2011).

Federal Law Enforcement in Georgia

As in all other states, federal law enforcement has a significant presence in Georgia. Offices for most federal agencies are located throughout the state, with many having central or regional offices in Atlanta as well as several other metropolitan areas. In addition, the largest presence of federal law enforcement agents can be found at the Federal Law Enforcement Training Center, the primary training facility for federal law enforcement.

Federal Law Enforcement Training Center

The Federal Law Enforcement Training Center (FLETC) is headquartered and has its main campus in Glynco, located on the east coast near Brunswick, equidistant between Savannah and Jacksonville, Florida. Glynco is not a recognized city, but rather the city and zip code servicing FLETC only. FLETC is currently part of the U.S. Department of Homeland Security, serving "as an interagency law enforcement training organization for over 80 Federal agencies" as well as providing services to local, state, tribal, and international law enforcement agencies. Partner organizations include 62 agencies from the executive branch, 3 agencies from the legislative branch, 2 agencies from the judicial branch, and 22 other agencies (FLETC, 2011).

Prior to the creation of FLETC, law enforcement training for federal agents was individualized for each agency and costly for the federal government. Studies in the late 1960s showed a vital need for a cost-effective and high-quality training curriculum that would serve all federal agencies in one central location, and include standardized course content delivered by professional instructors. In 1970, Congress authorized funds for the establishment of the Consolidated Federal Law Enforcement Training Center as a bureau of the Department of the Treasury, housed in temporary facilities in Washington, D.C. In May 1975, the former Glynco Naval Air Station was chosen as the permanent site for the training center, and the name shortened to FLETC. The first training began in September 1975. Since that time, FLETC has expanded to include facilities in Artesia, N.M., Charleston, S.C., Cheltenham, Md., as well as Gabarone, Botswana. On March 1, 2003, FLETC was formally transferred to the newly created Department of Homeland Security (FLETC, 2011).

State Law Enforcement in Georgia

Law enforcement at the state level in Georgia is varied and vast among numerous agencies. Duties among state law enforcement officers include patrol and traffic enforcement, criminal investigations, homeland security, and community relations.

Department of Natural Resources

The Department of Natural Resources (DNR) is responsible for the conservation and management of Georgia's natural and cultural resources. It is comprised of six divisions: Coast Resources; Environmental Protection; Historic Preservation; Parks, Recreation and Historic Sites; Sustainability; and Wildlife Resources. The legal authority for DNR includes air, soil, and water; all game species of animals, birds, and fish; all non-game species of animals, birds, and fish; all plants, whether common, endangered, or protected; and cultural, historic, or recreational resources within the state (Department of Natural Resources [DNR], 2011).

Environmental Protection Division

The Environmental Protection Division is responsible for bringing individuals, businesses, and government entities into compliance with environmental laws through the use of enforcement actions, such as consent and administrative orders. The Division is structured with seven district offices located throughout the state, and consists of three branches: air protection, land protection, and watershed protection. In addition, the Division handles hazardous waste that is generated or stored by government or businesses, and includes cleanup of contaminated sites (DNR, 2011).

Wildlife Resources Division

The Wildlife Resources Division is concerned with hunting, fishing, and boating within the state. Law enforcement within the Division focuses on protecting Georgia's wildlife populations, including game and nongame animals, threatened and endangered plants and animals, exotic animals, boating safety, litter and waste control, and other natural resource issues. In addition, conservation rangers provide hunter education and boating safety programs, while also conducting investigations into reported violations of wildlife laws, and hunting and boating accidents (DNR, 2011).

Department of Public Safety

The Georgia Department of Public Safety (DPS) is the largest state law enforcement agency, overseeing the day-to-day operations of the Capital Police, the Georgia State Patrol (GSP), and the Motor Carrier Compliance Division (MCCD). The DPS, created in 1937, is headed by a commissioner, who serves as the Chief Executive and holds the rank of Colonel in the Georgia State Patrol. The Deputy Commissioner, who holds the rank of lieutenant colonel in the Georgia State Patrol, currently oversees the daily operations of several divisions, including field operations for GSP, headquarters, special projects, capital police, comptroller, executive security, human resources, motor carrier compliance, operations review, planning, public information office, and training (Georgia Department of Public Safety [DPS], 2011a).

Legal Services and Special Investigations

Two units within the DPS are directly supervised by the Commissioner: Legal Services and Special Investigations. The Legal Services Unit has several purposes. It works with other state agencies in public safety-related matters; it processes requests for open records; it files Safety Responsibility claims to suspend driver licenses of those who damage GSP vehicles; it acts as liaison with the Department of Law in civil litigation matters; it drafts or reviews all proposed legislation impacting the DPS; and works with the Personnel Services staff to ensure compliance with state and federal labor laws (DPS, 2011b).

The Special Investigations Unit is comprised of four smaller units. The Internal Affairs Unit investigates allegations of misconduct made against DPS employees, as well as the misuse of radar speed-timing devices by any law enforcement agency in the state that has been certified by DPS. The Background Investigation Unit conducts background checks on all potential DPS employees. The Polygraph Unit assists the Internal Affairs and Background Investigation Units, providing polygraph examinations to employees, potential employees, and witnesses. The Permits Unit is responsible for the issuance of wholesale/retail firearms licenses (for handguns under 15 inches in length) and speed detection device permits (DPS, 2011b).

Capital Police

The Capital Police Services Unit provides primary security and law enforcement to the Capital Hill area. Enforcement includes preventing and detecting criminal behavior, protection of life and property, enforcing traffic regulations, investigating traffic crashes, and managing street closures throughout Capital Hill. "This includes the apprehension of criminals, traffic enforcement and protection of public and building security in the Capitol Hill area" (DPS, 2011c).

The Capital Square Security Unit is responsible for providing general security to Capital Square, including courtroom security for Georgia's Supreme Court and Court of Appeals, as well as security to elected officials, government employees, and visitors. The Unit "monitors entrances into these buildings by checking all State employees, guests and other personnel for valid identification; screens all incoming packages, deliveries and mail" (DPS, 2011c).

Georgia State Patrol

The Georgia State Patrol (GSP) is the most visible division within the Department of Public Safety. In the late 1930s, traffic fatalities and increased crime led to a call for a law enforcement agency with statewide arrest powers. In March 1937, the General Assembly created the Georgia State Patrol and in the summer of that year, the first Trooper School graduated 80 troopers. Since then, 86 Trooper Schools have been held. A leading law enforcement agency in the country, GSP was the first agency to place dash-mounted cameras in each of its patrol cars. In addition, all troopers are trained in the Pursuit Intervention Technique (P.I.T.) maneuver that allows troopers to end vehicle pursuits quickly and effectively (DPS, 2011a).

Field Operations for GSP includes several sections, employing 1,086 certified peace officers (Georgia Peace Officer Standards and Training [P.O.S.T.] Council, 2011). The troopers are divided into nine Troops (A-I). Each Troop is commanded by a captain, who is assisted by two lieutenants. Each Troop is comprised of a number of counties, with Troop C being the smallest, containing five counties surrounding Metro Atlanta, and Troop G being the largest with 23 counties. Each Troop is further divided into Posts (1–48). Each Post is commanded by a sergeant first class, who is assisted by one or more buck sergeants or corporals. Each Post is comprised of a number of counties, ranging from three to seven (DPS, 2011d).

Troop J is comprised of two specialty units. The troopers of the Safety Education Unit actively promote the safe operation of motor vehicles within their respective communities, by providing education and instruction to schools, civic groups, and various other community organizations. The troopers of the Implied Consent Unit maintain the breath-alcohol program for the state and work closely with the Forensics Science Division of the Georgia Bureau of Investigation in providing expert testimony in DUI cases (DPS, 2011d).

The Specialized Collision Reconstruction Team (SCRT) is trained to reconstruct and investigate fatal crashes so evidence can be properly and accurately presented in court. The SCRT consists of five teams located across the state to assist troopers with fatal crashes. Each team is equipped with the latest technology and on call 24 hours a day. The SCRT also assists other agencies in homicides, officer-involved shootings, fatal crashes, and large crime scene investigations when requested (DPS, 2011d).

The Special Weapons and Tactical (SWAT) team is comprised of GSP troopers who serve on the team part-time, being called from their regular duties when critical incidents occur. The SWAT team assists all law enforcement agencies throughout the state in handling and resolving critical incidents, such as hostage and barricaded subjects (DPS, 2011d).

The Criminal Interdiction Unit (CIU) provides assistance to local, state, and federal law enforcement agencies in the detection of drugs and the interdiction of drug trafficking. The CIU participates in the statewide effort to reduce drug trafficking and has been instrumental in seizing drugs, cash, and other assets from drug dealers and transporters (DPS, 2011d).

The Nighthawks DUI Task Force began in 2004 with ten of the most highly trained DUI officers in the state. These officers patrol the metro Atlanta area that includes Clayton, Cobb, DeKalb, Fulton, and Gwinnett counties, during peak DUI-related hours. The task force received the International Association of Chiefs of Police National Impairment Enforcement Award in 2005. In 2009, the DUI Nighthawks South Team was established in Bulloch County, to patrol the Savannah and Statesboro areas (DPS, 2011d).

The Georgia State Patrol Motorcycle Unit targets "speeding, seat belt violators, improper lane changes, following too closely and driving under the influence violators aggressively and judicially on the interstates of metro Atlanta" (DPS, 2011d). The goals of the Motorcycle Unit include increasing speed compliance on the interstate systems in the state; increasing seat belt compliance; reducing crashes by 20 percent; and targeting aggressive and DUI drivers (DPS, 2011d).

Executive Security Division

The Department of Public Safety is responsible for security details for the executive branch of Georgia state government. The Executive Security Unit provides physical security for the Governor's Mansion as well as personal security for residents. The Executive Protection Unit provides continuous personal security for the Governor, Lieutenant Governor, Speaker of the House, and their respective families (DPS, 2011e).

Motor Carrier Compliance Division

The Motor Carrier Compliance Division (MCCD) complies with the Federal Motor Carrier Safety Assistance Program and conducts safety inspections of commercial motor vehicles. The inspections include highway shipments of hazardous materials, safety performance audits on motor carriers, and commercial transit. The MCCD also governs vehicle size (height, length, and width) and vehicle weight (DPS, 2011f).

The MCCD is divided into nine regions, with 19 permanent inspection stations located throughout the state, primarily located on Interstate highways. Along with the visible inspection stations, under O.C.G.A. §40-16-2, the MCCD is also responsible for the enforcement of High Occupancy Vehicle (HOV) lanes. The 100+ miles of HOV lanes in metro Atlanta are provided for vehicles with two or more occupants, emergency vehicles, buses, and alternative fuel vehicles. The MCCD also inspects diesel powered vehicles, and assists with accidents, crashes, natural disasters, and community relations. In addition, all MCCD officers are certified peace officers with full arrest powers (DPS, 2011f).

Georgia Bureau of Investigation

The Georgia Bureau of Investigation (GBI) began in 1937 as part of the Georgia Department of Public Safety. Initially titled the Division of Criminal Identification, Detection, Prevention, and Investigation, it was the "plain clothes" division, while the Georgia State Patrol was the uniform division. "The initial charter authorized this division to maintain fingerprint and criminal history information and to employ agents as criminal investigators to assist local law enforcement officers throughout the state" (Georgia Bureau of Investigation [GBI], 2011a). In 1940, the name was changed to the current GBI.

In 1952, the Fulton County Crime Laboratory became part of the Department of Public Safety as the State Crime Laboratory, making it only the second statewide crime laboratory to be established in the United States. In 1972, under then Governor Jimmy Carter, an executive order was issued to create the Georgia Crime Information Center (GCIC). Because the GBI was responsible for maintaining fingerprints and criminal history information, the newly established GCIC became part of the Bureau. Additionally, Governor Carter proposed extensive changes to the organization of the executive branch of the state government. As a result, the GBI was separated from the Department of Public Safety and made an independent agency (GBI, 2011a).

The GBI is headed by a Director, who is appointed by the governor. The GBI consists of three divisions, each with numerous departments and units, that provide specialized service to the Criminal Justice System in Georgia. The GBI currently employs 306 certified peace officers (P.O.S.T. Council, 2011).

Investigative Division

The Investigative Division is the largest division within the GBI, comprised of more than 350 employees. The Division is divided into 15 regional investigative offices, each comprised of numerous counties, from seven to fourteen. Each region is staffed with two supervisors, an investigative assistant, and a number of special agents. In addition, each region employs at least one Child Abuse Specialist and one Crime Scene Specialist. The division's primary responsibility is to assist local law enforcement, when requested, with a variety of felony criminal investigations, including homicide, rape, armed robbery, child abuse, and fraud. In addition, special agents investigate crimes occurring on state-owned property (GBI, 2011b).

The Division operates six Regional Drug Enforcement Offices across the state in Canton, Carrollton, Milledgeville, Savannah, Sylvester, and Thomson. Each of these offices is responsible for drug law enforcement within designated areas of the state. In addition, the GBI works with the Criminal Justice Coordinating Council and local law enforcement agencies in 11 statewide Multi-Jurisdictional Drug Task Forces. With local law enforcement officers working the investigations, the GBI provides a supervisor for each task force, who provides supervisory and operational oversight (GBI, 2011b).

The GBI has also assigned agents to several other drug enforcement initiatives. The Atlanta High Intensity Drug Trafficking Area is comprised of local, state, and federal drug enforcement agents who work to identify and arrest regional drug traffickers operating in metro Atlanta, particularly in Cobb, DeKalb, Fulton, and Gwinnett counties. The Organized Crime Drug Enforcement Task

Forces Strike Force is focused on international drug cartels doing business in metro Atlanta (GBI, 2011b).

The Division also employs agents in a variety of specialized units: Child Exploitation and Computer Crimes Unit, Communications Center, Financial Investigations Unit, Georgia Information Sharing Analysis Center, Georgia Medicaid Fraud Control Unit, Major Theft Unit, Polygraph Unit, Special Operations Unit, and Training Unit. In addition, other services provided by the Division include the Bingo Unit, Body Recovery Team, Child Abduction Response Team, Crisis Intervention Team, Document and Benefit Fraud, Forensic Art, Identity Theft, Social Security Fraud, and Counter Terrorism Task Force (GBI, 2011b).

Division of Forensic Sciences

The Division of Forensic Sciences (DOFS) was established with the addition of the State Crime Laboratory in 1952. "Laboratory scientists and technicians in specialized disciplines collect, analyze, and interpret all aspects of physical evidence for officers, investigators, and District Attorneys throughout the state" (GBI, 2011c). The headquarters laboratory is located in Decatur, with regional laboratories located across the state. In addition, many individual departments provide specialized technology in forensic investigations (GBI, 2001c):

- Chemistry—analysis of evidence items for the presence or absence of controlled substances
- Firearms—examination of firearms and components, bullets and cartridges, distance determination tests, toolmarks, serial number restoration, and NIBIN database
- Forensic Biology—provides timely scientific analysis of biological evidence
- Implied Consent—oversees the state's breath alcohol testing program
- Latent Prints—identification and comparison of fingerprints and AFIS database
- Medical Examiners—provides forensic pathology under the authority of the Georgia Death Investigation Act
- Operations Support—evidence receiving, entry into LIMS, evidence transport, and storage/disposition of evidence
- Photography—photography services
- Quality System—ensures compliance with accreditation standards and DOFS quality standards
- Questioned Documents—examination of documents, handwriting, mechanical impressions, footwear and tire impressions, and photography services

- Toxicology—provides state and local law enforcement and medical examiners with vital information about human biological samples, specifically whether drugs, alcohol, or poisons played a role in the commission of a crime or death
- Trace Evidence—analyzes paint, plastic, hair, fiber, glass, fractured materials, general materials, and gunshot residue

Georgia Crime Information Center (GCIC)

The Georgia Crime Information Center (GCIC) supplies 24-hour access to a computerized database containing the criminal history, fingerprints, and criminal records of more than 2,600,000 individuals. The GCIC was the first state criminal history database to establish an Automated Fingerprint Identification System (AFIS), allowing the GCIC to receive electronic fingerprint submissions from more than 350 agencies. The GCIC currently receives an average of 1,000 electronic fingerprint transactions daily (GBI, 2011d).

In addition, the GCIC maintains several other databases. The Georgia Protective Order Registry began July 1, 2002 and stores protective orders issued by Superior Courts. The database provides victims and law enforcement officers with 24-hour access to over 43,000 orders. The Georgia Sexually Violent Offender Registry began in 1997, providing images and information on registered sex offenders. The link may be accessed at any time and is updated daily (GBI, 2011d).

Medical Examiner's Office

The Medical Examiner's Office provides forensic pathology services to 153 counties in Georgia. Death cases are reported by coroners, deputy coroners, and law enforcement agencies for a death occurring in one or more of the following circumstances:

- homicide, suicide, or suspicious unknown circumstances
- unlawful use of controlled substances, chemicals, or toxins
- while incarcerated or in custody of law enforcement
- apparently accidental or after an injury
- disease, injury or toxic agent during employment
- while not under care of physician during immediate period before death
- related to disease that could constitute threat to health of general public
- human remains disposed in offensive manner

Based on the examiner's investigation, there are five determinations for the manner of death:

- homicide—death by actions of another
- natural—death from disease or medical condition
- accidental—unintended death
- suicide—intentional death that is self-inflicted
- undetermined—little or no evidence to establish manner of death (GBI, 2011e).

Georgia Emergency Management Agency/ Homeland Security

The Georgia Emergency Management Agency/Homeland Security (GEMA) is the lead agency in the state for coordinated planning and response in emergency situations that require a multi-agency response and support. "GEMA's mission is to provide a comprehensive and aggressive all-hazards approach to homeland security initiatives, mitigation, preparedness, response, recovery, and special events in order to protect life and property and prevent and/or reduce negative impacts of terrorism and natural disasters in Georgia" (Georgia Emergency Management Agency/Homeland Security [GEMA], 2011).

In mirroring the Federal Emergency Management Agency (FEMA), GEMA provides preparedness, response, and recovery initiatives for Georgia in natural and man-made disasters and crises. Preparedness includes hurricanes, radiological preparedness, school safety, and terrorism. Response includes State Warning Point, an interactive communications interface that is linked to FEMA, state agencies, and all 159 counties and disseminates information rapidly and effectively. Alerts include the Emergency Alert System, Levi's Call (child abduction), Mattie's Call (disabled or elderly persons), and Kimberly's Call (violent criminals at large). Recovery includes individual assistance, disaster recovery centers, and public and local government assistance (GEMA, 2011).

Governor's Office of Highway Safety

The Governor's Office of Highway Safety (GOHS) is a multifaceted agency, working with local and state law enforcement, as well as community and civic organizations, with the goals of increasing awareness of highway safety and decreasing traffic crashes and fatalities on Georgia's roads. A major component of the GOHS is to collect and maintain statistical data on various aspects of highway safety. In addition, through the Traffic Enforcement Services division, the GOHS promotes numerous programs and provides funding for law enforcement initiatives that relate to highway safety. Programs include Operation Zero Tolerance (targeting DUI), Click It or Ticket! (targeting seat belt compliance), and Georgia H.E.A.T. (Highway Enforcement of Aggressive Traffic, targeting aggressive drivers) (Governor's Office of Highway Safety [GOHS], 2011).

The GOHS also provides educational and training programs for citizens. These include child passenger safety (car seat compliance), bicycle and pedestrian safety, motorcycle safety (laws and riding techniques), and the Georgia Young Adult Program (education to decrease injuries and fatalities among young drivers) (GOHS, 2011).

Metropolitan Atlanta Rapid Transit Authority

The Metropolitan Atlanta Rapid Transit Authority (MARTA) Police Department is a unique law enforcement agency in the state. As a transportation agency, the MARTA Police Department has jurisdiction throughout DeKalb and Fulton Counties, the current jurisdictions for MARTA's bus and rail lines. Established in 1977 with 26 officers, the department has grown to include various units and operational areas found in traditional law enforcement agencies (Metropolitan Atlanta Rapid Transit Authority [MARTA] Police Department, 2011).

The MARTA Police Department currently employs 310 certified peace officers (P.O.S.T. Council, 2011). These officers work in numerous operational departments, including criminal investigations, bomb assessment, explosive K-9 and disposal technicians, crisis negotiations, metro fugitive task force, bike patrol, juvenile crime prevention, gang liaison, communications, property and evidence, narcotics K-9, crime scene, emergency preparedness, community outreach, and joint terrorism task force.

The department was the first of currently four transit agencies in the country to achieve national certification through the Commission on Accreditation for Law Enforcement Agencies (CALEA) in 1996 and has since been reaccredited every three years. In addition, the department has achieved certification from the Georgia Association of Chiefs of Police (MARTA Police Department, 2011).

Additional State Law Enforcement Agencies

Numerous additional state agencies contain a law enforcement component or investigatory unit, employed with certified peace officers. These agencies include the Department of Agriculture, the Secretary of State, the Public Service Commission, the Georgia Public Safety Training Center, the Building Authority and Ports Authority, the Georgia Forestry Commission, the state Fire Marshal, and the Department of Revenue. In addition, Stone Mountain Park and the World Congress Center are popular tourist attractions where safety and security issues require law enforcement presence.

County Law Enforcement in Georgia

Georgia consists of 159 counties, each represented by a sheriff, the chief law enforcement officer, who is elected to serve four-year terms. The position of sheriff is governed by O.C.G.A. § 15-16-1, which stipulates the following qualifications for eligibility to hold the office of sheriff:

- citizen of the United States;
- resident of the county for at least two years immediately preceding the date of qualifying for election;
- registered voter;
- at least 25 years of age;
- obtained a high school degree or equivalent in educational training as established by the Georgia Peace Officer Standards and Training (P.O.S.T.) Council;
- no conviction for a felony or any offense involving moral turpitude in Georgia or any other state;
- fingerprinted in local, state, and national databases to disclose any criminal record;
- provided a complete written history of places of residence for the preceding six years;
- provided a complete written history of places of employment for the preceding six years; and
- registered peace officer as provided in O.C.G.A. § 35-8-10 or must obtain certification as a peace officer within six months of taking office.

"Georgia was one of the first states to mandate qualifications for those seeking the Office of Sheriff, the first state to mandate in-service training, and the first state to conduct specialized training for newly elected sheriffs" (Georgia Sheriff's Association, 2011a).

The oldest recognized law enforcement agency in Georgia, as well as one of the oldest in the country, is the Chatham County Sheriff's Office, established in 1732 in Savannah. The title of sheriff, however, was not adopted until 1788, after the title of Bailiff, held from 1732 to 1753, and Provost, held from 1754 to 1787. "The Office of the Sheriff is mandated by law to perform certain functions for the County. The Sheriff is also mandated to execute all warrants, civil processes, subpoenas, and writs delivered to him by the courts" (Chatham County Sheriff's Office, 2011a).

Sheriff's Office

The sheriff carries out law enforcement duties and responsibilities with assistance from deputy sheriffs. All deputy sheriffs must be certified as peace officers by the state (see Chapter 15). Deputy sheriffs have countywide jurisdiction and are able to make arrests for violations of county ordinances as well as state statutes. There are currently 17,242 certified deputy sheriffs throughout the state. An additional 2,013 certified peace officers work in communications units and 1,992 work in corrections. There are 242 peace officers working as county marshals in 20 offices statewide, while another 48 peace officers are employed with seven county fire departments (P.O.S.T. Council, 2011).

The typical sheriff's office in Georgia is comprised of numerous divisions, each with its own command structure, but all of which ultimately report to the sheriff. A military style, clear chain of command structure is utilized, and unlike other law enforcement agencies, employees of the sheriff's office work at the pleasure of the sheriff.

Administrative Division

The administrative division encompasses the office of the sheriff and his or her immediate staff. An undersheriff or chief deputy is the second in command, and assists the sheriff with operations and policies, as well as community relations. The next rank of major handles personnel matters and day-to-day operations. These include the maintenance of records, property and evidence collection and storage, equipment, and community relations (public information reports). In addition, the Division is also responsible for desk services, and is the point of contact for individuals visiting the sheriff's office.

Patrol Division

Comprising the largest section of the sheriff's office, the patrol division is also the most visible. Command of the division may be at the rank of major, captain, or lieutenant. The rank of sergeant or corporal will typically be the patrol squad supervisor. Patrol consists of rotating shifts to provide 24-hour service. Shifts vary by agency, with the 40-hour work week being served in numerous configurations. For example, a deputy may patrol eight hours, as one of three shifts per day, and work five days per week. A deputy may patrol ten hours, as one of several overlapping shifts per day, and work four days per week. Or a deputy may patrol 12 hours, as one of two shifts or four overlapping shifts per day, and work any number of configurations for work days and off days. In addition, deputies will typically rotate shifts on a regular basis, depending on the hours per shift. However, some agencies do offer permanent shifts. Deputies on the eight-hour rotation will typically have a shift from 7:00 a.m. to 3:00 p.m., 3:00 p.m. to 11:00 p.m., and 11:00 p.m. to 7:00 a.m. Deputies on the ten- and 12-hour shifts may begin at 7:00 a.m. or as early as 5:00 a.m.

The patrol division may also include specialized units, including traffic enforcement, K-9, crime prevention and safety, bicycle patrol, and special response teams. The K-9 unit assists patrol in various functions, including seeking criminals, narcotics detection, bomb detection, and search and rescue. The K-9 dogs may also be assigned to a specific unit, such as narcotics or jail operations.

Criminal Investigations

The criminal investigations unit may be commanded by a major, captain, or lieutenant. The purpose of this unit is to investigate crimes, both felony and misdemeanor, occurring within the county, as well as complaints received from county residents. Investigators may also receive additional specialized training in numerous areas of criminal investigation and evidence, including homicide, domestic violence, crimes against children, crime scene investigation, interviews and interrogations, and chain of custody. In addition, the unit may also be responsible for maintaining verifications of registered sex offenders living within the county.

Jail Operations

There are 147 jails and detention facilities operated by county sheriff's offices across the state. These units are commanded by various ranks, including captain, commander, colonel, major, and lieutenant. County jails house inmates who are awaiting trial, who have not received bail or able to supply a bond for release, or who have been sentenced to serve one year or less in a correctional facility. Correctional officers are required to be P.O.S.T. certified in corrections, which is a specific program of training and certification separate from peace officer certification.

Jail operations may also maintain a specialized unit for the purpose of cell extraction and other high-risk situations. Similar to patrol SWAT teams, these officers are typically trained in specialized areas, such as riot control, combat tactics, and specialized weapons. These teams may also conduct daily cell searches to ensure contraband is not introduced into the jail, as well as conduct investigations of incidents occurring within the jail (Lowndes County Sheriff's Office, 2011).

Court Services

The county, state, and specialty courts operating within each county need security, which is provided by deputy sheriffs, commanded by various ranks, including captain, commander, colonel, major, and lieutenant. Not only do deputies screen everyone who enters the courthouse or court complex, they also provide protection to judges and their staff, to visitors and participants attending court, and to juries during trial and deliberation. In Chatham County, in 2009, 1,165,375 individuals entered the Judicial and Juvenile Courthouses, where 1,072 prohibited items were confiscated (Chatham County Sheriff's Office, 2011b).

Deputies assigned to the court are also responsible for the movement and transportation of inmates and those incarcerated before trial. For example, in Gwinnett County, "more than 10,000 prisoners appear in court annually" (Gwinnett County Sheriff's Department, 2011). No case in recent history has shed more light on the enormous and often dangerous duty of inmate transport in Georgia, and across the nation, than the Brian Nichols shooting spree in March 2005. Nichols was being transported from a holding cell within the Fulton County Justice Tower to a courtroom to stand trial for rape. In the holding cell, as the deputy removed handcuffs so he could change into civilian clothes, Nichols overpowered and brutally attacked the deputy. He then moved to the courtroom where he killed the judge, a court reporter, and a sergeant with the Fulton County Sheriff's Office, and later, while on the run, he killed a federal law enforcement agent (Associated Press, 2008).

Special Operations

Sheriff's deputies may be employed in one of a variety of special operations units or teams that function as standalone squads apart from patrol, with deputies receiving specialized training and education. Some special operations are focused on high-risk law enforcement, such as SWAT (Special Weapons and Tactical) teams, fugitive units, drug and narcotics units, hostage/crisis negotiations units, bomb squads, surveillance units, vice squads, gang units, and many others.

Other special operations focus on community relations, including school resource officers, D.A.R.E. (Drug Abuse Resistance Education) and G.R.E.A.T. (Gang Resistance Education and Training) programs, Neighborhood Crime Watch units, Family Violence units, and more recently, civilian law enforcement academies. These deputies work closely with community leaders and civic groups while also providing a law enforcement presence.

Training is also a large part of any law enforcement agency. Many sheriff's offices employ training officers, while others maintain a training division or unit, whose job is to provide training and educational resources to all deputies in all divisions and to ensure training mandates are met. According to O.C.G.A. §35-8-21, during each calendar year, "any person employed or appointed as a peace officer shall complete 20 hours of training." Known as in-service training, the training officer or training division is able to provide and ensure mandated levels of training and/or competency within the agency, allowing for minimal disruption of duties while saving travel funds to state training facilities.

Emergency 911 Communications

Emergency 911 Communications (or E911 centers), established at the county level, are a critical aspect of any sheriff's office and/or county police department. E911 centers are the first point of contact for emergency calls from citizens and victims of crime. E911 centers are staffed with P.O.S.T. certified communications officers, and some agencies require dispatchers to also be certified as emergency medical dispatchers. Many E911 centers on the county level also process emergency calls for municipal police departments, fire departments, and emergency medical units.

County Police Departments

Twelve counties throughout the state have established county police departments, and these agencies currently employ 3,874 certified peace officers. (P.O.S.T. Council, 2011). Due to the rapid growth in population and industry of these counties, it was deemed necessary to develop a second county law enforcement agency to meet the demands of the communities they serve, most located in the metro Atlanta area. These departments have been established by the County Commission and serve as a separate entity to the sheriff's office. The Chief of Police is appointed by the Commission, rather than elected by the citizens of the county.

The typical arrangement for counties with two law enforcement agencies is for the county police department to patrol the unincorporated areas of the county, as well as engage in investigations, while the sheriff's office handles jail and court functions, and is responsible for serving warrants and civil papers.

The county police department is engaged in all aspects of law enforcement. Typical patrol divisions comprise the largest section of agency personnel, and include traditional traffic and patrol units. Many agencies also maintain a wide array of smaller specialty units, such as K-9 units, motorcycle units, SWAT (Special Weapons And Tactical) units, C.A.G.E. (Criminal Apprehension and Gang Enforcement) units, H.E.A.T. (Highway Enforcement of Aggressive Traffic) units, and Honor Guard (Henry County Police Department, 2011a).

The criminal investigations divisions of county police departments serve to investigate and assist with evidence collection and preservation for use in criminal prosecutions. A typical criminal investigations division includes officers assigned to specific crimes, such as crimes against persons, crimes against children, crimes against property, domestic violence, crime scene investigations, forensics, financial crimes, evidence, special victims units, and cold case units. Duties and responsibilities include: "identify and apprehend offenders; recover stolen property; gather, document and evaluate facts in reference to criminal activity; process crime scenes, recover and preserve evidence and property; and present evidence to various courts to seek a successful prosecution of the offender(s)" (Henry County Police Department, 2011b).

County Marshal Departments/Offices

County marshals and deputy marshals work in various capacities in each of the 159 counties. The marshal's office may be created for the purpose of serving the judiciary in the county, enforcing laws, court orders, and writs of state and local courts, as well as providing court security and assistance for other law enforcement agencies when needed. The mission statement of the Fulton County Marshal's Department (2011) is to "serve the public by enforcing the orders, writs and precepts of the State and Magistrate Courts of Fulton County, and other courts of component judicial authority, in a responsible, efficient, and cost-effective manner."

A county marshal department or office may also function as an additional law enforcement entity in the county, enforcing specific county ordinances and state codes. For example, the Fayette County Marshal's Office was created in 1989 by consolidating the former offices of Code Enforcement, Park Ranger, and Safety Director into one agency, and has subsequently added a Weight and Scales program in conjunction with the Georgia Department of Transportation, and a Marine Patrol Unit to enforce boating safety regulations on county reservoirs (Fayette County Marshal's Office, 2011).

Campus Police

Another aspect of county law enforcement involves county boards of education. Currently, 28 counties have created campus police departments for their K-12 county school boards, employing 451 peace officers. The campus police officers are employed and work for the school district or board of education (P.O.S.T. Council, 2011).

The purpose of the campus police is similar to agencies found on college and university campuses, with an emphasis on providing a safe and secure environment for students, teachers, administrators, and visitors to the schools in the district. These agencies are also structured as typical law enforcement agencies, with a chief, administrative staff, and line officers. Campus police officers are highly engaged with the administration, staff, and students of each campus, providing assistance in crime prevention, investigating criminal and gang activity, providing first responder assistance in emergency situations, monitoring visitors, and making routine patrols of facilities (Bibb County Campus Police, 2011).

Municipal Law Enforcement in Georgia

Municipal law enforcement in the State of Georgia is carried out by 13,106 certified peace officers working for city police departments. An additional 1,635 certified peace officers work with other municipal agencies, including communications, hospital and railroad police, and community and city fire departments (P.O.S.T. Council, 2011).

Municipal police departments are similar to their county counterparts, with agencies typically made up of various departments and units, each having specific duties and responsibilities. However, the chief of police is an appointed position, hired by the City Council. Police officers are employed by and work for the city or municipality, and must be certified as peace officers by the state. This provides a greater level of job security than county deputies. Police departments are created with a military style command structure, providing a clear chain of command.

Administrative Division

The administrative division, also known as support services, manages the administrative functions for various divisions or units within the department, including the patrol and investigative divisions. The Chief of Police is the top administrator, and may be assisted by one or more assistant or deputy chiefs, and others within the division holding the ranks of major, captain, or commander. The Division may be responsible for personnel matters, maintaining records and files, equipment and vehicle inventory, property and evidence collection and storage, and desk services, serving as the initial point of contact for individuals visiting the police department. The Division may also provide administrative oversight for training, accreditation and certification, public information, court services, crime prevention and crime stoppers, school resource officers and education programs, and homeland security.

Patrol Division

Uniform patrol is the most visible aspect of the police department. Command of the division may be at the rank of major, captain, or lieutenant. The rank of sergeant or corporal will typically be the patrol squad supervisor. The primary responsibility of the patrol division is to answer emergency and non-emergency calls for service. The patrol division works rotating shifts and rotating on/off days throughout the year. Various configurations are used, including 8-hour, 10-hour and 12-hour shifts, with some police departments also providing permanent shift schedules.

The patrol division may consist of specialized units connected to the patrol function. Bicycle patrols are used in many areas, particularly in neighborhoods, downtown areas, and in other places where it is impractical to patrol by car. Traffic units are also a standard feature of many police departments. These units strategically target speeders, reckless drivers and drunk drivers, while also assisting in crash investigations. For example, "the Selective Traffic Enforcement Program [STEP] is responsible for the investigation of fatality, severe injury, and leaving the scene accidents" (Marietta Police Department, 2011). Police dogs (K-9 units) are also on patrol, working with officers during traffic stops and check points for narcotics and bomb detection.

Officers with the patrol division may also be assigned to specific squads or units that require specialized training and education. These units include SWAT (Special Weapons and Tactical), hostage negotiations, motorcycle units, drug and narcotics interdiction, and gang apprehension.

Investigative Division

Criminal investigations are a critical part of law enforcement. There are numerous units within any investigative division, with the number and responsibilities of the units mostly dependent on the size of the agency and available resources.

Detectives investigate crimes that become known to the police through calls for service, police observation, or citizen complaints. Detectives are typically assigned to one or more specific crime units, and in some cases gain specialized training and education in those crimes. In smaller agencies, detectives may investigate all manner of crimes. The following, although not exhaustive, is a list of specific types of crime units.

- Persons crimes — crimes committed against a person, such as murder/homicide, assault, battery, robbery, sexual assault, kidnapping, and child molestation
- Property crimes — crimes committed against property, such as burglary, larceny, motor vehicle theft, financial crimes, and cyber crimes
- Street crimes — crimes committed in specific areas
- Narcotics — crimes committed in trafficking illegal narcotics
- Gangs — crimes involving gang related activities
- Financial crimes — crimes involving fraud, including identity theft, forgery, telemarketing fraud, credit card transaction fraud, and Internet fraud
- Forensics — involves collecting and preserving crime scene and other evidence, including crime lab testing and analysis
- Juvenile or Youth crime — crimes committed by juveniles
- Family violence — involves violence within the family or domestic relations
- Sex crimes — crimes involving a sexual component (rape)
- Fugitive squad — involves identifying and apprehending suspects with outstanding arrest warrants

Jail Division

In numerous municipalities across the state, the police department operates a city jail. The city jail may be commanded by a commander, major, or captain, with additional administrative staff of sergeants and corporals. City jail corrections officers are state certified, but may or may not be certified peace officers. Similar in function to the county jail, for example, "the City of Smyrna Jail is a full service jail housing both pre-trial and sentenced inmates of Smyrna and the City of Marietta." The jail "has sixty four beds" and the "current daily population average is 45, with an average length of stay of 3.5 days. Last year the City of Smyrna Jail processed 3,556 inmates" (Smyrna Police Department, 2011).

Emergency 911 Communications

Many larger municipal law enforcement agencies have established individual E911 centers, separate from the county. These communication centers function as the initial point of contact for victims and witnesses of crime and provide that vital line of communication when officers are handling calls for service. Employees must be P.O.S.T. certified communications officers and many agencies require emergency medical dispatcher certification. As an example, for a city of approximately 50,000 residents, Smyrna's E911 center "handles over 52,000 calls for service each year and more than 190,000 telephone calls are placed to the Center each year" (Smyrna Police Department, 2011).

Community Oriented Policing

In recent years, county and municipal law enforcement agencies have started adopting the community oriented policing (COP) model as the preferred organizational structure for their agencies. "Community policing is a philosophy that promotes organizational strategies, which support the systematic use of partnerships and problem-solving techniques, to proactively address the immediate conditions that give rise to public safety issues such as crime, social disorder, and fear of crime" (Office of Community Oriented Policing Services, 2009). The COP strategy has become popular in areas where rising crime rates, allegations of unethical behavior and misconduct, and/or scandals involving government officials have led to a distrust of law enforcement.

The primary feature of the COP strategy is that law enforcement officers are working on a personal level with the community, by getting out of patrol cars and talking with citizens, business owners, and local organizations in a joint effort to reduce and prevent crime. Law enforcement needs citizen cooperation, and officers actively engaging in community activities helps to strengthen communication and trust between them and citizens, allowing for more effective law enforcement.

Numerous joint law enforcement and community initiatives have been established across the county. Some examples include citizen crime watch neighborhoods, citizen law enforcement academies, McGruff and crime stoppers, National Night Out, school resource officers, D.A.R.E. and G.R.E.A.T. programs, residential security inspections, and educational programs about drugs, gangs, and safety in the workplace.

Accreditation

Law enforcement agencies at the local and state levels across the county work toward providing professional, public safety service to their communities. One aspect of this increase in professionalism is accreditation. Accreditation is a process whereby an agency will seek an outside organization to evaluate the agency and to provide guidance and instruction on how to maintain and improve, not only in the area of professionalism, but in all aspects of the delivery of service.

National Accreditation

The national accrediting body for law enforcement is the Commission on Accreditation for Law Enforcement Agencies (CALEA), created in 1979 through the joint efforts of the major law enforcement executive associations: International Association of Chiefs of Police, National Organization of Black Law Enforcement Executives, National Sheriff's Association, and Police Executive Research Forum (Commission on Accreditation for Law Enforcement Agencies [CALEA], 2011).

The CALEA accreditation is a voluntary opportunity for law enforcement agencies to demonstrate an established set of professional standards, which include developing a comprehensive set of written directives; developing a preparedness program to address critical incidents; improving community relationships; strengthening the agency's accountability; and limiting the agency's liability and risk exposure. CALEA's goals are to:

- "Strengthen crime prevention and control capabilities;
- Formalize essential management procedures;
- Establish fair and nondiscriminatory personnel practices;
- Improve service delivery;
- Solidify interagency cooperation and coordination; and
- Increase community and staff confidence in the agency" (CALEA, 2011).

The process of accreditation involves a self-assessment, an on-site assessment by CALEA assessors, and compliance and reaccreditation every three years. The fees for the CALEA accreditation process depend on the number of authorized full-time employees of the agency, which is defined as sworn and non-sworn personnel. The fee ranges from $7,425 for an agency with 1–24 personnel, to $18,900 for an agency with 1000+ personnel. In addition, agencies receiving initial accreditation will continue to pay the annual continuation fees, again, based on agency personnel, ranging from $3,320 to $5,615 (CALEA, 2011).

Of the more than 18,000 law enforcement agencies across the country, approximately 1,200 have met the requirements for national accreditation. Currently in the State of Georgia, numerous agencies on the state, county, and municipal levels have received or are in the process of receiving CALEA accreditation. On the state level, the Georgia Bureau of Investigation, Georgia State University Police Department, and MARTA Police Department have received accreditation, while the Georgia Tech Security and Police Department is in the accreditation process. Seven county sheriff's offices have received accreditation (Cherokee, Columbia, DeKalb, Forsyth, Fulton, Hall, and Monroe), while four others (Catoosa, Clarke, Clayton, and Floyd) are in the accreditation process. Six of the 12 county police departments have received accreditation (Athens-Clarke, Clayton, Cobb, DeKalb, Fulton, and Gwinnett) (CALEA, 2011). In addition, the Fulton County Marshal's Department, in 1995, "became the first Marshal's Department in the Country to be nationally accredited by the prestigious Commission on Accreditation for Law Enforcement Agencies (CALEA)" (Fulton County Marshal's Department, 2011).

There are currently 24 municipal police departments accredited through CALEA: Alpharetta, Atlanta, Columbus, Covington, Fayetteville, Forest Park, Gainesville, Garden City, Griffin, Johns Creek, Kennesaw, LaGrange, Macon, Marietta, Moultrie, Norcross, Peachtree City, Riverdale, Rome City, Roswell, Suwanee, Thomasville, Valdosta, and Waycross. Five additional municipal police departments (Conyers, Dalton, Milton, Sandy Springs, and Savannah-Chatham) are in the accreditation process (CALEA, 2011).

State Certification

The Georgia Association of Chiefs of Police provides an agency certification program for state and local law enforcement agencies. Similar to CALEA's accreditation process, the certification process involves six steps: application, policy development, assessment, joint committee review, awards ceremony, and monitoring compliance. Once certified, agencies are required to provide annual reports outlining continued compliance. "Certification status represents a significant professional achievement. Certification acknowledges the implementation of policies and procedures that are conceptually sound and operationally effective" (Georgia Association of Chiefs of Police [GACP], 2011a).

Obtaining state certification ensures, for the agency and the community, a set level of professionalism, which includes greater effectiveness, reducing liability, and enhancing community relations and public confidence in the agency. Athens-Clarke County Police Department became the first to achieve state certification, and since, 98 law enforcement agencies have achieved state certification through the GACP certification program. This includes 62 municipal agencies, 28 county agencies, and nine state agencies (GACP, 2011a).

Law Enforcement Support Organizations

Numerous law enforcement support organizations exist in Georgia, devoted to enhancing communication, providing educational opportunities, and supplementing agency benefits.

Georgia Association of Chiefs of Police

The Georgia Association of Chiefs of Police (GACP) was incorporated in 1962 "to promote cooperative, professional relationships throughout the state, to evaluate the standards of police institutions and the profession, to offer quality training and continuing education for administrators, and to provide opportunities for police executives to exchange information and experiences" (GACP, 2011b). The organization boasts an active membership of more than 1,000 law enforcement agency managers (rank of captain and above) from municipal and county police departments, college and university police departments, corporate and private security companies, state and federal agencies, and citizens who support law enforcement throughout the state. The GACP provides law enforcement representation in legislative and other government activities, including membership on the Georgia Homeland Security Taskforce (GACP, 2011b).

Georgia Sheriff's Association

The Georgia Sheriff's Association, a non-profit organization, was founded in 1957, with membership limited to the 159 elected sheriffs in the state. However, the association has more than 70,000 honorary members who provide financial support for programs and training. The purpose of the association is to "promote and improve law enforcement in Georgia, to provide training and education for sheriffs, deputy sheriffs and other sheriff's office staff, and to maintain an active voice in the Georgia General Assembly on matters relating to public safety, law enforcement and Georgia's criminal and juvenile justice systems" (GSA, 2011b).

The association is also the sponsor of the Georgia Sheriff's Youth Homes, whose purpose is to give at-risk and disadvantaged children, aged six to 16, structure and a stable home, while emphasizing education, training, and a strong work ethic. The first home was opened in 1960, in Hahira, as the Georgia Sheriff's Boys Ranch. Since that time, four additional homes have been opened across the state for both boys and girls, in Chatsworth, Dalton, LaGrange, and Nunez. Children accepted for placement in one of the youth homes attend public school, and are provided with spiritual and moral training, educational support through tutoring and summer learning programs, recreational and extra-curricular activities in school and the community, summer vacations with outdoor activities, and life skills training (Georgia Sheriff's Youth Homes, 2011).

Peace Officers' Annuity and Benefit Fund of Georgia

On February 1, 1950, then Governor Herman Talmadge signed into law an act from the General Assembly to create the Peace Officers' Annuity and Benefit (POAB) Fund of Georgia. The purpose of the act "was to provide revenue and a source of revenue for the purpose of paying annuities and benefits to the peace officers of the State of Georgia" (Peace Officers' Annuity and Benefit [POAB] Fund of Georgia, 2011).

Membership in POAB is limited to P.O.S.T. certified peace officers employed full-time by the state or by any county or municipal agency, including elected and appointed positions. Membership is governed by O.C.G.A. § 47-17-1, which specifically defines the term "peace officer."

Assets in the fund began with $6,653 on June 30, 1950, with 561 active members. With 1,830 active members and a retirement roll of 345, assets reached the $1,000,000 mark in 1955. At the end of the last fiscal year for the 20th century, on June 30, 1999, assets totaled $332,685,433, with 10,002 active members and a retirement roll of 1,806. Retirement benefits paid during this last fiscal year totaled $10,160,909. On June 30, 2007, assets totaled $485,000,000, with 12,971 active members and 2,967 on the retirement roll, and retirement benefits paid totaling $15,600,000 (POAB, 2011).

Peace Officers Association of Georgia

The Peace Officers Association of Georgia was incorporated on September 21, 1953. Part of the mission of the association is "to assist peace officers and their families, to provide for and encourage the education and training of peace officers, to improve the profession, (and) to improve and extend the service rendered by its members to the people of Georgia and its subdivisions" (Peace Officers Association of Georgia [POAG], 2011). The association works to initiate, endorse, and support legislation beneficial to peace officers, encourage an esprit de corps among members through social activities and recognition of officers, and ensure that education standards, ethics, and training for peace officers continue to be adhered to, promoted, and elevated. The association also holds an annual convention and sponsors the awards for Officer of the Year for Valor and Officer of the Year for Meritorious Service (POAG, 2011).

Conclusion

Law enforcement in the State of Georgia serves a vital function in the safety and security of residents and visitors. As with all states in the country, federal, state, and local law enforcement officers work tirelessly, and with the latest advancements in technology, and detection and apprehension techniques, law enforcement at all levels will continue to provide residents and visitors with the highest level of protection.

Chapter Review Questions

1. What is the purpose of the Federal Law Enforcement Training Center?
2. Discuss the various state law enforcement agencies, including their primary duties and responsibilities.
3. Discuss the various county law enforcement agencies, including their primary duties and responsibilities.
4. What is the Community Oriented Policing concept?
5. What is the Georgia Crime Information Center and why is this Center important to local and state law enforcement?

References

Associated Press. (December 13, 2008). Multiple Life Terms for Courthouse Killings in Atlanta. *New York Times.*

Bibb County Board of Education Campus Police. (2011). Campus Police. Retrieved from: http://schools.bibb.k12.ga.us.

Chatham County Sheriff's Office. (2011a). Our History. Retrieved from: http://chathamsheriff.org.

Chatham County Sheriff's Office. (2011b). Court Services Division. Retrieved from: http://www.chathamsheriff.org.

Commission on Accreditation for Law Enforcement Agencies (CALEA). (2011). Retrieved from: http://www.calea.org.

Fayette County Marshal's Office. (2011). Retrieved from: http://www.fayette countyga.gov.

Federal Law Enforcement Training Center. (2011). Retrieved from: http://www.fletc.gov.

Fulton County Marshal's Department. (2011). Retrieved from: http://www.georgiacourts.org.

Georgia Association of Chiefs of Police. (2011a). State Certification. Retrieved from: http://www.gachiefs.com.

Georgia Association of Chiefs of Police. (2011b). GACP History. Retrieved from: http://www.gachiefs.com.

Georgia Bureau of Investigation (GBI). (2011a). GBI History. Retrieved from: http://gbi.georgia.gov.

Georgia Bureau of Investigation (GBI). (2011b). Investigative Division. Retrieved from: http://investigative.gbi.georgia.gov.

Georgia Bureau of Investigation (GBI). (2011c). Division of Forensic Sciences. Retrieved from: http://dofs.gbi.georgia.gov.

Georgia Bureau of Investigation (GBI). (2011d). Georgia Crime Information Center. Retrieved from: http://gbi.georgia.gov.

Georgia Bureau of Investigation (GBI). (2011e). Medical Examiner's Office. Retrieved from: http://gbi.georgia.gov.

Georgia Department of Natural Resources (DNR). (2011). DNR Divisions. Retrieved from: http://www.gadnr.org.

Georgia Department of Public Safety (DPS). (2011a). History. Retrieved from: http://dps.georgia.gov.

Georgia Department of Public Safety (DPS). (2011b). Commissioner. Retrieved from: http://dps.georgia.gov.

Georgia Department of Public Safety (DPS). (2011c). Capital Police. Retrieved from: http://dps.georgia.gov.

Georgia Department of Public Safety (DPS). (2011d). Georgia State Patrol. Retrieved from: http://dps.georgia.gov.

Georgia Department of Public Safety (DPS). (2011e). Executive Security Division. Retrieved from: http://dps.georgia.gov.

Georgia Department of Public Safety (DPS). (2011f). Motor Carrier Compliance Division. Retrieved from: http://dps.georgia.gov.

Georgia Emergency Management Agency/Homeland Security. (2011). Retrieved from: http://www.gema.ga.gov.

Georgia Peace Officer Standards and Training (P.O.S.T.) Council. (2011). Peace Officer Population June 2011. Clarkdale, GA: P.O.S.T. Council.

Georgia Sheriff's Association. (2011a). Sheriff's Qualifications. Retrieved from: http://www.georgiasheriffs.org.

Georgia Sheriff's Association. (2011b). FAQs. Retrieved from: http://www.georgiasheriffs.org.

Georgia Sheriff's Youth Homes. (2011). About Us. Retrieved from: http://www. georgiasheriffs.org.

Governor's Office of Highway Safety. (2011). Retrieved from: http://www.gahigh waysafety.org.

Gwinnett County Sheriff's Department. (2011). Court Security. Retrieved from: http://www.gwinnettcountysheriff.com.

Henry County Police Department. (2011a). Uniform Patrol Division. Retrieved from: http://www.co.henry.ga.us.

Henry County Police Department. (2011b). Criminal Investigations Division. Retrieved from: http://www.co.henry.ga.us.

Lowndes County Sheriff's Office. (2011). Jail Operations. Retrieved from: http://www.lowndessheriff.com.

Marietta Police Department. (2011). Uniform Patrol Division. Retrieved from: http://www.mariettaga.gov.

Metropolitan Atlanta Rapid Transit Authority (MARTA). (2011). MARTA Police Department. Retrieved from: http://www.itsmarta.com.

O.C.G.A. §15-16-1. (2011). Official Code of Georgia Annotated.

O.C.G.A. §35-8-10. (2011). Official Code of Georgia Annotated.

O.C.G.A. §35-8-21. (2011). Official Code of Georgia Annotated.

O.C.G.A. §40-16-2. (2011). Official Code of Georgia Annotated.

O.C.G.A. §47-17-1. (2011). Official Code of Georgia Annotated.

Officer Down Memorial Page. (2011). Retrieved from: http://www.odmp.org.

Office of Community Oriented Policing Services. (2009). Community Policing Defined. Washington: U.S. Department of Justice.

Peace Officers' Annuity and Benefit Fund of Georgia. (2011). About Us. Retrieved from: http://poab.georgia.gov.

Peace Officers Association of Georgia. (2011). Mission Statement. Retrieved from: http://www.poag.org.

Smyrna Police Department. (2011). Jail. Retrieved from: http://www.ci.smyrna. ga.us.

CHAPTER 7

GEORGIA'S COURTS

Learning Objectives

After reading the chapter, students will be able to:

- Explain the roles of the 11th Circuit Court of Appeals and U.S. District Courts in Georgia.
- Identify and describe the various personnel working with the Supreme Court of Georgia.
- Describe the state level and local level courts in Georgia.
- Describe the roles of the Attorney General of Georgia, district attorney, and solicitor general.
- Describe the role of the public defender.
- Explain how the Office of Georgia Capital Defenders assists with death penalty cases.

Key Terms

Administrative Office of the
  Courts of Georgia
Attorney General of Georgia
Clerk
District Attorney
Georgia Accountability Courts
Georgia Court of Appeals
Georgia Public Defenders
Judicial Council of Georgia
Judiciary
Judiciary Act of 1789
Juvenile Courts
Law Assistants

Magistrate Courts
Municipal Courts
Office of Georgia Capital
  Defenders
Probate Courts
Solicitor General
State Bar of Georgia
State Courts
Superior Courts
Supreme Court of Georgia
United States Court of Appeals
United States District Courts

The judicial organization of the State of Georgia is rich in history at the state and local levels, as well as at the federal level. The role of the courts has been ever expanding since Georgia became a state in 1788. The Georgia Constitution, dating back to 1777, provides a judicial system for the state. Although most of Georgia's courts are at the local level, the Constitution establishes the provisions for local and state courts, including both state and individual rights pertaining to the judiciary.

In following the provisions of the federal Bill of Rights, the Georgia Constitution of 1983, in Article I, Paragraph XI, provides that "(a) The right to trial by jury shall remain inviolate, except that the court shall render judgment without the verdict of a jury in all civil cases where no issuable defense is filed and where a jury is not demanded in writing by either party. In criminal cases, the defendant shall have a public and speedy trial by an impartial jury; and the jury shall be the judges of the law and the facts. (b) A trial jury shall consist of 12 persons; but the General Assembly may prescribe any number, not less than six, to constitute a trial jury in courts of limited jurisdiction and in superior courts in misdemeanor cases. (c) The General Assembly shall provide by law for the selection and compensation of persons to serve as grand jurors and trial jurors." In addition, Paragraph XII authorizes that "No person shall be deprived of the right to prosecute or defend, either in person or by an attorney, that person's own cause in any of the courts of this state," while Paragraph XVIII provides that "No person shall be put in jeopardy of life or liberty more than once for the same offense except when a new trial has been granted after conviction or in case of mistrial" (Georgia Constitution of 1983).

Federal Courts in Georgia

Federal courts have had a presence in the State of Georgia since the passage of the Judiciary Act of 1789, when Georgia was established as a single judicial district with one judgeship, while being assigned to the Southern Circuit. Currently, the State of Georgia resides in the Eleventh Circuit for the U.S. Court of Appeals and is divided into three districts for the U.S. District Courts.

U.S. Court of Appeals in Georgia

Federal level appeals initiating in the U.S. District Courts within the State of Georgia were first heard in U.S. Circuit Courts, beginning in 1789. Between the years 1789 and 1912, the federal Congress expanded and altered the role of the Circuit Courts and Georgia's position within the federal judiciary. Numerous acts and reorganizations moved Georgia from its initial Southern Circuit in 1789 to the Fifth Circuit in 1801, to the Sixth Circuit in 1802, to the Southern District of Georgia in 1848, while providing a U.S. District Court to hear appeals for the Northern District. Georgia moved back to the Fifth Circuit in 1862, followed by the creation of a Circuit Court for the Northern District of Georgia in 1872. The Judiciary Act of 1891 created the U.S. Courts of Appeals and removed appellate jurisdiction of the Circuit Courts (the Circuit Courts continued as trial courts until their eventual abolishment in 1912) (Federal Judicial Center [FJC], 2011).

The Judiciary Act of 1891 established nine U.S. Courts of Appeals, one for each of the judicial circuits, with Georgia being placed in the Fifth Circuit. Georgia remained in the Fifth Circuit until the latest reorganization, in 1980, with the Fifth Circuit Court of Appeals Reorganization Act. The Act split the Fifth Circuit into two, maintaining a smaller Fifth Circuit with Mississippi, Louisiana, Texas, and the Canal Zone, and a new Eleventh Circuit containing the states of Georgia, Florida, and Alabama (FJC, 2011).

The Eleventh Circuit Court of Appeals "is the busiest federal appellate court in the United States with its twelve authorized judgeships" (United States Court of Appeals, Eleventh Circuit, 2011). The Circuit is comprised of nine U.S. District Courts, three in each state, with three-fourths of the cases being decided on the briefs submitted, while the remaining cases include oral arguments. The oral arguments are typically held in the Elbert P. Tuttle United States Court of Appeals Building in Atlanta, but are also held in Jacksonville and Miami, Florida, and Montgomery, Alabama (United States Court of Appeals, Eleventh Circuit, 2011).

U.S. District Courts

The U.S. District Courts serve as federal trial courts of original jurisdiction, hearing criminal cases that involve violations of federal law and civil cases within federal jurisdiction. The State of Georgia is divided into three federal districts: Northern, Middle, and Southern. As with the U.S. Circuit Courts, the federal Congress has been continuously expanding and altering the structure of the District Courts with periodic increases in the number of judgeships in each district (FJC, 2011).

The Northern District of Georgia was created by Congress in 1849 and currently serves 46 counties in northwestern Georgia. The district is further divided into four divisions—Atlanta, Gainesville, Newnan and Rome—with court being held in each division. The Court consists of 11 judges, with assistance from eight senior judges and nine full-time magistrate judges (United States District Court, Northern District of Georgia, 2011).

The Middle District of Georgia currently serves 70 counties and is further divided into five divisions—Albany, Athens, Columbus, Macon, and Valdosta—with court being held in each division. The Court consists of three judges, one Chief Judge, one Senior Judge, and three magistrate judges (United States District Court, Middle District of Georgia, 2011).

The Southern District of Georgia currently serves 43 counties in southeastern Georgia. The district is further divided into six divisions—Augusta, Brunswick, Dublin, Savannah, Statesboro, and Waycross—with court being held in each division. The Court consists of eight judges; three located in Augusta, two located in Brunswick, and three located in Savannah (United States District Court, Southern District of Georgia, 2011).

State Court System of Georgia

Currently, "the judicial power of the state is vested in seven levels or classes of courts. The Georgia court system has two appellate-level courts: the Supreme Court of Georgia and the Court of Appeals of Georgia. There are five classes of trial-level courts: the superior, state, juvenile, probate, and magistrate courts. In addition, approximately 400 municipal and/or special courts operate at the local level" (New Georgia Encyclopedia, 2011). "Each county is to have at least one superior court, magistrate court, probate court, and where needed a state court and a juvenile court. In the absence of a state court or a juvenile court, the superior court exercises that jurisdiction" (Supreme Court of Georgia [SCG], 2011).

The Administrative Office of the Courts of Georgia (AOC) handles much of the communication between the state courts and serves as liaison to the community and state. The AOC consists of six divisions. The Court Services Division works to provide judges and court personnel with education, training, planning, policy development, jury management, and public publications, including the annual publication of the Georgia Courts Directory. The Financial Administration Division, established by O.C.G.A. § 15-5-24, provides accounting, payroll, and fiscal support in order to properly secure the assets of the judiciary and public funds. The General Counsel Division provides administrative legal advice while regulating court reporters, interpreters, and misdemeanor probation providers. The Governmental Affairs Division works with various committees of the state General Assembly to ensure accurate and timely communications regarding information pertinent to the judiciary. The Information Technology Division is working to fully automate the courts throughout the state, which includes integration of data collaboration and

Figure 7.1 Diagram of the Georgia Court System

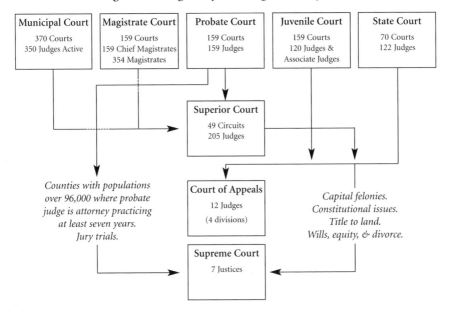

more effective communication throughout Georgia's courts. The Planning and Research Division provides information, analyses, and workload assessments for legislators to determine the appropriate number of judgeships and budgets to ensure an effective delivery of justice to the citizens of Georgia (Administrative Office of the Courts of Georgia [AOC], 2011).

Supreme Court of Georgia

For its first 57 years, the State of Georgia was the only state in America to operate without an appellate court, in particular a state supreme court. In other words, there was no court at the state level to review the cases and decisions of the state and local trial courts. In 1835, the constitution of Georgia was amended to authorize the creation of a Supreme Court. However, it was not until ten years later that the State of Georgia General Assembly acted to establish an appellate court. "Prior to 1845 a new trial before a new jury in the local court was the only procedure available for the correction of judicial error" (SCG, 2011). In addition, "Once established, the Georgia Supreme Court was unusual in that it was required to hear all cases and resolve them within a given time. In other states the appellate courts, like the U.S. Supreme Court, have some leeway in deciding what cases they will hear" (New Georgia Encyclopedia, 2011).

When the Supreme Court was created, three justices were chosen by the General Assembly to serve on the Court. Joseph Henry Lumpkin was appointed the first chief justice and served in that capacity until his death in 1867. Lumpkin was influential in Georgia law and judiciary, cofounding the University of Georgia law school, and, in 1833, serving on a commission that created Georgia's first penal code. Eugenius A. Nisbet served as a state representative, a senator, and a member of the U.S. House of Representatives before being appointed as a justice. Hiram Warner was the only newly appointed justice to have judicial experience, having been elected the first judge of the Coweta Judicial Circuit, and who later became the second chief justice (New Georgia Encyclopedia, 2011).

In 1845, the judicial system of the state consisted of 11 superior court circuits. Between 1845 and 1865, the Supreme Court justices travelled throughout the state during the year, holding court in nine different locations. The travel each year involved the justices paying their own expenses from a yearly salary of $2,500 and traveling over 1,000 miles, with only 300 miles by railroad. The decisions of the Supreme Court were handed down orally from the bench; only later were decisions written. The Constitution of 1865 ended the travel of the justices as the Court was to be located at the seat of government, which, in 1868, moved from Milledgeville to the current location of Atlanta (SCG, 2011)

In 1896, the Georgia Constitution was amended to provide three more justices to the Court, while also providing that the citizens of the state would elect the justices and chief justice. The Constitution of 1945 added a seventh justice (SCG, 2011).

The Constitution of 1983 articulates the Supreme Court as a court of review, with exclusive and general appellate jurisdiction in the following cases:

Exclusive Appellate Jurisdiction

- all cases involving construction of a treaty, or Constitution of Georgia or the United States, and all cases which question the constitutionality of a law, ordinance, or constitutional provision
- all cases contesting an election

General Appellate Jurisdiction

- all cases involving title to land
- all cases involving equity
- all cases involving habeas corpus
- all cases involving wills
- all cases involving divorce and alimony

- all cases involving extraordinary remedies
- all cases certified to the Court by the Court of Appeals
- all cases involving a sentence of death imposed or possibly imposed

In addition, the Supreme Court may review a question of law from any state or federal appellate court, and by certiorari any case from the Court of Appeals deemed of gravity or of great public importance (SCG, 2011).

In 2009, a total of 1,979 cases were filed with the Georgia Supreme Court. Of those, 554 were direct appeals, of which 333 were heard and decided by opinion, while 564 were petitions for certiorari (a document seeking judicial review), of which 56 were granted and heard. Appeals for habeas corpus (a legal action in which an inmate is contesting the legality of detention) counted for 393 of the cases, of which 32 were granted (SCG, 2011).

Officers of the Court

Within the Supreme Court of Georgia, there are officers who work with and/or for the justices.

The Clerk is appointed by the Court to serve a term of six years. The Clerk is considered the administrative officer of the Court and is responsible for handling the Court's records and in keeping the minutes of all Court hearings. With the approval of the Court, the Clerk may appoint deputy clerks. The Clerk may be removed from the appointment for neglect of duties, improper conduct, or incapacity (SCG, 2011).

Law Assistants are appointed by individual justices and serve at their pleasure. The Law Assistants assist the justices in conducting research and in preparing opinions of decisions of the Court. The Law Assistants must be licensed to practice law in the State of Georgia, but are not allowed to actively practice law while working for the Court (SCG, 2011).

The Reporter, appointed by the Court, serves as the official reporter for both the Supreme Court and the Court of Appeals. The Reporter's duties involve publishing the opinions of both courts. In addition, the Reporter may appoint an Assistant Reporter (SCG, 2011).

Operation of the Court

The Court hears oral arguments throughout the year, except in the months of August and December. The Clerk will prepare the calendar of cases which will be heard by the Court. "Each case accepted for review by the Supreme Court is assigned to one of the seven justices for preparation of a preliminary opinion (decision) for circulation to all other justices. The justices review trial transcripts, case records and the accompanying legal briefs prepared by attorneys. An opinion is adopted or rejected by the Court after thorough discussion by all the justices in conference" (AOC, 2011).

State Bar of Georgia and Office of Bar Admissions

The Supreme Court of Georgia has the responsibility of establishing the standards for admitting attorneys into the practice of law in the state. Within this responsibility, the Court has created several administrative agencies who are responsible for overseeing the practice of law.

The Court created the State Bar of Georgia in 1963 as an administrative arm of the Court. The purpose of the State Bar is to foster among its members the principles of duty and service to the public; to improve the administration of justice; and to advance the science of law (SCG, 2011). In order to actively practice law in the state, one is required to be a member of the State Bar. Currently, there are 33,906 active members in good standing, 8,045 inactive members in good standing, 996 emeritus members, 12 affiliate members, 64 student members, and 5 foreign law consultants (State Bar of Georgia [SBG], 2011).

The Office of Bar Admissions was created as the administrative office for both the Board to Determine Fitness of Bar Applicants and the State Board of Bar Examiners. The Board to Determine Fitness of Bar Applicants, comprised of both practicing attorneys and lay persons, conducts background investigations of all persons applying for admission to practice law in the state. The Board makes recommendations to the State Board of Bar Examiners for those applicants possessing the appropriate moral fitness and character to practice law. This recommendation becomes part of the application to take the Bar examination.

The State Board of Bar Examiners is responsible for reviewing and grading the Georgia Bar Examination, and consists of five attorneys, appointed by the Court. The examination is administered twice a year and the fees paid to take the examination are placed in the State Treasury.

Judicial Council of Georgia

The Judicial Council of Georgia was established in 1973, under O.C.G.A. § 15-5-20, and became an administrative arm of the Supreme Court in 1978. The AOC serves as the staff to the Council. The Council "is the state-level judicial agency charged with developing policies for administering and improving the courts" (SCG, 2011). The Council currently convenes with 25 members, representing both appellate and trial courts throughout the state. "The chief justice and presiding justice of the Supreme Court act as the chairperson and vice-chairperson, respectively. The chief judge and another judge of the Court of Appeals; the presidents and presidents-elect of the superior, state, juvenile, probate and magistrate court councils; the president of the Council of Municipal Court Judges; and the ten superior court district administrative judges complete council membership" (SCG, 2011).

Judicial Qualifications Commission

The purpose of the Judicial Qualifications Commission is to discipline, remove, or cause an involuntary retirement of active judges in the state. The Commission reviews the activities of judges and makes recommendations to the Supreme Court, who has the final order to discipline or remove judges from the bench. According to the 1983 Constitution of the State of Georgia, a judge "may be removed, suspended or otherwise disciplined for willful misconduct in office, willful and persistent failure to perform the duties of office, habitual intemperance, conviction of a crime involving moral turpitude, or for conduct prejudicial to the administration of justice which brings the judicial office into disrepute." Furthermore, any judge "may be retired for disability which constitutes a serious and likely permanent interference with the performance of the duties of office" (SCG, 2011). The Commission consists of seven members: two currently serving judges selected by the Supreme Court; three attorneys, with a minimum of ten years of practice in law in the state, elected by the Board of Governors of the State Bar of Georgia; and two citizens appointed by the Governor (SCG, 2011).

The Chief Justice's Commission on Professionalism

Due to a perceived decline in the professionalism of the legal profession, the Supreme Court of Georgia and the State Bar of Georgia joined efforts to raise the level of professionalism of both lawyers and judges in the state. "The Commission, the first such body of its kind in the country, has as its primary charge ensuring that the practice of law remains a high calling, enlisted in the service not only of the client, but the public good as well" (SCG, 2011). The membership of the Commission includes the Chief Justice of the Supreme Court, who serves as chair, as well as representatives of the judiciary, the State Bar, the four ABA-approved law schools in the state, and the public (SCG, 2011).

Equity Commission

The Equity Commission was created in 1995 by combining the Supreme Court Committee for Gender Equality (created in 1992) and the Commission on Racial and Ethnic Bias (created in 1993). Through Gender Equity, the Commission works to develop education and training programs for new judges and the public; serves as a resource for various media outlets; advocates legislation and develops mechanisms for processing complaints; and provides a resource for revising curriculum in Georgia law schools. Through Racial and Ethnic Bias, the Commission gathers public perception on the judicial system's treatment of minority and ethnic groups; studies the administration and personnel policies of the courts; investigates the impact of bias on justice processes; and reports findings to the Supreme Court (SCG, 2011).

Georgia Court of Appeals

The Georgia Court of Appeals was established in 1906 by an amendment to the Georgia Constitution, 61 years after the establishment of the Supreme Court.

Due to the ever increasing caseload for the Supreme Court, the State Bar Association, at its annual meeting in 1895, proposed the creation of a court of appeals. However, no constitutional amendment was placed on the ballot for election. The idea of a court of appeals was again proposed at the 1902 annual meeting of the State Bar Association, with the organization creating a committee to evaluate the issue further. A formal bill was proposed in October 1902 in the General Assembly, where it languished until 1906. On July 31, 1906, a bill to amend the state constitution was finally approved, with the amendment being ratified in the general election of October 3, 1906. The amendment appointed each appellate court as a court of final jurisdiction, with the Supreme Court having exclusive jurisdiction in capital felony cases (Court of Appeals of Georgia [COA], 2011).

The election of the first judges to form the first bench of the Court of Appeals was held in November 1906. Of the 16 candidates, the three receiving the most votes were seated as Judges—Benjamin H. Hill, Arthur G. Powell, and Richard B. Russell. In an order by the Supreme Court dated December 1906, 155 pending civil cases were transferred to the new court, with an additional 24 criminal cases and one additional civil case transferred to the new court by a Supreme Court order dated January 1907. In addition to the newly seated judges, Marian Bloodworth became the Court's first female employee, serving as a court stenographer (COA, 2011).

With the advent of the two appellate courts now hearing cases, the caseload continued to expand. In a constitutional amendment in 1916, the Supreme Court was limited in the class of cases over which it would have jurisdiction, while the Court of Appeals expanded in jurisdiction and number of judges, moving from three to six. In addition, the judges would now sit in two divisions, with each acting independently in hearing and deciding cases (COA, 2011).

The next major shift for the Court was a 1956 constitutional amendment, which provided that the two appellate courts would have direct review of juvenile court judgments. However, in the 1968 case of *Powell v. Gregg* (224 Ga. 226), the Supreme Court determined that juvenile court cases were solely within the purview of the Court of Appeals. In addition, a 1977 state statute transferred jurisdiction of appeals involving armed robbery, rape, and kidnapping where the death penalty is not imposed from the Supreme Court to the Court of Appeals, and transferred jurisdiction in cases involving contested elections and validity of legislative enactments of municipalities from the Court of Appeals to the Supreme Court (COA, 2011).

In 1960, the number of Court of Appeals judges was increased to seven, and in 1961, the number was again increased to nine, creating three divisions with three judges, with one division handling all criminal appeals. The single division hearing criminal appeals remained until 1967. In 1996, the number of judges was increased to ten, while 1999 brought the addition of two more judges, thus creating the current system of four divisions with three judges each (COA, 2011). The judges are elected to serve a term of six years. The 1983 Georgia Constitution requires that "they shall have been admitted to practice law for seven years and provides that the General Assembly may provide by law for additional qualifications, including a minimum residency requirement" (SCG, 2011).

Both appellate courts have functioned effectively for over 100 years, and both consult the State Bar in creating rules of the respective courts, while each acts independently in creating its own operating procedures. Of the 91 justices having served on the Supreme Court and the 70 judges having served on the Court of Appeals, 15 have served on both courts, with Richard B. Russell being the only individual to serve as the Chief Justice and Chief Judge on both courts (COA, 2011).

Superior Courts

The Superior Courts in the State of Georgia serve as the general jurisdiction trial courts. The state is divided into ten judicial districts, which are further divided into 49 judicial circuits, with 205 superior court judges presiding. The Superior Court "has exclusive, constitutional authority over felony cases, divorce, equity and cases regarding title to land" and exclusive jurisdiction over "such matters as declaratory judgments, habeas corpus, mandamus, quo warranto and prohibition" (AOC, 2011).

Each of the 159 counties in the state has its own Superior Court; however, one judge may preside in more than one county. In addition, each circuit has a chief judge to handle administrative tasks for the circuit. (AOC, 2011). Superior Court judges are elected in circuit-wide races to four-year terms on a nonpartisan basis and must be at least 30 years old, be a citizen of Georgia for at least three years, and have practiced law for at least seven years. The Court must hold session in each county at least twice a year (New Georgia Encyclopedia, 2011).

Council of Superior Court Judges

The Council "assists the Superior Court Judges and the Judicial Circuits by providing administrative support, research, programming, court automation and communications" (The Council of Superior Court Judges [CSCJ], 2011). The Council also provides public service information via its website on topics related to the Superior Court, including how to find the local Superior Court, as well as Georgia Legal Aid, Jury Basics, contact information for corrections and parole, and state agency listings (CSCJ, 2011).

State Courts

A 1970 legislative act established that existing countywide courts of limited jurisdiction be designated State Courts. "State courts may exercise jurisdiction over all misdemeanor violations, including traffic cases, and all civil actions, regardless of the amount claimed, unless the superior court has exclusive jurisdiction" (AOC, 2011). Currently designated in 70 counties, State Courts are also authorized to hold preliminary hearings and hearings on applications for search and arrest warrants, and the Georgia Constitution grants them authority to review lower court decisions as provided by law (AOC, 2011).

Judges presiding in State Court are elected in countywide, nonpartisan elections to four-year terms and must be at least 25 years old, be admitted to practice law for at least seven years, and have lived in the state for at least three years. Of the 122 active State Court judges, approximately half are full-time and half are part-time, with part-time judges being allowed to continue the practice of law in courts other than their own (AOC, 2011).

Council of State Court Judges

The Council was created by the General Assembly in O.C.G.A. §15-7-26 "to effectuate the constitutional and statutory responsibilities conferred upon it by law and to further the improvement of the State Courts, the quality and expertise of the judges thereof, and the administration of justice" (Council of State Court Judges, 2011). The Council strives to further its mission each year by developing a strategic plan to increase the quality and expertise of its judges, to maintain the impartiality of the courts, and to ensure the fair and efficient administration of justice (Council of State Court Judges, 2011).

Probate Courts

Probate courts exist in each of the 159 counties in the state, with one judge presiding in each court. The probate courts "exercise exclusive, original jurisdiction in the probate of wills, administration of estates, appointment of guardians and involuntary hospitalization of incapacitated adults and other individuals" (AOC, 2011). All probate court judges administer oaths of office and issue marriage and firearms licenses. In addition, probate courts may hold preliminary and habeas corpus hearings, and hear certain misdemeanor and traffic cases, as well as violations of state game and fish laws in counties where no state court exists. Probate Court judges may also serve as election supervisors and make appointments to certain local public offices (AOC, 2011).

Probate judges are elected in countywide, partisan elections to four-year terms, and must be at least 25 years old, a high school graduate, a U.S. citizen, and a resident of the county for at least two years. In counties with a population over 96,000, judges must be at least 30 years old and have practiced law for at least seven years (AOC, 2011).

Council of Probate Court Judges

The Council was created by O.C.G.A. § 15-9-15, and is composed of the judges of the probate courts of the state. The purpose of the Council is "to effectuate the constitutional and statutory responsibilities conferred on it by law and to further the improvement of the probate courts and the administration of justice" (Council of Probate Court Judges, 2011).

Magistrate Courts

The 1983 Georgia Constitution created Magistrate Courts from the existing Justice of the Peace and Small Claims courts. "Magistrate court jurisdiction includes civil claims of $15,000 or less, dispossessory writs, county ordinance violations, misdemeanor deposit account fraud (bad checks), preliminary hearings, issuance of summons, arrest warrants, and search warrants" (Judicial Branch, 2011). Magistrate Courts may also grant bail though jury trials are not held. In cases where a defendant specifically requests in writing for a jury trial, the case will be transferred to a state or superior court (AOC, 2011).

Magistrate Courts exist in each of the 159 counties in the state, presided over by a chief magistrate, who assigns cases, sets court sessions and policy for the court, and, with the consent of the superior court judges, appoints other magistrates (currently 354). Most chief magistrates are elected to four-year terms in countywide, partisan elections, while other chief magistrates are appointed pursuant to local legislation. To be appointed as a magistrate, an individual must be at least 25 years of age, have a high school diploma or equivalent, and be a resident of the county for at least one year. The terms for magistrates appointed by the chief magistrate run concurrently with the term of the chief. The number of magistrates, in addition to the chief magistrate, is typically set by the superior court judges of the county (AOC, 2011).

Council of Magistrate Court Judges

The Council, created by state statute, is designed "to effectuate the constitutional and statutory responsibilities conferred upon it by law, to further the improvement of the magistrate courts and the administration of justice, to assist the chief magistrates, magistrates, and senior magistrates throughout the state in the execution of their duties, and to promote and assist in the training of chief magistrates, magistrates, and senior magistrates" (Council of Magistrate Court Judges, 2011). The Council also provides public information, including court and judge directories and links to other courts within the state.

Juvenile Courts

Juvenile Courts exist in each of the 159 counties in the state. Juvenile Courts have exclusive, original jurisdiction over "delinquent children under the age of 17 and deprived or unruly children under the age of 18," and "over minors committing traffic violations or enlisting in the military services, consent to marriage for minors, and cases involving the Interstate Compact on Juveniles" (AOC, 2011). In addition, Juvenile Courts have concurrent jurisdiction with Superior Courts in proceedings to terminate parental rights, in custody and child support cases, and in cases involving capital felonies, while Superior Court has original jurisdiction over juveniles who commit certain serious felonies (AOC, 2011).

Juvenile Court judges serve four-year terms and are appointed by the Superior Court judges of the circuit. Judges must be at least 30 years old, have practiced law for at least five years, and be a resident of the state for at least three years (AOC, 2011).

Council of Juvenile Court Judges

The Council is comprised of all Juvenile Court judges, including both full and part-time judges. The mission of the Council is to provide "support to juvenile courts through legal research services, legislative tracking, and specialized programs to assist in protecting the best interests of children and the state" (Council of Juvenile Court Judges, 2011).

Municipal Courts

Municipal Courts operate under various names with various jurisdictions throughout the state, hearing cases involving violations of municipal ordinances, issuing criminal warrants, and conducting preliminary hearings. In addition, Municipal Courts may have concurrent jurisdiction in cases involving shoplifting and possession of one ounce or less or marijuana (AOC, 2011). "Municipal courts are the busiest courts in Georgia with more than 400 judges managing more than 800,000 cases per year" (Council of Municipal Court Judges, 2011).

The qualifications and terms of office for judges presiding in Municipal Courts are set by local legislation.

Council of Municipal Court Judges

The Council was created by O.C.G.A. § 36-32-40 to assist Municipal Court judges in the execution of their duties and to promote and provide professional training. All judges presiding in municipal and special courts are members of the Council. In addition, the Council provides continuing education opportunities, publications, legislative advocacy, and court support services (Council of Municipal Court Judges, 2011).

Georgia Accountability Courts

Georgia Accountability Courts "promote personal responsibility by holding the participant accountable for his/her actions and behaviors" (Georgia Accountability Courts [GAC], 2011). The purpose of the Accountability Courts is to provide a team approach, whereby the judge, prosecutor, defense attorney, law enforcement, treatment provider, and others involved in the case work together to create supervision, support, and encouragement for each offender (GAC, 2011).

There are currently more than 90 Accountability Courts operating in 74 counties throughout the state, with each class of court serving a unique target population, and having a specific jurisdiction. The elements and functioning of these courts are based on the first adult drug court model that was developed in Dade County, Florida. Of the more than 90 Accountability Courts, 72 are specifically drug courts, as follows (GAC, 2011):

- 31 Adult Felony Drug Courts with Superior Court jurisdiction
- 1 Felony Drug-DUI Court with Superior Court jurisdiction
- 1 Felony Drug-Mental Health Court with Superior Court jurisdiction
- 18 DUI Courts with State Court jurisdiction
- 12 Juvenile Drug Courts with Juvenile Court jurisdiction
- 9 Family Dependency Treatment Courts with Juvenile Court jurisdiction

Other courts within the Accountability Courts serve populations involved with Child Support and Veterans. Individuals being processed through these courts "must go through intensive treatment, attend regular court sessions before the judge, submit to frequent random alcohol and drug testing, maintain employment, be financially responsible, support their families, pay fees, and in some cases, attend school" (GAC, 2011).

Prosecuting Attorneys in the State of Georgia

The State of Georgia is represented in numerous courts and in various cases throughout the state by prosecuting attorneys. All prosecuting attorneys have graduated from an accredited law school and are members of the Georgia State Bar.

Attorney General of Georgia

The State of Georgia has recognized the office of state Attorney General for more than 250 years, with the 53rd individual currently serving in that capacity. The first formally appointed Attorney General, William Clifton, arrived in Savannah from England in 1754 and began drafting a plan for Georgia's court system, which provided the basis for Georgia's current judicial system. The Georgia Constitution of 1868 "made the Attorney General a constitutional officer, and he became the legal adviser to the Governor and the other departments of state government" (Office of Attorney General of Georgia, 2011).

"The mission of the Department of Law is to serve the citizens of the State of Georgia by providing legal representation of the highest quality to the agencies, officers and employees of state government and by honorably and vigorously carrying out the constitutional and statutory responsibilities of the Attorney General" (Office of Attorney General of Georgia, 2011). The authority and obligations of the Attorney General are delineated in the Georgia Constitution and in the Official Code of Georgia. The duties include:

- serving as attorney and legal advisor for all state agencies, departments, authorities, and the governor;
- providing opinions on legal questions pertaining to the State or its agencies;
- representing the State in all capital felony appeals before the Georgia Supreme Court;
- representing the State in all civil cases before any court;
- representing the State in all cases appearing before the United States Supreme Court;
- prosecuting public corruption cases where criminal charges are filed against any person or business for illegal activity when dealing with the State;
- conducting special investigations into questionable activity involving any state agency or department or person or business having dealings with the State;
- initiating civil or criminal actions in the name of the State when requested by the governor; and
- preparing all contracts and agreements regarding any matter in which the State is involved (Office of the Attorney General of Georgia, 2011).

The Georgia Department of Law, Office of the Attorney General, is comprised of various divisions. The five legal divisions are as follows: Regulated Industries and Professions Division, Commercial Transactions and Litigation Division, Criminal Justice Division, General Litigation Division, and Government Services and Employment Division. The operations division is divided into the following areas: computer services, financial services, and human resources. In addition, the Attorney General Division includes the Special Prosecutions Unit, Counsel to the Attorney General, and Communications Office (Office of the Attorney General of Georgia, 2011).

District Attorney

The State of Georgia is divided into 49 judicial circuits, with each circuit comprised of one to eight counties. The District Attorney is the chief prosecuting officer for the State in each of the circuits. Each District Attorney represents the State in both criminal trial and appellate cases in Superior Court as well as delinquency cases in Juvenile Court. Each District Attorney is an elected constitutional officer who is elected circuit-wide to four-year terms, works for the judicial branch of the State government, and must have been an active member of the State Bar of Georgia for three years prior to election. In addition, a full-time staff of assistant district attorneys, investigators, and victim assistance and administrative personnel assist the District Attorney in each circuit (Prosecuting Attorney's Council of Georgia, 2011).

Solicitor-General

The Solicitor-General is an elected county officer who represents the State in misdemeanor criminal trial and appellate cases heard in the State Court. In 64 of the 159 counties in the State, the Solicitor-General prosecutes misdemeanor cases in which the maximum punishment is a sentence of 12 months to be served in jail. In 20 counties, the Solicitor-General is a full-time official, with a staff of assistants, investigators, and administrative personnel, while Solicitor-Generals in the remaining 44 counties serve as part-time officials in addition to practicing private law. In the remaining counties that do not have a State Court, and in Chatham, Dougherty, Miller, and Rockdale Counties, the District Attorney prosecutes misdemeanor criminal cases (Prosecuting Attorney's Council of Georgia, 2011).

Georgia's Public Defenders

According to the Georgia Constitution of 1983, Article I, Paragraph XIV provides that "Every person charged with an offense against the laws of this state shall have the privilege and benefit of counsel; shall be furnished with a copy of the accusation or indictment and, on demand, with a list of the witnesses on whose testimony such charge is founded; shall have compulsory process to obtain the testimony of that person's own witnesses; and shall be confronted with the witnesses testifying against such person."

As required by the Supreme Court in *Gideon v. Wainwright* (372 U.S. 335 [1963]) and *Argersinger v. Hamlin* (407 U.S. 25 [1972]), defendants who are indigent (meaning unable to afford an attorney) must be provided the assistance of an attorney in all crucial stages of the criminal justice process. The Georgia Indigent Defense Act, signed into law in May 2003, created a statewide public defender system for indigent cases in Superior Court and in all juvenile delinquency cases, providing funds for all personnel and various other expenses. Other courts, meeting certain criteria, may contract with the public defender system for services, but must use local funds.

Circuit Public Defenders are appointed by a Public Defender Supervisory Panel in 43 of the 49 judicial circuits in the State. The remaining six judicial circuits opted out of the state system and provide their own Public Defender offices, funded by the individual circuits. Public Defenders are responsible for providing legal defense to all indigent persons charged with a criminal offense, and must be at least 25 years of age, have practiced law in the Superior Courts for at least three years, and be a member in good standing of the Georgia State Bar (Georgia Public Defender Standards Council, 2011).

The Office of the Georgia Capital Defender was created as a trial resource center for attorneys handling death penalty cases. The Office provides assistance and training to local attorneys appointed as defense counsel for defendants charged with a capital offense; provides service as co-counsel in trial and direct appeal of death penalty cases; and accepts appointment for direct representation as lead counsel in death penalty cases based on individual circumstances of the case (Georgia Capital Defenders, 2011).

The Georgia Public Defender Standards Council was created with the Georgia Indigent Defense Act of 2003 to oversee the public defender system. The Council functions as an independent agency within the executive branch of the State. Its mission is to "to ensure, independently of political considerations or private interests, that each client whose cause has been entrusted to a circuit public defender receives zealous, adequate, effective, timely, and ethical legal representation," to provide "all such legal services in a cost efficient manner" and "to conduct that representation in such a way that the criminal justice system operates effectively to achieve justice" (Georgia Public Defender Standards Council, 2011).

Conclusion

The court system within the State of Georgia is vast and complex, yet similar in structure and organization to other state court systems. Residing within the Eleventh Circuit for the U.S. Court of Appeals and comprising three federal districts, the State and the capital City of Atlanta serve as a central location for federal prosecutions, making it the busiest circuit in the federal system. In addition, the State has been active and persistent in providing effective legal representation for indigent defendants at criminal trials in Superior Court and for juvenile delinquency cases.

Chapter Review Questions

1. What roles do the 11th Circuit Court of Appeals and the U.S. District Courts play in the judicial process in Georgia?
2. What are the different state courts in Georgia?

3. What courts are on the local level and what types of cases are heard in these courts?
4. What kinds of cases are tried by the Attorney General of Georgia, district attorneys, and solicitor generals?
5. What is the role of the public defender in Georgia? How does the Office of Georgia Capital Defenders assist in death penalty cases?

References

Administrative Office of the Courts of Georgia (AOC). (2011). Services and Responsibilities. Retrieved from: http://www.georgiacourts.org.
Argersinger v. Hamlin, 407 U.S. 25 (1972)
Council of Juvenile Court Judges. (2011). Council Profile. Retrieved from: http://w2.georgiacourts.org.
Council of Magistrate Court Judges. (2011). Public Information. Retrieved from: http://www.georgiacourts.org.
Council of Municipal Court Judges. (2011). About the Council. Retrieved from: http://www.georgiacourts.org.
Council of Probate Court Judges. (2011). Welcome. Retrieved from: http://w2.georgiacourts.org.
Council of State Court Judges. (2011). The Council. Retrieved from: http://www.statecourt.georgiacourts.gov.
Council of Superior Court Judges (CSCJ). (2011). About CSCJ. Retrieved from: http://www.cscj.org.
Court of Appeals of Georgia (COA). (2011). History. Retrieved from: http://www.gaappeals.us.
Federal Judicial Center. (2011). History of the Federal Judiciary. Retrieved from: http://www.fjc.gov/
Georgia Accountability Courts (GAC). (2011). About. Retrieved from: http://w2.georgiacourts.org.
Georgia Capital Defenders. (2011). Home. Retrieved from: http://www.gacapdef.org.
Georgia Constitution of 1983. Retrieved from: http://georgiainfo.galileo.usg.edu.
Georgia Public Defender Standards Council. (2011). Home. Retrieved from: http://www.gpdsc.org.
Gideon v. Wainwright, 372 U.S. 335 (1963)
New Georgia Encyclopedia. (2011). Judicial Branch. Retrieved from: http://www.georgiaencyclopedia.org.
O.C.G.A. § 15-5-20. (2011). Official Code of Georgia Annotated.

O.C.G.A. § 15-5-24. (2011). Official Code of Georgia Annotated.

O.C.G.A. § 15-7-26. (2011). Official Code of Georgia Annotated.

O.C.G.A. § 15-9-15. (2011). Official Code of Georgia Annotated.

O.C.G.A. § 36-32-40. (2011). Official Code of Georgia Annotated.

Office of Attorney General of Georgia. (2011). History. Retrieved from: http://law.ga.gov.

Prosecuting Attorney's Council of Georgia. (2011). Search. Retrieved from: http://www.pacga.org.

Powell v. Gregg, 224 Ga. 226, 161 S.E.2.d 265 (1968)

State Bar of Georgia (SBG). (2011). Membership Statistics. Retrieved from: http://www.gabar.org.

Supreme Court of Georgia (SCG). (2011). History. Retrieved from: http://www.gasupreme.us.

Supreme Court of Georgia. In *New Georgia Encyclopedia*. Retrieved from: http://www.georgiaencyclopedia.org.

United States Court of Appeals, Eleventh Circuit. (2011). About the Court. Retrieved from: http://www.ca11.uscourts.gov.

United States District Court, Middle District of Georgia. (2011). Home. Retrieved from: http://www.gamd.uscourts.gov.

United States District Court, Northern District of Georgia. (2011). About Us. Retrieved from: http://www.gand.uscourts.gov.

United States District Court, Southern District of Georgia. (2011). Home. Retrieved from: http://www.gasd.uscourts.gov.

CHAPTER 8

CORRECTIONS IN GEORGIA

Learning Objectives

After reading the chapter, students will be able to:

- Explain the role of federal prisons in the state.
- Discuss the history of state prisons in Georgia.
- Discuss the various classifications for inmates in state correctional facilities.
- Discuss the different types of correctional facilities in the state.
- Explain the role of the death penalty in Georgia's correctional system.
- Describe local corrections and the role it plays in Georgia.
- Discuss probation and the role it plays in Georgia's correctional system.

Key Terms

Boot Camp	Medium Security
Chain Gang	Minimum Security
Classification	Podular Design
Close Security	Pre-Release Center
Correctional Emergency	Private Prison
Response Team	Probation
County Prison	Probation Detention Center
Day Reporting Center	Reentry Initiatives and Services
Death Penalty	State Board of Pardons and
Federal Bureau of Prisons	Paroles
Georgia Department of	State Prisons
Corrections	Transitional Center
Inmate Under Death Sentence	Victim Services
Jail	

Corrections within the State of Georgia consists of federal, state, and local institutions, housing defendants awaiting trial, housing inmates serving court sentences, and housing inmates on death row. Corrections also includes officers working within the institutions as well as probation officers supervising convicted persons and parole officers supervising inmates released from correctional institutions.

Federal Bureau of Prisons

The Federal Bureau of Prisons (BOP) "was established in 1930 to provide more progressive and humane care for Federal inmates, to professionalize the prison service, and to ensure consistent and centralized administration of the 11 Federal prisons in operation at the time" (BOP, 2011). The BOP currently maintains 116 institutions, a headquarters central office, six regional offices, two staff training centers, and 22 community corrections offices. "The regional offices and Central Office provide administrative oversight and support to Bureau facilities and community corrections offices. In turn, community corrections offices oversee residential reentry centers and home confinement programs" (BOP, 2011). There are approximately 210,000 federal inmates, with approximately 80 percent housed in BOP-operated institutions, and the remaining housed in privately managed or community-based institutions and local jails (BOP, 2011).

Currently in the State of Georgia, the BOP operates two low security facilities, two medium security facilities, and one community corrections facility. In addition, the Southeast Regional Office is located in Atlanta. The low security facilities, D. Ray James in Folkston and McRae, operate with a double-fenced perimeter, dormitory and cubicle style housing, and strong work components. In addition, both institutions are part of the approximately 15 percent of the BOP's inmate population confined in institutions operated by private corrections companies. "Contract facilities help the Bureau manage its population and are especially useful for meeting the needs of low security, specialized populations like sentenced criminal aliens. Staff of the Correctional Programs Division in the Central Office provide oversight for privately-operated facilities" (BOP, 2011). In addition, the BOP has contracts with several county jails and detention facilities to house inmates, assisting the counties in saving operating funds.

The medium security facilities have several housing and work components. The Federal Correctional Institution at Jesup houses approximately 1,150 male inmates and includes a satellite low facility housing approximately 605 male inmates, and a minimum security facility housing approximately 150 male inmates. The United State Penitentiary in Atlanta, opened in 1902, houses approximately 2,500 male inmates, and includes a detention center for pre-trial and holdover inmates, as well as a satellite camp for minimum security male inmates (adjacent to the main facility that provides inmate labor to the main institution) (BOP, 2011).

State of Georgia Department of Corrections

The mission of the Georgia Department of Corrections (GDC) states that it "protects and serves the public as a professional organization by effectively managing offenders while helping to provide a safe and secure environment for the citizens of Georgia" (2011a). The core values of the GDC are Loyalty, Duty, Respect, Selfless Service, Honor, Integrity, and Personal Courage. The vision for the Department includes the recognition of being "the best corrections system in the nation at protecting citizens from convicted offenders and at providing effective opportunities for offenders to achieve positive change. We are a leader and partner in making Georgia a safer, healthier, better educated, growing, and best managed state" (GDC, 2011a). The vision is accomplished by:

- Ensuring public safety;
- Operating safe and secure facilities;
- Providing effective community supervision of offenders;
- Creating opportunities for restoration to offenders;
- Ensuring the rights of victims;
- Partnering with public, private, and faith-based organizations;
- Sustaining core values of Loyalty, Duty, Respect, Selfless Service, Honor, Integrity, and Personal Courage; and
- Ensuring the well being of employees and their families (GDC, 2011a).

History of State Corrections in Georgia

In 1811, the General Assembly delegated funds for the first state prison to be built in Milledgeville, then the state capital. The prison was completed and opened in 1815, across the street from the Governor's Mansion. It housed all white offenders, both male and female. A hospital was added in 1832 and in 1844, workshops were constructed, all forming an octagon shape.

In 1864, Governor Joe Brown offered pardons to all male inmates to fight for the Confederacy. The female inmates burned and attempted to destroy the prison, with General Sherman finishing the job during his march through Georgia. Following the Civil War, in 1874, Federal Governor Ruger authorized the convict lease system, whereby state prisoners were leased to private individuals and companies for labor services, bringing the state about $10 per year.

The convict lease system was maintained until 1897, when the General Assembly abandoned the system in favor of one created by the state prison board commission. The General Assembly authorized $50,000 to build a prison farm for men, women, and boys. The prison farm, built near Milledgeville, was surrounded by stockades and contained a gin, a corn grinding mill, a depot, a warehouse, and was one of the largest agricultural undertakings by the state.

The chain gangs began in 1903 as the state prison board commission contracted with individuals and corporations to assist counties in the construction of public highways, railroads, and other public service projects. The prisoners, working on various projects throughout the state in the chain gangs, were housed in prison camps, and by 1929, there were 140 active prison camps. Prisoners working in the chain gang wore black and white striped uniforms and were expected to perform physical labor while in leg chains. Although the chain gangs would develop a reputation for brutality, it was not until 1932 that national attention was given to the prison system in Georgia. However, another ten years would pass before more national attention, in the form of an article in *Life Magazine*, would force then Governor Ellis Arnall to begin an investigation of the state prison system.

The investigation led to reform in all aspects of the state prison system. The chain gangs were replaced with a system that had a more humane treatment and rehabilitative focus. By the end of the 20th century, Georgia boasted the eighth largest prison system in the country (Chamber of Commerce, 2011).

Today's Correctional System

In FY 2009, the GDC operated with a total funding budget of $1,043,637,575. The largest component of this budget was personal services, at 53.6 percent. The second largest component was health, at 20 percent, with regular operating costs only comprising 12 percent of the total budget (GDC, 2010a).

In FY 2009, the inmate population within the GDC was 54,049. Table 8.1 shows the number of inmates convicted of specific crimes. Table 8.2 shows the number of inmates by age, gender and race.

Classifications

The GDC uses three security classifications for its correctional facilities which indicate the security level of inmates: close, medium, and minimum. The purpose of the classification is the proper assignment of inmates to specific facilities, based on the sentence, nature of the offense, criminal history, history of violence, and the medical and treatment needs of the individual in-

Table 8.1 Number of Inmates by Offenses

Offenses	# of Inmates
Violent	23,867
Sexual	7,837
Property	10,755
Drug	9,236
Habit/DUI	136
Others	2,218
Murder	5,221
Rape	1,833
Armed Robbery	5,180
Kidnapping	1,640
Aggravated Sodomy	222
Aggravated Sexual Battery	182
Aggravated Child Molestation	1,359

(GDC, 2010a)

Table 8.2 Inmates by Age, Gender, and Race

Age	# of Inmates
Under 20	1,111
20–29	16,856
30–39	15,953
40–49	12,752
50–59	5,713
60–69	1,321
70+	239
Not reported	104
Gender	
Male	50,331
Female	3,718
Race	
White	20,050
Black	33,557
Indian	70
Asian	68
Not reported	304

(GDC, 2010a)

mate. Once an offender is classified and placed in a certain facility, reclassification will occur at specific time intervals, typically every 12 months or when circumstances justify a review of classification (GDC, 2011b).

Close Security classification indicates that an inmate poses a serious escape risk, has a history of assaults, is considered dangerous, and may have a detainer on file for the commission of other serious crimes (a detainer is a request by a law enforcement agency to hold the inmate pending further charges or actions). Inmates at Close Security facilities may never leave the prison and require supervision by a correctional officer at all times (GDC, 2011b).

Medium Security classification is currently the largest category of inmates. This classification indicates that an inmate will have no major adjustment problems, and that although the inmate may work outside of the prison, constant supervision is required (GDC, 2011b).

Minimum Security classification indicates that an inmate poses a minimal escape risk, is able to abide by prison regulations, and poses a minimal threat to the community. Inmates in this classification often work outside the prison under minimal supervision, have proven to be trustworthy and cooperative, and have no drug or alcohol problems. In addition, inmates assigned to Minimum Security are eligible for transitional centers (GDC, 2011b).

Agency Divisions

The Commissioner, whose job is the overall supervision of the agency, heads the GDC and is assisted by numerous assistants and directors. Within the Administration Division are the following seven sections, whose main functions are to provide financial and asset management: Budget Services, Business Management, Business Processes, Care and Custody, Financial Services, Fiscal Audits, and Purchasing (GDC, 2011c).

The Corrections Division "is responsible for the direct supervision of all offenders sentenced to the Georgia Department of Corrections" (GDC, 2011d). Within this division, numerous prisons, centers, offices, and boot camps exist throughout the state, housing approximately 60,000 offenders, while another 150,000 probationers are supervised within the community or probation facilities.

The Operations, Planning and Training Division, created in 2004 to provide support and professional services to the GDC, consists of the following nine sections: Communications Center, Engineering and Construction Services, Fire Services, Office of Health Services, Office of Information Technology, Institutional Training, Planning and Strategic Management, Reentry Services, and Safety Officer (GDC, 2011d).

Correctional Facilities

The State of Georgia Department of Corrections operates numerous correctional facilities throughout the state. The facilities differ in terms of inmate classification, operational management, function, and cost.

State Prisons

The GDC operates 29 state prisons, which house violent, repeat offenders, as well as nonviolent offenders who have exhausted all other options for punishment. Two of the state prisons are assigned for women. Offenders may be sentenced directly to prison by a judge or may be placed in prison due to revocation proceedings.

Inmates within the various state prisons who are physically and mentally capable of work are assigned to work details. These details may be related to the daily operations of the institution, such as cooking, cleaning, laundry, or general repairs, or may be specialized details. These specialized details include (GDC, 2011b):

- Community Work Details—low security offenders build, refurbish, and maintain prison and community buildings; clean public buildings and schools; perform roadwork; and work at landfills and recycling centers.
- Correctional Industries—approximately 1,800 inmates receive on-the-job training in fields such as metal fabrication, printing and screen printing, license plates, footwear, optics, woodworking, upholstery, garment and chemical production.
- Fire Services—specially selected minimum security inmates are chosen to work in prison fire stations and respond to prison and rural fire emergencies.
- Food and Farm Operations—more than 5,000 inmates work on prison farms and work in preserving, preparing, and serving foods.
- Offender Construction—carefully supervised, skilled inmates serve construction needs of the GDC, other state agencies, and the community. Inmates are housed temporarily in nearby facilities while working on renovation or remodeling jobs across the state.

Inmates Under Death Sentence

The State of Georgia is currently one of 36 states, along with the federal government, to provide the death penalty for convicted felons. Under Georgia law, only the crimes of murder, rape, and kidnapping are punishable by a sentence of death.

The state has carried out executions since 1735, when the first person to be legally executed was Alice Ryley, a white female who was hanged for the murder of her master (GDC, 2010b). Prior to 1862, the crime of murder received a mandatory death sentence. However, the Georgia Code of 1861 provided for life in prison, given at the discretion of the jury (Wilkes, 2009).

Execution by hanging was carried out by the sheriff of the county or judicial circuit where the crime occurred, and continued until the last two hangings were held on May 20, 1925. "It is estimated that over 500 legal hangings occurred in Georgia between 1725 and 1925" (GDC, 2010b).

On August 16, 1924, the General Assembly passed an act to abolish hanging, substituting electrocution and providing one central location for all executions (the last hangings were allowed to occur in 1925 because the crimes were committed before the effective date of the new law). The first electric chair was built in 1924 and was located at Georgia State Prison in Milledgeville. Electrocutions, 162 in total, occurred at Milledgeville through 1937, when, in 1938, the electric chair moved to the new Georgia State Prison built in Reidsville (GDC, 2010b).

The first execution in Reidsville occurred May 6, 1938. A total of 256 executions were eventually carried out until 1964, when the U.S. Supreme Court suspended all executions. Of the 256 executions, one inmate was female, with the oldest inmate at 72 and the youngest at 16 years of age (GDC, 2010b).

In the 1972 case of *Furman v. Georgia*, the U.S. Supreme Court struck down existing death penalty laws as unconstitutional. In March 1973, the General Assembly approved a new death penalty statute, but it was not until the 1976 case of *Gregg v. Georgia* that the Supreme Court upheld the Georgia law as constitutional (GDC, 2010b).

In 1980, executions were moved again, this time to the Georgia Diagnostic and Classification Prison in Jackson. A new electric chair was built for this facility, with the old chair remaining on display in Reidsville (GDC, 2010b).

At the turn of the century, another change occurred, this time eliminating electrocution as the mode of execution and implementing lethal injection for all new death sentences, effective May 1, 2000. However, in October 2001, the Georgia Supreme Court declared that execution by electrocution violates the 8th Amendment provision against cruel and unusual punishment, and lethal injection became the only mode of execution (GDC, 2010b).

Today, the GDC houses male inmates under death sentence and carries out state ordered executions at the Georgia Diagnostic and Classification State Prison in Jackson, while female inmates under death sentence are housed at Metro State Prison in Atlanta. The Georgia Constitution stipulates that the Georgia

Table 8.3 Age and Race of Males Under Death Sentence

Age	White	Black
20–29	1	0
30–39	15	10
40–49	15	22
50–59	16	13
60–69	4	3
TOTAL	51	48

(GDC, 2011g)

Board of Pardons and Paroles will make all appeals or requests for clemency (GDC, 2010b).

As of January 2, 2011, there are 100 inmates residing on death row—51 white males, 48 black males, and 1 white female. The oldest inmate on death row is currently 68 years old and the youngest is currently 28 years old. Two inmates have been residing on death row for almost 34 years, with the newest inmate placed on death row in July 2010 (GDC, 2011g). Table 8.3 illustrates the ages and races of male inmates under death sentence.

Private Prisons

The GDC is currently in contract with Corrections Corporation of America for two state prisons: Coffee Correctional Facility in Nicholls and Wheeler Correctional Facility in Alamo. The facilities were built and opened in 1998 by Corrections Corporation of America, who maintains daily operations of the facilities. The contract includes a GDC Private Prison Monitor who works on site to ensure all contract provisions are met regarding safety, security, and sanitation. These prisons operate in the same manner as other state prisons, with inmates working full-time details and having opportunities for education and counseling programs. In addition, as required by contract, both prisons are accredited by the American Correctional Association and the Medical Association of Georgia (GDC, 2011b).

Boot Camps

The Probation Boot Camp, located at the Al Burruss Correctional Training Center in Forsyth, near Macon, houses approximately 100 male felons. Inmates can be sent directly to the facility from a court sentence or as a result of a revocation action. The boot camp consists of a highly structured military regimen program and requires inmates to work during the day in the facility or to perform public service work within the local community. In addition, risk reduction programs are provided in the evening (GDC, 2011d).

The Offender Boot Camp, located at Coastal State Prison in Garden City, near Savannah, houses approximately 255 male felons. The State Board of Pardons and Paroles chooses inmates from those sentenced to prison to attend the three- to four-month boot camp program. If the inmate successfully completes the boot camp program, he will be released on parole, regardless of the length of the original court sentence. Like the Probation Boot Camp, this camp is a highly structured military regimen program, requiring inmates to work during the day in the facility or to perform public service work within the local community. In addition, rehabilitative programs are provided during the evening (GDC, 2011d).

Convicted felons who are considered for the Probation or Offender Boot Camp must:

- be between 17 and 35 years of age at the time of sentencing;
- have no previous incarceration in an adult penal institution;
- be serving no less than nine months or more than five years in prison;
- have no known contagious or communicable disease;
- have no known physical limitation that would exclude strenuous labor or physical activity; and
- have no known medical disorder or retardation that would prevent strenuous physical activity or intensive interaction in any program (GDC, 2011b).

The Boot Camp Plus program serves drug offenders only. The offenders assigned to this program may have had one prior felony conviction, but will only qualify for the program if the current sentence is a drug charge only. Convicted felons eligible for the Boot Camp Plus program must:

- be between 17 and 40 years of age at the time of sentencing;
- be serving no less than 25 months or more than five years in prison;
- have no known contagious or communicable disease;
- have no known physical limitation that would exclude strenuous labor or physical activity; and
- have no known medical disorder or retardation that would prevent strenuous physical activity or intensive interaction in any program (GDC, 2011b).

In order to be eligible for a Boot Camp program, the offender cannot have been convicted of any of the following offenses, either currently or in the past:

Aggravated Assault, Battery, Child Molestation, Sodomy or Stalking; Armed Robbery; Arson; First Degree Child Molestation; Criminal Gang Activity; Cruelty to Children; Enticing a Child for Indecent Purposes; Feticide; Hijacking of Motor Vehicle; Homicide by Vehicle (Felony); Incest; Involuntary Manslaughter; Kidnapping; Murder; Possession of a Firearm (if current offense); Possession of any Drug with Intent to Distribute; Rape; Residential Burglary (may have had probated sentence); Robbery (all types); Sale of any type of Drug; Serious Injury by Vehicle (may have had probated sentence); Sexual Exploitation of Children; Statutory Rape; Trafficking of any Controlled Substance; or Voluntary Manslaughter (GDC, 2011b).

County Prisons

The GDC has established interagency agreements with 23 counties within the state to lease 5,020 beds in county work camps, also called county prisons. These prisons' low-security, long-term inmates provide unpaid, but highly skilled work for the counties in which they are housed. The county prisons allow inmates to "assist in the maintenance of roads and parks; work at local landfills; serve on local fire crews; assist with small construction projects for government agencies, and assist local government agencies as needed" (GDC, 2011d).

Pre-Release Centers

The GDC has six Pre-Release Centers, one housing female inmates, all hosted by a state prison. The centers are designed to work with inmates who are within five years of release, for the purpose of assisting in the re-entry of those inmates into the community. The centers provide a secure environment, emphasize work, and provide the inmate with work experience within the community prior to release (GDC, 2011b).

The mission of the centers is to reduce recidivism, thus increasing safety to the community, by assisting in finding suitable housing and meaningful employment for the inmates. The goal is to provide work opportunities to enhance the inmate's work ethic (GDC, 2011b).

Transitional Centers

The GDC operates 15 transitional centers throughout the state, housing 2,986 inmates, of which 347 are women, and all are hosted by a state prison. The purpose of the transitional center is to provide selected inmates with a program to slowly integrate them back into society by obtaining employment and enhancing their prospects for stability upon release. "Research has shown that offenders who have the opportunity to re-enter the community after a stay in a transitional center are up to a third more likely to succeed in maintaining a crime-free life" (GDC, 2011d).

Inmates are referred to a transitional center by either prison staff or the Georgia Board of Pardons and Paroles. The decision to place an inmate within a center is based upon, in part, the inmate's criminal history and behavior while in prison. Once assigned, the inmate is required to go through a 30-day orientation period, during which time the inmate will attend classes in preparation for employment, as well as participate in programs and assignments that contribute to the upkeep of the center. Classes include drug and alcohol education, communication skills, financial management, and employment instruction.

When the inmate has completed the orientation period, work release is sought through a paid job within the community. A job coordinator will screen the inmate for certain jobs, and will assist employers with problems or issues. Employers provide periodic performance reports to the job coordinator to measure the inmate's progress in the work force.

Once the inmate has gained employment, 30 percent of the salary must be given to the transitional center for room and board, but this is not to exceed $90 weekly. Inmates also pay federal, state, and local taxes. If the inmate has minor children, family support is required, and with the exception of a small allowance for transportation and incidentals, all other funds are held until the inmate is released from the center. The fees collected by the transitional centers amount to over $1.2 million in annual revenue to the state. Inmates typically stay an average of nine to 12 months, and are then either released on parole or released to the community if the sentence has been fulfilled. Not only do transitional centers provide employment and re-integration for the inmate, but the citizens of Georgia also benefit from the revenue (GDC, 2011b).

In addition, transitional centers house low risk maintenance workers who are assigned to maintain the facility and/or other state facilities in the community. These inmates do not earn wages, but have access to programs in the center, and typically stay for longer periods than work release inmates. For example, of the inmates housed at the Atlanta Transitional Center, about half are classified as maintenance workers who provide details to the Governor's Mansion, the State Capital Complex, and the Georgia State Patrol Headquarters (GDC, 2011d).

Reentry Initiative and Services

The State of Georgia and the GDC are actively engaged in various forms of reentry services for Georgia's prison population. Because of the high recidi-

vism rates for inmates within the state, the GDC begins providing reentry services to inmates at the point of entry into GDC supervision. The goals of reentry include assisting the inmate to be a productive member of his/her family
and community, providing links to services necessary for the successful transition back to the community, addressing the inmate's needs and identifying
community resources to meet those needs, enhancing community safety by
reducing recidivism, and promoting collaborative partnerships that support
the inmate's reentry into the community (GDC, 2010a).

Reentry services include programs targeted toward specific aspects of an inmate's life while in prison and then moving toward release. Programs include:

- Chaplaincy program—providing religious service and counseling for all
  faiths.
- Faith and Character-Based program—a 12-month curriculum for personal and spiritual growth and development.
- Reentry Partnership Housing program—a collaborative effort with local
  individuals and agencies to provide housing to released offenders who
  have no other housing alternative upon release.
- Risk Reduction Services—providing programs designed to change criminal thinking and reduce criminal behavior.
- Volunteer Services—involving community stakeholders in order to provide services and mentoring to support the successful transition from
  prison to the community (GDC, 2010a).

The GDC offers specific vocational education and training programs, whose
goals are to decrease recidivism by providing inmates with job skills for gain-
ful employment. The programs are: auto body repair; building maintenance;
cabinetry/carpentry; computer office/technology; construction; cosmetology/
barbering; equine rescue program; food preparation/culinary arts; graphic
arts/printing; masonry/tile setting; service industry; and welding (GDC,
2010a).

Transitional Centers are the preferred method of preparing inmates for reentry into the community, although the limited number of beds available in these
centers make them a viable option for only a small percentage of inmates.
Therefore "in house" transitional dormitories have been created within the
state prisons for inmates who are within 12 months of their release date. These
transitional dormitories grant the inmates isolation from the general prison
population so the inmates can receive and participate in intensive training, focusing on reentry. Programs include education, job skills, and substance abuse
treatment (GDC, 2011d).

State Board of Pardons and Paroles

The State Board of Pardons and Paroles in Georgia is part of the executive branch and is "constitutionally authorized to grant paroles, pardons, reprieves, remissions, commutations, and to restore civil and political rights" (State Board of Pardons and Paroles [PAP], 2011). Parole was first provided in Georgia in 1908 by the General Assembly, authorizing the Prison Commission to implement a system of parole or conditional pardons. However, the system was limited in funding and staff. In February 1943, the General Assembly enacted legislation to create the State Board of Pardons and Paroles as an independent agency. In August 1943, Georgia voters ratified an amendment to the Georgia Constitution, establishing the Parole Board's authority and the appointment of Board members by the governor for seven-year terms. The initial Board consisted of three members, but was expanded to its present size of five members by Constitutional amendment in 1973 (PAP, 2011).

The Board continuously strives to improve its professionalism and accountability. Beginning in 1970, parole officers are required to obtain a four-year college degree. In 1979, the Board established the Parole Decision Guidelines, known as the "grid system," which measure an inmate's severity of criminal behavior with the likelihood of success on parole. The guidelines have improved the parole decision process, allowing for more consistent, soundly based, and understandable decisions (PAP, 2011).

Since 1983, parole officers must be state certified peace officers by the Peace Officers Standards and Training (P.O.S.T.) Council, and maintain annual training requirements. In 1993, the Board doubled the required training to ensure parole officers are receiving the more up-to-date training offered. In addition, the Field Services division (community parole supervision) of the Board has maintained continuous accreditation by the American Correctional Association since 1994, making it one of only four parole field organizations in the country to achieve accreditation (PAP, 2011).

Supervision

"Protection of the public and the successful reintegration of the offender back into the community are the hallmarks of parole supervision" (PAP, 2011). Parole officers work under the supervision of the Board and agency managers. In fiscal year 2010, the parolee population for the state was 22,403. In terms of successful completion of parole supervision, "performance measures associated with supervision of these cases reveal that 69% of parolees successfully completed their period of parole supervision. This compares very favorably to the 49% national average of parolees who successfully complete parole supervision" (PAP, 2011).

The success rate of parole supervision is in large part due to the dedication of parole officers. In fiscal year 2010, parole officers made 477,527 contacts with parolees as part of the surveillance component of supervision and collected more than $3,000,000 in parole supervision fines, placed in the state treasury. In addition, the Board requires extensive investigation of personal and criminal backgrounds be conducted on all potential parolees. These investigations are handled by parole officers, with 58,250 conducted in fiscal year 2010 (PAP, 2011).

In addition, the Interstate Compact Unit oversees the placement and transfer of all parolees into and out of the state. The Unit arranges supervision of transferring parolees, responds to parole violations, handles extraditions, and responds to the needs of victims. The unit is also responsible for maintaining the files of all Conditional Transfers to federal, out-of-state, and Immigration and Naturalization Service Detainers. "The State Board of Pardons and Paroles Interstate Compact Unit is one of the most efficient in the nation. Georgia Parole is a member of the Interstate Commission of Adult Offender Supervision (ICAOS). This organization is responsible for creating and maintaining the rules of the Interstate Compact Agreement. The ICAOS is comprised of all 50 states, the District of Columbia, Puerto Rico and the Virgin Islands" (PAP, 2011).

Victim Services

The Board has historically and continuously been keenly aware of the impact of crime on victims and survivors. In 2005, the Board joined with the Georgia Department of Corrections to combine victim services with the Corrections and Parole Board Office of Victim Services. This merger has allowed for more effective services and opportunities to accommodate victims. The office works with victims to ensure their views and concerns are heard by the Board members prior to parole decisions. In addition, the office works with victims and families to answer questions and keep them informed of the parole process and decisions (PAP, 2011).

Victim Impact Statements (VIPs) allow all victims and survivors to express to the Board how the crime has affected them and their families. The VIPs may be completed by the victim or for the victim by a family member or attorney. It provides detailed information on the crime and its aftermath. In addition, the Board has established the Victim Information Program (V.I.P.), a 24-hour, automated information system, providing victims and families access to information about the offender. The V.I.P. also provides automated notification to the victim and/or family if the offender is released from custody (PAP, 2011).

Probation Supervision

"In FY 2008, the probation population was 148,629 probationers under supervision. The average Standard/Administrative caseload in Georgia is 250 probationers per officer. This ratio is significantly higher than the national average caseload size" (GDC, 2011e). Each judicial circuit has at least one probation officer and there are currently 113 offices located throughout the state. The most common offense committed by those placed on probation is drug-related (possession, sale, manufacture, distribution, and trafficking), with property crime being the second most common offense (GDC, 2011e).

Probationers are assessed and supervised according to their level of risk for re-offending. All probationers, as a condition of probation, must agree to allow probation officers to visit their home and workplace, while others, as a condition of the court order, must submit to drug testing. Probation officers may also require their probationers to report directly to the probation office at various times throughout their probation period. In addition, all probationers are required to submit to evaluations and testing related to rehabilitation, while also participating in and completing rehabilitative program as directed by the GDC.

Probation officers provide supervision to all probationers. All state probation officers are P.O.S.T. certified peace officers and have statewide arrest powers. In addition to general stipulations for contact and supervision, some probationers require additional direct contact by probation officers. Intensive Probation Supervision (IPS) requires high levels of surveillance and intervention. Probationers may be placed on IPS as a direct sentencing option or as a result of revocation or sentence modification. Mandated employment and curfews are critical elements of IPS supervision, while probation officers may also order house arrest, and make contact with IPS probationers 24 hours a day (GDC, 2011e).

Specialized Probation Supervision (SPS) is a program specifically designed for sex offenders. Each of the 49 judicial circuits has at least one probation officer specially trained to supervise these probationers. The SPS probationers are supervised in a highly restrictive and structured environment, where travel and computer access are severely limited and monitored, while probationers are required to keep the SPS probation officer apprised of physical whereabouts and activities at all times (GDC, 2011e).

SPS probationers are required to undergo treatment by providers who are certified by the state and GDC, which includes a specialized treatment regimen to properly address the deviant behavior. For certain sex crimes, probationers are required to provide DNA samples, maintained by the Georgia

Bureau of Investigation in a statewide database. The samples assist in identifying repeat offenders as well as eliminating suspects (GDC, 2011e).

In 1996, the Georgia Bureau of Investigation created the Sex Offender Registry, requiring all persons convicted of a sex-related offense to register. The Registry contains photos, names, addresses, identifying information (scars, tattoos, etc.), offense, state and date of conviction, and the date of the last verification of address. In 1999, probation officers received the technology to digitally send photos and information from the field office directly to the database, saving time in updating probationer information. The database is free and accessible for all citizens and interested persons through the Georgia Bureau of Investigation website or the GDC public website (GDC, 2011e).

In addition to the extensive supervision by probation officers, probationers under SPS may also be required to have Global Positioning Monitors, designed to establish the distance between probationers' residences and the places where potential victims may gather. If a probationer establishes a residence close to potential victims, the officers have the opportunity to intervene and relocate the probationer so he/she does not reoffend (GDC, 2011e).

Provisions of court ordered probation may also require probationers to perform community service, requiring the probationer to perform unpaid labor for a specified number of hours. In Georgia, the service requirement can consist of picking up trash along roadways, landscaping around public buildings, or may involve more skilled labor, such as mechanical work, remodeling, electrical wiring, plumbing, or painting public buildings. In addition, community service hours may consist of assisting the community in cleanup after natural disasters (GDC, 2011e).

Probation officers are also required to collect court and state fees from their probationers. Along with the stipulations for supervision, offenders placed on probation are required to pay $23 per month, in accordance with Georgia Code O.C.G.A. §42-8-34. Of this amount, $9 goes to the Georgia Crime Victims Emergency Fund. Additionally, once placed on probation, a one-time fee of $50 for felons and $25 for misdemeanants goes to the Georgia Bureau of Investigation Crime Lab. Probationers pay other fees required by the court, including restitution, to the probation officer, with the funds then being sent to the court or victim (GDC, 2011e).

Probationer Profile

The following tables provide a numerical count of offenders being placed on probation in calendar year 2010 (indicating a total of 39,417 **new** probationers in 2010. Table 8.4 illustrates the age of the probationers by gender.

Table 8.4 Age of Probationers by Gender

Age	Male	Female
13–19	4,970	920
20–29	10,535	2,740
30–39	7,493	2,253
40–49	5,515	1,546
50–59	2,380	507
60–69	423	67
70+	59	3
Not reported	5	1
TOTAL	31,380	8,037

(GDC, 2011f)

Table 8.5 illustrates the race of the probationers by gender.

Table 8.5 Race of Probations by Gender

Race	Male	Female
White	11,929	4,309
Black	17,967	3,543
Hispanic	1,202	136
Asian	101	18
Native American	19	7
Other	153	27
Unknown	9	0
TOTAL	31,380	8,037

(GDC, 2011f)

Table 8.6 illustrates the offenses of the probationers by gender.

Table 8.6 Offenses of Probationers by Gender

Offenses	Male	Female
Violent	5,442	883
Sexual Crime	1,336	34
Property	9,942	3,659
Drug	7,442	2,176
Habit/DUI	224	39
Other	1,988	458
Not reported	5,006	788
TOTAL	31,380	8,037

(GDC, 2011f)

Probation Detention Centers

The GDC currently operates ten probation detention centers, housing over 2,000 probationers, with approximately 230 beds for female probationers. The centers are designated as minimum security, housing probationers for a period of 60 to 120 days, for the purpose of providing short-term confinement in a secure, safe, and work-oriented environment. Offenders are either placed on probation and sent to a center as a sentencing option, or are sent to a center as a result of a revocation proceeding. In addition, probationers who require more security than community supervision or a diversion center can provide, but who are also not eligible for a boot camp, are sent to these centers (GDC, 2011b).

The probation detention centers are highly structured and regimented, with schedules that include participation in programming designed to facilitate the successful reintegration into the community. Programming includes academic education, employment preparation, group counseling, personal health, primary health care, and substance abuse prevention (GDC, 2011b).

Work details include supervised, unpaid employment in the surrounding communities, as most centers have contracts with local government entities and the Georgia Department of Transportation. In addition, some probationers work to maintain the centers, while a select few are assigned to jobs supervised by other governmental agencies (GDC, 2011b).

Court Services

State probation officers are assigned in each of the 49 judicial circuits throughout the state and actively work in the courtroom with the Superior Court judges to provide information, make recommendations, and prepare legal documents required in sentencing and revocation processes. The Statewide Probation Act of 1956 created probation as a statutory alternative to incarceration, and it has since become the most frequently used sentencing option throughout the state. It is recognized as a critical component of the correctional system, and officers supervise probationers according to court ordered conditions, while providing documentation and feedback to the court as necessary (GDC, 2011d).

Day Reporting Centers

Day reporting centers provide intensive substance abuse treatment for approximately 100 probationers. There are currently 13 centers located throughout the state. Although more costly than traditional field probation, the centers function at a fraction of the cost of residential treatment. Programs at these centers include adult basic education, cognitive restructuring, community service, employment enhancement, intensive supervision, and substance abuse counseling (GDC, 2011e).

Probationers assigned to the centers are required to be employed upon completion of the initial orientation, assessment, diagnostics, and programming. Probationers failing to complete the provisions of the center are subject to revocation proceedings (GDC, 2011e).

Juveniles in Adult Prisons

In the State of Georgia, the age of adulthood is 16. However, it is possible for a juvenile to be transferred to an adult court for trial, with sentencing to be served in an adult prison at the age of 13 (O.C.G.A. §15-11-30.2). Currently, there are 104 inmates under the age of 18 serving in GDC state prisons, including two females (GDC, 2011h).

Table 8.7 illustrates the age of male juveniles currently serving in adult prisons. Included in the table is the age at admission into the correctional facility. Table 8.8 illustrates the race of male juveniles currently serving in adult prisons.

Table 8.7 Age of Inmates at Admission

Age	# of Inmates	Age at Admission
14	1	4
15	4	10
16	11	13
17	86	75

(GDC, 2011h)

Table 8.8 Race of Juveniles Serving In Adult Prisons

Race	# of Inmates
White	12
Black	85
Hispanic	4
Other	1

(GDC, 2011h)

Although not a large number of juveniles are serving in adult prisons, the GDC is experiencing the same trend found across the country of more juveniles committing serious offenses and being waived to stand trial in adult courts. This is shown in the four juveniles, aged 14, who were tried and sentenced as adults within the first five months of 2011. This is in contrast to the one 14-year-old sentenced to adult prison in the first decade of this century, in 2005 (GDC, 2011h).

Special Operations

There are several special operations units that function within the GDC to support the supervision of inmates. The units are located within specific correctional facilities and are able to provide support to the Corrections Division (GDC, 2011d).

GDC Tactical Squads

The GDC currently has 23 tactical squads located at various facilities across the state. Each squad is comprised of 12 correctional officers who have received extensive training and education in chemical munitions, firearms, hostage situations, riot and crowd control, as well as other less than lethal munitions. In addition, the tactical squads are responsible for hostage negotiations and rescue.

Canine (K-9) Units

GDC canine units are based at several strategically located facilities across the state. These units assist the GDC with offender tracking, as well as narcotics and explosive detection. In addition, these units assist local, state, and federal law enforcement when requested.

Correctional Emergency Response Team (CERT)

The GDC currently has 27 correctional emergency response teams located at various facilities across the state. Each CERT team consists of a team leader and five correctional officers, and has received intensive training and education on managing non-compliant inmates to ensure effective facility operations. In addition, each CERT team has received extensive training in escorts and transports, inmate searches, interview and interrogation techniques, cell extractions, chemical munitions, and security threat groups.

Inter-Agency Liaison

The GDC serves a vital role in Georgia's law enforcement and criminal justice system. The Inter-Agency Liaison serves on various task forces and represents the GDC in state and national policy meetings. For example, through the liaison, the GDC committed staff and other support to assist in natural disaster reliefs across the country.

Local Corrections

Jails and detention facilities serve several purposes in Georgia, which is similar to other jails across the country. An individual who has been convicted of a crime and sentenced to a year or less will serve the sentence in a jail. Jails serve as holding facilities for those individuals awaiting trial, and are used to confine individuals who will serve as witnesses in a trial if it is deemed there is a threat or other reason why they would not appear at the trial. Jails are also used for the temporary detention of individuals who are deemed in need to supervision when there are no other available facilities (Reid, 2007).

There are 159 county sheriff offices in the state. Currently, 147 county sheriff's offices are operating jails, housing more than 42,000 inmates. "In addition to protecting the public and jail staff from dangerous criminals, federal and state laws require that sheriffs must provide for the safety, health, and welfare of inmates housed in county jails" (Georgia Sheriff's Association, 2011). Due to budget, size, and other constraints, twelve counties currently do not operate local jails, but instead rent space from neighboring sheriff's offices (Baker, Chattahoochee, Clay, Echols, Glascock, Lanier, Long, Quitman, Stewart, Taliaferro, Webster, and Warren).

In addition to county jails, there are a number of municipal police departments that operate their own city jails. Functioning in the same manner as county jails, these city jails house inmates who are awaiting trial or serving sentences of up to one year. In both county and city jails, correctional officers must be state certified in corrections, with some officers also certified in law enforcement.

Inmates in county and city jails may participate in work or labor details, which provide low-risk inmates an opportunity to work on maintenance projects within the facility and work in various operations functions, such as food service, cleaning, laundry, etc. Details may also include supervised labor in the community, including highway clean up and maintenance projects, providing service to the community without labor costs. "During 2010, these inmates contributed more than 84,000 man hours to the county. Figuring at minimum wage, these services saved local taxpayers an estimated $55,200.00" (Crisp County Sheriff's Office, 2011).

Jail Designs

Jails and detention facilities differ in size and design, based upon the funding and needs of the community when built. More newly designed and built jails focus on a podular design, where the interior cells open to a common area, and the correctional officer's desk and control console are placed within the common area. This means the officer is working within the living area of the cell block, or pod, and has direct supervision and access to all inmates. This newer design creates a self-contained control area that allows for increased contact between inmates and officers, while decreasing the need to move inmates among different areas of the jail, thus increasing security. An older, but still in use design has a similar layout to the podular design, but the officer's control desk is located in a secure room, providing indirect supervision, also called remote surveillance.

Correctional officers working within the pods are not armed, but carry radios equipped with an emergency button, signaling central control of an emergency situation. Strong and effective communication skills are a must for corrections officers since there is no physical barrier between them and the inmates. In addition, video cameras are placed in strategic locations throughout the jail, to ensure all space is visible at all times. Central control is also able to lock and unlock specific doors when needed.

Georgia Statutes

One aspect of jail operations is to determine the nationality of individuals charged with a state crime. O.C.G.A. §42-4-14 states that "when any person is confined, for any period, in the jail of a county or municipality or a jail operated by a regional jail authority in compliance with Article 36 of the Vienna Convention on Consular Relations, a reasonable effort shall be made to determine the nationality of the person so confined." Additionally, "When any foreign national is confined, for any period, in a county or municipal jail, a reasonable effort shall be made to verify that such foreign national has been lawfully admitted to the United States and if lawfully admitted, that such lawful status has not expired." If the foreign national is found to be in the country illegally, jail personnel are required to contact the U.S. Department of Homeland Security.

Jails and detention facilities are also required to follow safety and security measures as set forth in Georgia law. According to O.C.G.A. §42-4-31, "(a) It shall be unlawful for any person having charge of or responsibility for any detention facility to incarcerate any person in the detention facility unless a full-time jailer is on duty at the detention facility at all times while a person is incarcerated therein." Section (c) requires that "the officer in charge of a detention facility shall have the facility inspected semiannually by an officer from the state fire marshal's office or an officer selected by the Safety Fire Commissioner." Furthermore, "There shall be at least two separate keys for all locks at a detention facility, with one set in use and all duplicate keys safely stored under the control of a jailer or other administrative employee for emergency use" (O.C.G.A. §42-4-31). As an additional safety measure, all security personnel are required to be familiar with locking and unlocking cell doors and fire escapes to ensure an immediate release of inmates during an emergency.

Probation Supervision

Probation supervision at the local level is handled by private probation companies who contract with local jurisdictions. According to O.C.G.A. §42-8-100, the chief judge of any court within the county is authorized to contract with corporations, enterprises, or agencies to provide probation supervision, counseling, and collection services for all monies to be paid by the defendant placed on probation for ordinance violations or misdemeanors. In addition, O.C.G.A. §42-8-101 created the County and Municipal Probation Advisory Council, assigned to the Administrative Office of the Courts (AOC).

The Council is comprised of judges from various state and local courts, the commissioner of corrections, a sheriff, a county commissioner, a mayor, a public probation officer, and a private probation officer, all appointed by the governor. The purpose of the Council is to develop rules and regulations for: reviewing and implementing uniform professional standards for private probation officers and contracts with probation services; establishing a 40-hour orientation for newly hired private probation officers and a 20-hour yearly continuing education; enforcing contracts and imposing sanctions and fines; establishing registration for private corporations, enterprises, or agencies providing probation services; and requiring criminal record checks of all private probation officers (O.C.G.A. §42-8-101).

The Council has currently approved 34 private probation companies to provide services to the courts throughout the state. Unlike state probation officers who supervise felons, private probation officers supervise only misdemeanors. In addition, private probation officers are not required to be certified peace officers by the P.O.S.T. Council. However, O.C.G.A. §42-8-102 has established the following standards for employment as a private probation officer:

- must be 21 years of age;
- must have completed a standard two-year college course of study or have four years of law enforcement experience;
- must complete a 40-hour initial orientation program upon employment and receive 20 hours of continuing education annually;
- must not have been convicted of a felony or sufficient misdemeanors to establish a pattern of disregard for the law;
- must not have been convicted or pled guilty or nolo contendere to any misdemeanor involving moral turpitude within five years preceding date of employment;
- must not have an outstanding warrant for arrest; and
- must not have a pending charge of felony, domestic violence, or misdemeanor involving moral turpitude (2011).

Because private probation officers are not P.O.S.T. certified peace officers, they do not have the authority to arrest or carry weapons for supervision. If the private probation officer deems a probationer to be in violation of the terms of probation, the officer will complete an affidavit and present it to the supervising judge of the county, who will determine whether probable cause exists for the issuance of an arrest warrant for violation of probation. If the warrant is issued, it will be served by the local sheriff's office in the county in which the violation occurred.

Conclusion

Correctional systems in the State of Georgia have seen many changes in the two centuries since the General Assembly approved the building of the first state prison in 1811. Corrections on all levels continues to be a vital part of the criminal justice system, especially in a time when citizens of the state, and Americans in general, are calling for harsher sanctions and punishments for criminals. The correctional systems operating in the state work toward a common goal of protecting citizens by effectively managing offenders. With an increased emphasis on professionalism and innovative initiatives, corrections in Georgia will continue to lead the nation.

Chapter Review Questions

1. Describe the history of corrections in the State of Georgia, including chain gangs.
2. What are the classifications given to inmates and why are these important?

3. What are the different types of correctional facilities for state inmates?
4. Why is jail design an important part of local corrections?
5. What is probation? How does it meet the needs of Georgia's correctional system?

References

Chamber of Commerce, Turner County. (2011). History of the Prison System in Georgia. Retrieved from: http://www.jailmuseum.com.

Crisp County Sheriff's Office. (2011). Detention Division. Retrieved from: http://www.crispcountysheriff.com.

Federal Bureau of Prisons (BOP). (2011). Federal Prison Facilities in Georgia. Retrieved from: http://www.bop.gov.

Georgia Department of Corrections (GDC). (2011a). About GDC. Retrieved from: http://www.dcor.state.ga.us.

Georgia Department of Corrections (GDC). (2011b). Facility Descriptions. Atlanta: State of Georgia.

Georgia Department of Corrections (GDC). (2011c). Administration Division. Retrieved from: http://www.dcor.state.ga.us.

Georgia Department of Corrections (GDC). (2011d). Corrections Division. Retrieved from: http://www.dcor.state.ga.us.

Georgia Department of Corrections (GDC). (2011e). Probation Supervision. Retrieved from: http://www.dcor.state.ga.us.

Georgia Department of Corrections (GDC). (2011f). Probationer Statistical Profile: Probation Starts During CY2010. Atlanta: State of Georgia.

Georgia Department of Corrections (GDC). (2011g). Office of Planning and Analysis: Inmates Under Death Sentence (UDS). Atlanta: State of Georgia.

Georgia Department of Corrections (GDC). (2011h). Inmate Statistical Profile: Juveniles in Adult Prison System, June (2011). Atlanta: State of Georgia.

Georgia Department of Corrections (GDC). (2010a). FY 2009 Annual Report. Atlanta: State of Georgia.

Georgia Department of Corrections (GDC). (2010b). Office of Planning and Analysis: The Death Penalty. Atlanta: State of Georgia.

Georgia Sheriff's Association. (2011). Jail Services. Retrieved from: http://www.georgiasheriffs.org.

O.C.G.A. § 15-11-30.2. (2011). Official Code of Georgia Annotated.

O.C.G.A. § 42-4-14. (2011). Official Code of Georgia Annotated.

O.C.G.A. § 42-4-31. (2011). Official Code of Georgia Annotated.

O.C.G.A. §42-8-34. (2011). Official Code of Georgia Annotated.

O.C.G.A. §42-8-100. (2011). Official Code of Georgia Annotated.

O.C.G.A. §42-8-101. (2011). Official Code of Georgia Annotated.

O.C.G.A. §42-8-102. (2011). Official Code of Georgia Annotated.

Reid, Sue Titus. (2007). Criminal Justice, 8th Ed. Cincinnati, OH: Atomic Dog Publishing.

State Board of Pardons and Paroles (PAP). (2011). Retrieved from: http://www.pap.state.ga.us.

Wilkes, Donald E. (2009). Sentence to Death. Retrieved from: http://www.law.uga.edu.

CHAPTER 9

GEORGIA'S JUVENILES

Learning Objectives

After reading the chapter, students will be able to:

- Explain the history of the Juvenile Justice System in Georgia.
- Define key concepts used in the Juvenile Justice System.
- Explain the various stages of process through the system.
- Discuss the options at a disposition hearing.
- Identify and explain the duties and responsibilities of the Juvenile Court personnel.
- Describe juvenile justice statistics for the State of Georgia.

Key Terms

Adjudicatory Hearing	Exclusive Original Jurisdiction
Aftercare	Intake
Child	Juvenile Justice
Commitment	Non-Secure Residential
Concurrent Jurisdiction	Treatment
Delinquent Act	Probable Cause
Delinquent Child	Regional Youth Detention Center
Department of Juvenile Justice	Sealing Records
Designated Felony	Secure Detention
Detention Hearing	Status Offender
Disposition Hearing	Unique Youth Served
Diversion	Unruly Child
Exclusive Jurisdiction	Youth Detention Center

The mission of the Georgia Department of Juvenile Justice (DJJ) is "to protect and serve the citizens of Georgia by holding youthful offenders accountable for their actions through the delivery of treatment services and sanctions in appropriate settings and by establishing youth in their communities as productive and law abiding citizens" (Georgia Department of Juvenile Justice [DJJ], 2011a).

The purpose of the DJJ is to provide "supervision, detention and a wide range of treatment and educational services for youths referred to the Department by the Juvenile Courts" and to provide "assistance or delinquency prevention services for at-risk youths through collaborative efforts with other public, private and community entities" (DJJ, 2011b). More than 4,300 employees manage programs, facilities, and services for the more than 52,000 juveniles who are placed under DJJ supervision each year (DJJ, 2011b).

History of Juvenile Justice in Georgia

Juvenile justice has more than 100 years of history in the State of Georgia. The first juvenile facility, the Georgia State Reformatory, was built in 1905 in Milledgeville, the state capital from 1804 to 1868, to house delinquent boys formerly housed in the adult penitentiary. During the 1930s, two more reformatories were built, one to house females and one to house African-American males (DJJ, 2011c). The Georgia General Assembly enacted the first juvenile code in 1933, which defined the objectives of juvenile proceedings: to assist, protect, and restore children whose well-being is threatened; to provide care, guidance, and control conducive to the child's welfare and the best interests of the state; and to secure care equivalent to what the parents should have given to the child (O.C.G.A. § 15-11-1).

But it was not until 1963 that a distinct unit on the state level devoted to juvenile justice was established. The Youth Services unit was created within the Division of Family and Children Services (DFACS), then part of the Department of Social Services. At this time, the three reformatories were re-designated as state training schools, and a fourth training school was opened in 1964, providing long-term custody of delinquent youth (DJJ, 2011c).

In 1967 and 1968, Youth Services built and opened six Regional Youth Detention Centers (RYDCs), for the purpose of providing secure facilities for juveniles in custody within an hour's drive of any point in Georgia. The RYDCs are secure, short-term centers for juveniles awaiting trial in either Juvenile Court or Superior Court. In addition, some juveniles are held in RYDCs awaiting a community-based placement more conducive to his or her assessed needs.

By the end of the 1960s, each of the RYDCs provided 30 beds for juveniles, creating a total capacity of 180 beds between all six centers (DJJ, 2011c).

During the 1970s, Youth Services raised the RYDC capacity to 406 beds with the establishment of eight new or redesigned RYDCs. In addition, in 1971, Youth Services established the first Community Treatment Center, providing juveniles with a safe place during after school hours (DJJ, 2011c).

The Georgia General Assembly passed the Governmental Reorganization Act of 1972. The Act consolidated several departments, including DFACS, of which Youth Services remained, and the Department of Public Health, into the Department of Human Resources (DHR). In addition, the Board of Human Resources was created to oversee the DHR (Georgia Department of Human Resources [DHR], 2011).

Also in 1972, the DHR expanded Youth Services to its own area within DHR and renamed it Division of Youth Services. In addition, the Georgia General Assembly enacted law that required the re-designation of the four training schools into Youth Development Campuses (YDCs) (DJJ, 2011c). The YDCs are long-term rehabilitation facilities for juveniles sentenced or committed to the custody of DJJ by juvenile courts (DJJ, 2011d).

In 1977, the Georgia General Assembly passed Senate Bill 100, providing specific guidelines to differentiate status offenders from delinquents and enforcing 24-hour intake on a statewide basis. Drastic changes in the juvenile justice system were required to meet the mandates. In 1979, a classification system similar to the one used by the Georgia Department of Corrections for adult offenders was implemented. The Determinate Sentencing system classifies juveniles into four categories, with multiple and habitual offenders receiving increased sentence lengths (DJJ, 2011c).

During the 1980s, Youth Services continued to increase capacity for both facilities. The decade ended with the addition of nine new or redesigned RYDCs and 673 beds, and with the YDCs having a new capacity of 680 beds. In 1981, the state passed the Designated Felony Act, which increased the sentence length from two to five years for violent offenders. And, in 1982, constitutional and legislative provisions to create a statewide juvenile court system were approved by the Georgia General Assembly (DJJ, 2011c).

The 1990s saw the largest growth in the DJJ, with the continued increase in RYDC capacity, which ended the decade with 1,050 beds, and the continued increase in YDC capacity to 2,254 beds. In 1992, Youth Services, by provision of the Georgia General Assembly, is revamped into the Department of Children and Youth Services (DCYS), a stand-alone functioning state department. In 1995, the Georgia General Assembly enacted Senate Bill 440, which provided that youth aged 13 or older who commit one of the identified "seven deadly sins"—murder, voluntary manslaughter, rape, aggravated sodomy, aggravated child molestation, aggravated sexual battery, and armed robbery with a firearm—are to be tried as an adult, and upon conviction, will serve the sentence in a YDC. In addition, the Bill created the Short Term Program (STP), a short-term Boot Camp program for juveniles confined for 60 to 90 days in a YDC rather than a commitment. In 1997, another name change created the current Department of Juvenile Justice (DJJ, 2011c).

The first decade of the 21st century saw many RYDCs and YDCs open and close across the state. By the end of 2009, the capacity of RYDCs had increased to 1,287 beds, while the capacity of YDCs decreased almost 45 percent to 1,260 beds. In 2005, Cohn RYDC opened in the name of Muscogee County Chief Juvenile Court Judge Aaron Cohn, at that time the country's longest sitting juvenile court judge. The boot camp style program fell out of favor in the middle part of the decade, and in 2005, the Georgia General Assembly enacted Senate Bill 134, changing the structure of the STP while reducing the maximum sentence from 90 days to 60 days. Also in 2005, the Southern Association of Colleges and Schools (SACS) accredited the DJJ schools. In 2006, the Georgia General Assembly enacted Senate Bill 136, providing bail options for juveniles, at the discretion of the judge and prosecutor (DJJ, 2011c).

The second decade of the new millennium showed a continued support for the DJJ. In October 2010, the DJJ marked an historical first when the DJJ schools received dual accreditation from SACS and the Correctional Education Association (CEA). Although each individual school within the DJJ system had been previously accredited by SACS, this recommendation recognized accreditation for the entire system, which includes 28 schools. "The Georgia Department of Juvenile Justice is Georgia's 181st school district. All DJJ teachers are certified. Students in short-term RYDCs and long-term YDCs both receive 330 minutes of instruction each day year round. Students in DJJ schools can achieve a GED, high school diploma or special education diploma. All academic and vocational credits awarded are transferable with the youth upon a return to the community" (DJJ, 2011h).

Federal Oversight of Juvenile Justice

Along with the expansive growth of the Juvenile Justice System and the Department of Juvenile Justice came notification, in March 1997, that the United States Department of Justice intended to investigate the DJJ. After the governor's pledge for full cooperation, the Department of Justice investigated all aspects of DJJ operations, including inspections of DJJ facilities, from March 1997 to February 1998 (Times Free Press, 2009).

In February 1998, the Department of Justice's Civil Rights Division notified the governor that conditions in DJJ's facilities violated the constitutional and federal statutory rights of juveniles in DJJ. These findings prompted the creation of a Memorandum of Agreement (MOA) between the DJJ and the Department of Justice, stipulating the appointment of an independent MOA monitor to investigate and complete reports for both parties every six months. The MOA involved evaluation and monitoring in six areas: education services, investigations, medical, mental health, protection-from-harm, and quality assurance (Times Free Press, 2009).

The Department of Justice began monitoring and investigation activities in February 1998. After four years, in August 2002, the DJJ filed a motion to dismiss with prejudice the initial complaint filed by the Department of Justice. As a result of the motion, the DJJ and Department of Justice agreed that the MOA's monitor would complete audits by the end of 2003, and the final MOA report would be issued in early 2004 (Times Free Press, 2009).

In October 2003, DJJ's education services were found to be in compliance and released from the MOA. In March 2004, the 14th and final report from the MOA monitor was completed. In January 2005, the Department of Justice determined the quality assurance and investigations functions were in compliance and were released from the MOA. In the same month, DJJ notified the Department of Justice of its readiness to complete the final evaluation for MOA compliance (Times Free Press, 2009).

In April 2005, the Department of Justice began verification tours for completing the final review, but suspended the tours over concerns regarding DJJ documents under review. In November 2006, an investigation by the United States Attorney's Office determined no systematic problems with the DJJ documents. As a result of these findings, in April 2007, the DJJ and Department of Justice negotiated the completion of the MOA, with a modified MOA signed in July 2008 requiring final inspections to be completed within nine months. In September 2008, final review and verification tours for the medical, mental health, and protection-from-harm portions of the MOA began, with monitors completing final reviews in December 2008 (Times Free Press, 2009).

The final report, written April 14, 2009 by the lead monitor for the Department of Justice, Dr. David Roush, indicated substantial improvement in DJJ operations over the past ten years. Dr. Roush "singled out DJJ's Office of Medical Services and Office of Behavioral Health Services, which he wrote are used as models for juvenile justice systems nationwide" (Office of the Governor, 2009).

As a result of the federal monitoring and the MOA process, many significant and permanent changes were made to the DJJ and its operations. Training for staff has been upgraded and standardized. All DJJ facilities have dramatically increased direct care staffing, including counselors and juvenile correctional officers. In addition, DJJ's Office of Continuous Improvement now monitors the system to ensure accountability and compliance (Office of the Governor, 2009).

Governor Sonny Perdue, in a press release dated May 18, 2009, stated that "the MOA proved to be a catalyst for positive change in Georgia's juvenile justice system. Before the MOA, DJJ's facilities operated well above capacity, and many necessary services were lacking. Now, DJJ's facilities function within their rated capacity, the agency's school system is accredited by the Southern Association of Colleges and Schools (SACS), and the department has offices dedicated to medical and mental health care and has greatly increased youths' access to both services" (Office of the Governor, 2009).

Jurisdiction of the Juvenile Court

The jurisdiction of the juvenile court, and thus the Department of Juvenile Justice, is defined in O.C.G.A. § 15-11-28, which provides for three different types of jurisdiction of juveniles.

Exclusive Original Jurisdiction of Juvenile Court (O.C.G.A. § 15-11-28(a))

The juvenile court has exclusive original jurisdiction over all juveniles who are alleged to be delinquent, unruly, or deprived; are in need of treatment or commitment as a mentally ill or mentally retarded child; are alleged to have committed a juvenile traffic offense; or who have been placed under the supervision of the court or on probation, provided such jurisdiction began prior to the juvenile's 17th birthday. In addition, the juvenile court also has exclusive original jurisdiction in proceedings involving judicial consent to marriage, employment or enlistment in the armed services; the Interstate Compact on Juveniles; termination of parental rights; an unemancipated juvenile's decision to seek an abortion; and reports brought by a local board of education.

Concurrent Jurisdiction with Superior Court (O.C.G.A. § 15-11-28(b)(1))

The juvenile court has concurrent jurisdiction with the superior court when a juvenile is alleged to have committed a delinquent act which would be considered a crime if tried in a superior court, and for which the juvenile may be punished by loss of life, imprisonment for life without parole, or confinement for life in a penal institution.

Exclusive Jurisdiction of the Superior Court (O.C.G.A. § 15-11-28(b)(2)(A))

The superior court has exclusive jurisdiction over the trial of any juvenile who is 13 to 17 years of age and who is alleged to have committed any of the following offenses: murder; voluntary manslaughter; rape; aggravated sodomy; aggravated child molestation; aggravated sexual battery; or armed robbery if committed with a firearm. In addition, the superior court may, after an investigation and for extraordinary cause, transfer a case back to juvenile court, for offenses for which the punishment is not loss of life, life in prison without parole, or confinement for life in a penal institution. In doing so, the superior court's jurisdiction will be terminated.

Juvenile Justice Terms and Definitions

Juvenile Justice is comprised of distinct terms and processes. Although it functions today in much the same way as the adult criminal justice system, the terms used and definitions of those terms are what distinguish juveniles from adults. Definitions of juveniles used by the Department of Juvenile Justice are given in O.C.G.A. § 15-11-2. In addition, the state designates specific offenses as felonies for juveniles in O.C.G.A. § 15-11-63.

Child (O.C.G.A. § 15-11-2(2))

A person is defined as a child if he or she is under the age of 17; is under the age of 21 and committed a delinquent act before the age of 17 and was placed under the supervision of the court or on probation; or is under the age of 18, if alleged to be a deprived child or status offender.

Delinquent Act (O.C.G.A. § 15-11-2(6))

A delinquent act is defined as a designated crime by this state, another state, federal law, or local ordinance, and is not a juvenile traffic offense; disobeying the terms of supervision contained in a court order; or failing to appear as required by a citation issued for violation of Code Section 3-3-23 (underage possession of alcohol).

Delinquent Child (O.C.G.A. § 15-11-2(7))

A delinquent child is defined as a juvenile who has committed a delinquent act and is in need of treatment or rehabilitation.

Status Offender (O.C.G.A. § 15-11-2(11))

A status offender is defined as a juvenile who is charged with or adjudicated of an offense, which would not be a crime if committed by an adult. Such offenses include, but are not limited to, truancy, running away from home, incorrigibility, and unruly behavior.

Unruly Child (O.C.G.A. § 15-11-2(12))

An unruly child is defined as a juvenile who is habitually and without justification truant from school; is habitually disobedient to his or her parent, guardian, or other custodian and is ungovernable; has committed an offense applicable only to a child; deserts his or her home without the consent of a parent or legal custodian; wanders or loiters on the street, highway, or any public place between 12:00 midnight and 5:00 a.m.; disobeys the terms of supervision contained in a court order in which the child was adjudicated unruly; patronizes any bar where alcoholic beverages are sold without being in the company of a parent or legal guardian or possesses alcoholic beverages; is in need of supervision, treatment, or rehabilitation; or has committed a delinquent act and is in need of supervision, but not of treatment or rehabilitation.

Designated Felony (O.C.G.A. § 15-11-63, Uniform Juvenile Court Rule 15.2)

A Designated Felony Act is an act that:

a) constitutes a second or subsequent offense, committed by a person who is 13 to 17 years of age, under subsection (b) of O.C.G.A. § 16-11-132, which makes it unlawful for a person under 18 years of age to possess or have under such person's control a handgun;

b) if done by an adult would be one or more of the following crimes:
   - kidnapping
   - first degree arson
   - aggravated assault
   - second degree arson
   - aggravated battery
   - robbery
   - armed robbery not involving a firearm
   - battery
   - attempted murder
   - attempted kidnapping
   - carrying or possessing a weapon (while at a school building or school function, or on school property or a bus)
   - hijacking a motor vehicle
   - any violation of O.C.G.A. § 16-7-82, § 16-7-84, or § 16-7-86, relating to offenses involving destructive devices
   - any act which would constitute a felony if committed by an adult, if the juvenile has been previously adjudicated delinquent three or more times for acts which would constitute a felony if committed by an adult
   - any violation of O.C.G.A. § 16-13-31, related to trafficking in cocaine, illegal drugs, marijuana, or methamphetamine
   - any criminal violation of O.C.G.A. § 16-14-4, relating to racketeering
   - any violation of O.C.G.A. § 16-10-52, relating to escape, if the juvenile as been previously adjudicated delinquent to have committed a designated felony;

c) constitutes a second or subsequent adjudication of delinquency for violation of O.C.G.A. § 16-7-85 or O.C.G.A. § 16-7-87, relating to the manufacture, possession, transport, distribution, or use of a hoax device, or the obstruction of certain officials in the detection, disarming, or destruction of a destructive device;

d) constitutes an offense within the exclusive jurisdiction of the superior court under O.C.G.A. § 15-11-28, but which is transferred by the superior court to the juvenile court for adjudication, or for extraordinary cause by the district attorney;

e) constitutes a second or subsequent violation of O.C.G.A. § 16-8-2 through § 16-8-9, relating to theft, if the property was a motor vehicle.

The Juvenile Justice Process

The juvenile justice process in the State of Georgia functions to ensure the well-being of every child in the state, and the facilities and quality of programs reflect the DJJ's "commitment to helping troubled youth develop critical life competency skills" (DJJ, 2011e).

Intake and Custody

There are several ways in which a juvenile may come to the attention of the DJJ—a written complaint or a petition may be filed against a juvenile, a juvenile may be transferred from another court, a law enforcement officer may issue a uniform traffic citation, or a Georgia Natural Resources/Game and Fish Division Notice of Summons may be issued. All of these situations lead to the first step in the juvenile justice process: intake (Administrative Office of the Courts of Georgia [AOCG], 2011).

In the State of Georgia, the majority of juveniles come to the attention of the DJJ through a written complaint. When a complaint is filed, a Juvenile Probation Parole Specialist (JPPS) will review the information and meet with the juvenile and his or her parent(s) and/or legal guardian(s) within 30 days of the complaint filing date. Once the intake process is completed, the JPPS will do one of the following:

- informally adjust the case;
- file a petition with the juvenile court for adjudicatory proceedings;
- divert the case to services outside the court; or
- recommend that the case be dismissed.

The intake process is available 24 hours a day, every day of the year. For most of the state, the DJJ provides intake services, while several counties operate independent courts, providing their own intake staff and services (DJJ, 2011e).

Prior to the filing of a petition, for acts deemed not serious in nature or alleged to be unruly, but amenable to informal handling, the JPPS may decide to informally adjust the case if certain prerequisites are met, through an informal hearing with the juvenile and his or her parent(s) and/or legal guardian(s). If this occurs, an Informal Adjustment Agreement is prepared, valid for up to three months, with an extension of an additional three months available by court order (DJJ, 2011f).

In order for an informal adjustment to occur, the following prerequisites must be met, as defined in O.C.G.A. § 15-11-69:

- the admitted facts in the case provide the juvenile court with jurisdiction over the juvenile;
- counsel and advice without adjudication is in the best interest of the juvenile and the public;
- the juvenile and his or her parent(s) and/or legal guardian(s) consent to the informal adjustment, knowing consent is not mandatory; and
- the case shall not be subject to informal adjustment for a designated felony defined in O.C.G.A. § 15-11-63 without the prior written approval of the district attorney or authorized representative (AOCG, 2011).

There are several options within the Informal Adjustment Agreement that the JPPS may select from:

- Council and Adjustment—When a satisfactory adjustment of the problem has been accomplished through counseling with the juvenile and his or her parent(s) and/or legal guardian(s) during the informal hearing, the informal adjustment is considered complete.
- Counsel and Advice—When there is a need for follow-up services by the JPPS on a less formal basis than would be provided on probation. The juvenile will be placed on counsel and advice for a period of up to three months from the day of the informal hearing. In addition, the juvenile is not to be detained.
- Referral to Counseling Resource—When the juvenile is placed on counsel and advice, pending the successful completion of the recommended counseling.
- Individualized Agreements—When the JPPS deems, based on the appropriateness of the offense and circumstances, that an individualized agreement is in the best interest of the juvenile. The agreement may in-

clude a letter of apology, book report, essay, traffic school, or volunteer work with a community service organization (AOCG, 2011).

When law enforcement officials take a juvenile into custody, the parent(s) and/or legal guardian(s) are notified of the detainment. A risk assessment is completed by the JPPS to evaluate the potential risk of re-offending and the risk of failure to appear for the court hearing, for the purpose of determining if the juvenile should be released immediately to the custody of his or her parent(s) and/or guardian(s), or detained. If it is determined that the juvenile should be detained, arrangements are then made to transport the juvenile to an RYDC or an alternative placement, such as a shelter (DJJ, 2011e). If the juvenile is not detained but the JPPS determines the case should proceed through further prosecution other than informal adjustment, a petition must be filed within 30 days from the date of the juvenile's release (AOCG, 2011).

Probable Cause/Detention Hearing

The second step in the juvenile justice process concerns the determination of probable cause to move the case forward through a formal petition and continued detention. If a juvenile is alleged to be delinquent or deprived, a probable cause hearing for juveniles detained on a warrantless arrest must be held within 48 hours from the moment of placement in detention or shelter care; otherwise, the detention hearing must be held within 72 hours. The juvenile is brought before the juvenile court judge, whereby the judge will review the findings from the JPPS, consider bail as an option, and determine if further detention is warranted (DJJ, 2011e).

The DJJ allows for taking a juvenile into custody and detention prior to a juvenile court hearing if secure detention is required to protect the juvenile or property of others; if the juvenile may abscond or may be removed from the jurisdiction of the court; if the juvenile has no parent or guardian or other person able to provide supervision and care and return the juvenile to the court when required; or if an order for detention or shelter care has been made by the court (DJJ, 2011f).

If the judge determines that there is probable cause to petition the juvenile court, the filing of the petition must be done within 72 hours on delinquent and unruly cases and within five days on deprived cases. Once the petition is filed, the court date for the formal adjudicatory hearing is set, to occur within 10 days from the petition filing date if the juvenile is to remain in detention. If the juvenile is not in detention, the formal adjudicatory hearing will be set within 60 days of the petition filing date (AOCG, 2011).

During the probable cause hearing and prior to the filing of the petition, based upon the evidence and investigation, the judge may opt to move to informally adjust or divert the case if it is deemed that adjudication is not in the best interest of the child and the public (DJJ, 2011e).

Adjudicatory Hearing

The third step in the juvenile justice process is the adjudicatory hearing, which is held to determine the facts of the case and the appropriate course of action. At this hearing, the judge will determine if the allegations outlined in the petition are true. If the allegations are determined to be false, the judge will dismiss the case. If the allegations are determined to be true, the judge will move to conduct a dispositional hearing (DJJ, 2011e).

Dispositional Hearing and Commitment

The fourth step in the juvenile justice process is the dispositional hearing, which may occur immediately following the adjudicatory hearing or at a later time. The purpose of the hearing is to determine the need for supervision, treatment, and rehabilitation of the juvenile. The disposition of the juvenile results in one of the following actions:

- placing the juvenile on probation;
- committing the juvenile to the custody of the DJJ;
- declaring the juvenile a designated felon, as defined by the designated felon statute;
- confining the juvenile to a maximum of 30 days in a YDC or in a treatment program provided by the DJJ or juvenile court;
- referring the case to the Department of Family and Children Services (DFCS);
- declaring the juvenile mentally incompetent to stand trial; or
- transferring the case to superior court.

If it is deemed appropriate for the juvenile to be committed to the custody of the DJJ, a screening process will occur within 10 days of the commitment date, to determine the juvenile's risk to the public and treatment needs, and to make a recommendation for placement. The process is conducted by a screening committee, comprised of at least four DJJ staff, usually including an RYDC counselor and an assessment classification specialist, as well as professionals from other child service agencies, including the Division of Community Corrections and, where appropriate, the DFCS and mental health (DJJ, 2011e).

The screening committee may recommend an alternative placement is in the best interest of the juvenile, such as a group home or wilderness program, and placement efforts will begin immediately (DJJ, 2011e). If a non-secure alternative placement is decided, one of three community detention programs may be utilized: attention homes, which consist of bed spaces located with private families, group homes or other institutions; in-home services, which allow the juvenile to remain at home while awaiting court hearings; or electronic monitoring, which uses technology and monitoring equipment to allow the juvenile to remain in the community (DJJ, 2011f).

If the screening committee determines that placement in a YDC is in the best interest of the juvenile, placement will occur as soon as a bed in a YDC becomes available. The commitment order is valid for two years (DJJ, 2011e). However, most juveniles are committed when probation and/or other court services have failed to prevent the juvenile from returning to the court on a new offense or violation of probation (DJJ, 2011f).

Designated felony commitments occur when a juvenile has been adjudicated as having committed certain felony acts, which indicate the juvenile requires restrictive custody. The custody, as determined by the juvenile court judge, ranges from 12 to 60 months, to be served in a YDC. In addition, the juvenile will not be discharged until at least one year of custody has occurred. These commitments have restrictions on terminations and reduce the level of intensive supervision on aftercare. The commitment orders are valid for five years or until the juvenile reaches the age of 21 (DJJ, 2011f).

In addition, any juvenile who has been convicted and sentenced as an adult will be placed in a YDC until he or she reaches the age of 17. At that time, the juvenile will be transferred to the Georgia Department of Corrections to serve the remainder of the original sentence (DJJ, 2011f).

Aftercare

Once a juvenile has been processed, committed, and detained by the DJJ and is ready to return home and to the community, he or she may be placed on aftercare, whose purpose is to provide the juvenile with a smooth transition into the community through supervision, counseling, and networking with appropriate agencies (DJJ, 2011f). "Aftercare is a nonjudicial administrative status granted to a child who is under an order of commitment to the Department of Juvenile Justice and has been released from confinement under the supervision of an employee of the Department" (AOCG, 2011). If the juvenile commits an additional delinquent or unruly offense while on aftercare, the case will be brought before the juvenile court. If the juvenile violates a condition of aftercare that is not a delinquent or unruly offense, the case will not be brought before the juvenile court. A violation of aftercare is not considered an offense and is to be handled administratively by the DJJ (AOCG, 2011).

Sealing Records

Under O.C.G.A. § 15-11-79.2, the records of juvenile proceedings may be sealed if the petition or complaint is dismissed or the case is handled through informal adjustment. In addition, if the juvenile is adjudicated delinquent or unruly, or on the court's own motion, and after a hearing, the records may be sealed under the following circumstances:

- if the court finds that two years have passed since the final discharge of the child;
- if the juvenile has not been convicted of a felony or misdemeanor involving moral turpitude and no criminal or delinquent proceeding is pending; or
- if the juvenile has been rehabilitated.

A reasonable notice of the hearing must be provided to the district attorney, the authority granting discharge if the final discharge was from an institution or parole, and the law enforcement officers or department having custody of the files. Once the order has been approved, the proceeding will be treated as if had never occurred. This means that all references to the proceeding shall be deleted and that the juvenile, the court, the law enforcement officers, and the departments must properly reply that no record exists with respect to the juvenile if any inquiry is made. Further inspection of sealed files is only permitted by an order of the court. In addition, the court may elect to seal any record containing information that would identify a victim of any act that would constitute a sexual offense if committed by an adult under O.C.G.A. § 16-6.

Officers of the Court and Court Personnel

The officers and personnel of the juvenile courts in the State of Georgia are governed by O.C.G.A. § 15-11 (Part 2) Juvenile Proceedings. The code provides that a juvenile court will be created in every county of the state, with each court assigned and attached to the superior court of the county for administrative purposes. In addition, the code provides definitions and explains the appointments of judges and associate judges, training, and duties pertaining to juvenile proceedings.

For FY 2011, there are currently 159 juvenile courts, one located in each county of the state, with 149 judges presiding. Each juvenile court judge serves as a member of the Council of Juvenile Court Judges of Georgia, which includes 53 full-time juvenile court judges, 40 part-time juvenile court judges, 13 full-time associate juvenile court judges, 16 part-time associate juvenile court judges, 4 superior court judges exercising juvenile court jurisdiction, 14 pro tempore judges, and 9 senior judges (Council of Juvenile Court Judges of Georgia [CJCJ], 2011). The mission of the Council is to provide "support to juvenile courts through legal research services, legislative tracking, and specialized programs to assist in protecting the best interests of children and the state" (CJCJ, 2011).

Appointment of Juvenile Court Judges

The State of Georgia is divided into ten district circuits, which are further divided into judicial circuits. Each circuit comprises one to 27 counties. For purposes of the juvenile court, the judge or majority of judges of the superior court in each judicial circuit will appoint one or more qualified persons to serve as judges of the juvenile courts of the circuit. The superior court judge(s) will determine the total number of circuit-wide juvenile court judgeships and will determine if the judges will serve in a full-time or part-time capacity, or a combination of both full-time and part-time. All persons appointed as juvenile court judges have the authority to preside over each juvenile court in each county of the judicial circuit, thus providing circuit-wide jurisdiction. If no person is appointed as a juvenile court judge in a judicial circuit, the superior court judge(s) will assume the duties of the juvenile court in all counties in the circuit. Each juvenile court judge appointed shall serve a term of four years. The compensation of juvenile court judges is set by the superior court with the approval of the governing authority of the county in which the judge will preside, with the benefits being offered by the governing authority of the judge's county of residence (O.C.G.A. § 15-11-18).

To qualify for a juvenile court judgeship, an individual must be at least 30 years of age, be a citizen of the state for at least three years, and have practiced law for at least five years. Juvenile court judges are eligible for reappointment. If more than one juvenile court judge is appointed, one will be designated as the presiding judge. Although practicing law is a qualification for juvenile court judgeship, it is unlawful for a full-time juvenile court judge to practice law outside of his or her judgeship. In addition, it is unlawful for a part-time juvenile court judge to engage directly or indirectly in the practice of law in his or her own court or in any case or proceeding in any other court where his or her own court has pending jurisdiction or has had jurisdiction. It is also unlawful for a juvenile court judge to give counsel, either directly or indirectly, on any matter before his or her court, except as called upon while performing the duties of the juvenile court judge (O.C.G.A. § 15-11-18).

Appointment of Associate Juvenile Court Judges

The juvenile court judge in each court may appoint one or more persons to serve as a full-time or part-time associate juvenile court judge. The associate judge serves at the pleasure of the judge, with compensation being approved and paid by the governing authority of the county. Each associate judge must meet the same qualifications for judgeship as the juvenile court judge. The judge will determine which cases are presided by the associate judge. A party of any proceeding, except detention or probable cause hearings, may file a written request within five days of receiving a copy of the order by the associate judge for the proceeding, requesting a rehearing with the judge, whereby the judge will determine if a rehearing will be ordered (O.C.G.A. § 15-11-21).

The juvenile court judge in each court may also appoint one or more persons to serve as a full-time or part-time associate juvenile court traffic judge. The associate traffic judge must be a member of the State Bar of Georgia or otherwise qualified by experience and training, with the compensation being approved and paid by the governing authority of the county (O.C.G.A. § 15-11-22).

Appointment of Juvenile Court Personnel

The juvenile court judge has the authority to appoint clerks and other personnel necessary for the effective operation of the court, with the compensation being approved and paid by the governing authority of the county. Employees shall be appointed from a list of eligible persons from the local merit boards or from lists established by competitive examinations conducted by the court. In addition, the judge may remove any appointed employee for cause, with the reasons stated in writing (O.C.G.A. § 15-11-24).

The juvenile court judge has the authority to appoint one or more probation officers, with the compensation being approved and paid by the governing authority of the county (O.C.G.A. § 15-11-24.1). The juvenile probation officer will conduct investigations, and make reports and recommendations to the court; receive and examine complaints and charges of delinquency, unruly

conduct, or deprivation of a juvenile; supervise and assist a juvenile on probation or in protective supervision; make appropriate referrals to private or
public community agencies; and take a juvenile into custody and detain him
or her under supervision if there is reasonable cause to believe the juvenile's health
or safety or that of another is in imminent danger. Otherwise, the juvenile
may abscond or be removed from the jurisdiction of the court (O.C.G.A. § 15-
11-24.2).

Juvenile Justice Statistics

The Department of Juvenile Justice maintains statistical data on both funding and services to juveniles. The following is a snapshot of the available data.

Statewide Budget

In FY 2011, the final budget for the Department of Juvenile Justice was
$310,501,877. This represents a decrease of $302,662 from the final budget in
FY 2010, mostly due to a drop in state funding for the DJJ. In terms of program funding, the largest portion of the budget was for secure detention
(RYDCs), at 34.7 percent. The second largest portion was for secure commitment (YDCs), at 23.4 percent. Community supervision was at 19.6 percent, community non-secure services were at 13.4 percent, and administration was at
8.9 percent, constituting the remainder of the budget (DJJ, 2011g).

Arrests for Uniform Crime Report (UCR) Index Crimes

In 2009, juveniles comprised roughly 18 percent of individuals arrested in
the State of Georgia for committing a classified Index Crime: murder, forcible
rape, robbery, aggravated assault, burglary, larceny, motor vehicle theft, and
arson. Table 9.1 shows the juvenile arrests in comparison to the total arrests for
each crime in 2009.

Juveniles Served

The total number of juveniles served by the Department of Juvenile Justice
is measured in numerous categories, across the fiscal year of 2009. Table 9.2
illustrates FY 2009 DJJ statewide totals for juveniles served.

Table 9.1 Juvenile Arrests versus Total Arrests

Crime	# of Juveniles	Total Crimes
Murder	35	444
Forcible Rape	32	365
Robbery	441	3,085
Aggravated Assault	1,258	9,302
Burglary	2,011	7,438
Larceny	6,176	36,179
Motor Vehicle Theft	552	1,831
Arson	70	215
Total	10,575	58,859

(GBI, 2010)

Table 9.2 Juveniles Served in FY 2009

Legal Status	Placement	Unique Youth Served	Admission	Release
Intake	At Home	22,506	25,415	25,473
	Non-Secure Detention	468	483	481
	Secure Detention RYDC	11,324	16,725	16,740
	Total	31,225	37,704	37,775
Diver/Inform	At Home	19,895	20,676	21,900
	Non-Secure Res Treat	626	655	666
	Total	20,111	19,932	21,167
Probation	At Home	13,680	10,592	10,727
	Non-Secure Res Treat	798	741	724
	Total	13,831	10,555	10,673
STP	Non-Secure Res Treat	131	115	128
	RYDC	3,404	3,768	3,848
	YDC	2,575	2,549	2,695
	Total	3,938	4,086	4,325
Commitment	At Home	5,072	4,136	3,986
	Non-Secure Res Treat	1,762	1,539	1,652
	RYDC Await Placement	2,748	3,865	3,829
	YDC	1,73	978	977
	Total	6,449	2,359	2,285
Statewide TOTAL		47,780	36,240	37,829

- Diver/Inform—Diversion/Informal Process; STP—Short Term Program; Non-Secure Res Treat—Non-Secure Residential Treatment (DJJ, 2011i).
- Unique Youth Served—If there are no juveniles in DJJ yesterday and one juvenile enters today, there is one juvenile served.
- Admissions—If a juvenile enters intake in the current fiscal year, there is one admission to intake. If the same juvenile's legal status in the same fiscal year changes to probation, there is one admission to probation. Overall, this means one admission to intake and one admission to probation for the fiscal year.
- Releases—If a juvenile leaves intake to go to probation in the current fiscal year, there is one release from intake. If the same juvenile in the same fiscal year is released from probation, there is one release from probation. Overall, this means one release from intake and one release from probation for the fiscal year (DJJ, 2011i).

Juvenile Characteristics

The following tables illustrate the characteristics of Unique Youth Served in DJJ for FY 2009. Table 9.3 shows legal status by gender, Table 9.4 shows legal status by ethnicity, and Table 9.5 shows legal status by age. Intake includes placement at home awaiting adjudication, in non-secure detention, or in secure detention in an RYDC. Diversion/Informal includes placement at home or in non-secure residential treatment. Probation includes placement at home or in non-secure residential treatment. Short Term Program includes placement in non-secure residential treatment, in an RYDC, or in a YDC. Commitment includes placement at home, in non-secure residential treatment, in an RYDC awaiting placement, or in a YDC.

Conclusion

The Juvenile Justice System in the State of Georgia functions like most other juvenile systems throughout the country. The system, first implemented in 1905 with the building of the Georgia State Reformatory, has seen dramatic changes in its laws, programs, and fundamental focus. The creation of the Department of Juvenile Justice has streamlined the juvenile justice process and allowed for more timely intervention and rehabilitation of Georgia's juveniles. Despite budget cuts and program eliminations, the Department of Juvenile Justice continues to address the issues of juvenile delinquency and crime by forming innovative approaches to recidivism and by providing Georgia's ju-

Table 9.3 Legal Status by Gender

Legal Status	Male	Female
Intake	20,745	10,480
Diversion/Informal	13,120	6,991
Probation	10,060	3,771
Short Term Program	3,213	725
Commitment	5,324	1,125

(DJJ, 2011i)

Table 9.4 Legal Status by Race

Legal Status	White	Black	Hispanic	Other
Intake	12,492	16,512	1,675	546
Diversion/Informal	7,296	11,285	1,106	424
Probation	6,005	7,059	573	194
Short Term Program	981	2,656	220	81
Commitment	1,332	4,583	402	132

(DJJ, 2011i)

Table 9.5 Legal Status by Age

Legal Status	12 & Under	13–15	16 & Up
Intake	2,843	16,195	13,242
Diversion/Informal	1,594	9,773	9,176
Probation	771	6,980	6,567
Short Term Program	71	2,094	1,857
Commitment	85	2,164	4,266

(DJJ, 2011i)

veniles with education, discipline, and support to thrive and become productive adults.

Chapter Review Questions

1. Describe the history of the Juvenile Justice System in Georgia.
2. Define the following terms: child, delinquent act, delinquent child, status offender, unruly child, and designated felony.
3. What happens at intake? Why is it so important to establish probable cause?

4.   What are the disposition options available in Juvenile Court?
5.   What are some of the characteristics of juveniles currently in the Juvenile Justice System in Georgia?

References

Administrative Office of the Courts of Georgia (AOCG). (2011). Uniform Rules: Juvenile Courts of the State of Georgia. Atlanta, GA: State of Georgia.
Council of Juvenile Court Judges of Georgia (CJCJ). (2011). Council Profile. Retrieved from: http://w2.georgiacourts.org.
Georgia Bureau of Investigation (GBI). (2010). 2009 Summary Report: Uniform Crime Reporting (UCR) Program. Atlanta: State of Georgia.
Georgia Department of Human Resources (DHR). (2011). Fact Sheet. Retrieved from: http://www.dhr.georgia.gov.
Georgia Department of Juvenile Justice (DJJ). (2011a). About Us: The Mission. Retrieved from: http://www.djj.state.ga.us.
Georgia Department of Juvenile Justice (DJJ). (2011b). About Us: Overview. Retrieved from: http://www.djj.state.ga.us.
Georgia Department of Juvenile Justice (DJJ). (2011c). A Brief History of the Department of Juvenile Justice. Retrieved from: http://www.djj.state.ga.us.
Georgia Department of Juvenile Justice (DJJ). (2011d). Facilities and Programs: Overview. Retrieved from: http://www.djj.state.ga.us.
Georgia Department of Juvenile Justice (DJJ). (2011e). The Juvenile Justice Process. Retrieved from: http://www.djj.state.ga.us.
Georgia Department of Juvenile Justice (DJJ). (2011f). Juvenile Justice Terms/Definitions. Retrieved from: http://www.djj.state.ga.us.
Georgia Department of Juvenile Justice (DJJ). (2011g). Statistics. Retrieved from: http://www.djj.state.ga.us.
Georgia Department of Juvenile Justice (DJJ). (2011h). DJJ School System to Receive Dual Accreditation. Retrieved from: http://www.djj.state.ga.us.
Georgia Department of Juvenile Justice (DJJ). (2011i). Statewide Statistics. Retrieved from: http://www.djj.state.ga.us.
O.C.G.A. § 15-11. (2011). Official Code of Georgia Annotated.
O.C.G.A. § 15-11-1. (2011). Official Code of Georgia Annotated.
O.C.G.A. § 15-11-2. (2011). Official Code of Georgia Annotated.
O.C.G.A. § 15-11-18. (2011). Official Code of Georgia Annotated.
O.C.G.A. § 15-11-21. (2011). Official Code of Georgia Annotated.
O.C.G.A. § 15-11-22. (2011). Official Code of Georgia Annotated.
O.C.G.A. § 15-11-24. (2011). Official Code of Georgia Annotated.

O.C.G.A. § 15-11-24.1. (2011). Official Code of Georgia Annotated.

O.C.G.A. § 15-11-24.2. (2011). Official Code of Georgia Annotated.

O.C.G.A. § 15-11-28. (2011). Official Code of Georgia Annotated.

O.C.G.A. § 15-11-63. (2011). Official Code of Georgia Annotated.

O.C.G.A. § 15-11-69. (2011). Official Code of Georgia Annotated.

O.C.G.A. § 15-11-79.2. (2011). Official Code of Georgia Annotated.

O.C.G.A. § 16-6. (2011). Official Code of Georgia Annotated.

O.C.G.A. § 16-7-82. (2011). Official Code of Georgia Annotated.

O.C.G.A. § 16-7-84. (2011). Official Code of Georgia Annotated.

O.C.G.A. § 16-7-85. (2011). Official Code of Georgia Annotated.

O.C.G.A. § 16-7-86. (2011). Official Code of Georgia Annotated.

O.C.G.A. § 16-7-87. (2011). Official Code of Georgia Annotated.

O.C.G.A. § 16-8-2. (2001). Official Code of Georgia Annotated.

O.C.G.A. § 16-8-9. (2011). Official Code of Georgia Annotated.

O.C.G.A. § 16-10-52. (2011). Official Code of Georgia Annotated.

O.C.G.A. § 16-13-31. (2011). Official Code of Georgia Annotated.

O.C.G.A. § 16-14-4. (2011). Official Code of Georgia Annotated.

Office of the Governor. (2009). Juvenile Justice Released from Federal Monitoring. Atlanta: Office of the Governor, Office of Communications.

Times Free Press. (2009). Memorandum of Agreement Timeline. Retrieved from: http://media.timesfreepress.com.

CHAPTER 10

TRAINING AND EDUCATING CRIMINAL JUSTICE PERSONNEL

Learning Objectives

After reading the chapter, students will be able to:

- Explain the purpose and scope of the Georgia Peace Officer Standards and Training Council.
- Explain the reason for state mandated training and in-service training for criminal justice personnel in the state.
- Identify and differentiate between the various state training topics for criminal justice personnel in the state.
- Discuss criminal justice higher education and the importance of accreditation.

Key Terms

Accreditation
Basic Mandate Certification
Georgia Peace Officer Standards and Training (P.O.S.T.) Council
In-Service Training
Technical College System of Georgia
University System of Georgia
Voluntary Certification

Criminal justice training and education flourish throughout the State of Georgia. The Georgia Peace Officer Standards and Training (P.O.S.T.) Council oversees the training of both local and state criminal justice personnel. Criminal justice education can be found at various levels of post-secondary education institutions, both public and private, including junior/community colleges, technical schools, and senior colleges.

The Georgia P.O.S.T. Council

The Council was established in 1970 by the Georgia General Assembly, under O.C.G.A. §35-8-3, and is administratively assigned to the Department of Public Safety. The mission of the Council is "to provide the citizens of Georgia with qualified, professionally trained, ethical and competent peace officers and criminal justice professionals" (Georgia Peace Officer Standards and Training [P.O.S.T.] Council, 2011). The Council "is responsible for the certification and regulation of Georgia's peace officers and other various public safety personnel," while also "establishing the minimum training standards and curriculum of the personnel certified by the agency" (P.O.S.T. Council, 2011).

The Council consists of 19 voting members and is supported by an advisory board. The following individuals comprise the 19 voting members: a member who is not the Attorney General; President of the Georgia Association of Chiefs of Police; President of the Georgia Sheriff's Association; President of the Georgia Municipal Association; President of the Association of County Commissioners of Georgia; President of the Peace Officers Association of Georgia; Chairman of the State Board of Pardons and Paroles; Commissioner of Corrections; President of the Georgia Prison Wardens' Association; Commissioner of Public Safety; a chief of police; a county sheriff; two municipal police officers other than a chief of police; a city manager or mayor; a county commissioner; two members who are peace officers; and Director of Investigations for the Georgia Bureau of Investigation. Individuals not identified for specific positions are appointed by the governor, for terms ranging from two to four years (P.O.S.T. Council, 2011).

The Council advisory members are appointed by the Council, serve in a non-voting capacity on the Council, and are chosen to represent a cross-section of the state criminal justice system. Members are identified from eight areas: Department of Juvenile Justice; Legislative; State Officers; Academician; Association Directors; Marshal; Campus Law Enforcement; and Communications (P.O.S.T. Council, 2011).

The Council has three main divisions. The first is the Certification and Training Division, whose primary function is to "ensure compliance, by agencies and peace officers, of qualifications and training requirements enumerated in the P.O.S.T. Act and to bring action against those agencies and officers in noncompliance" (P.O.S.T. Council, 2011). The second is the Operations Division, whose primary function is the development, evaluation, and management of peace officer training, including development of curriculum and examinations, administration of required examinations, and development of instructor training courses. The third is the Investigations Division, which handles the discretionary authority given to the Council by O.C.G.A. §35-8-7.1 to discipline officers. Disciplinary action includes revocation of certification, suspension of certification, probation, or other sanctions as provided by law (P.O.S.T. Council, 2011).

P.O.S.T. Certifications

The Georgia P.O.S.T. Council (2011) provides mandatory and voluntary certification to local and state criminal justice personnel. According to O.C.G.A. §35-8-8 (2011), individuals wishing to be employed and trained as peace officers must meet the following requirements:

- be at least 18 years of age;
- be a United States citizen;
- have a high school diploma or its equivalent;
- have not been convicted by any state or the federal government for a crime for which the punishment could have been imprisonment in a state or federal prison;
- have not been convicted of a sufficient misdemeanor that establishes a pattern of disregard for the law;
- be fingerprinted to determine the existence of any criminal record, as identified by the Georgia Bureau of Investigation and the Federal Bureau of Investigation;
- possess good moral character determined by an investigation under the procedures established by the Council;
- have an oral interview with the hiring agency to determine the applicant's background, appearance, and ability to communicate;
- be found to be free from any physical, emotional, or mental conditions which might adversely affect exercising the powers and duties of a peace officer; and
- successfully complete an academy entrance examination administered by the Council.

The Georgia Public Safety Training Center (GPSTC), located in Forsyth, is the training center for state criminal justice personnel, housing training units for the Department of Juvenile Justice, Department of Natural Resources, Department of Public Safety Motor Carrier Compliance Division, Georgia Bureau of Investigation, Georgia Emergency Management Agency, Georgia State Patrol, and State Board of Pardons and Paroles. The Center is also home to the Georgia Firefighter Standards and Training Council, providing the training needs of all fire and safety related services through the Georgia Fire Academy.

The Georgia Corrections Academy was created by the Georgia Department of Corrections (GDC), and is located on the campus of Tift College, in Forsyth. This is also the location of the GDC State Offices South. The Academy is responsible for both basic mandate certification and advanced training for correctional facility and probation operations throughout the state (Georgia Department of Corrections [GDC], 2011).

Basic mandate certification is conducted at GPSTC and at various locations throughout the state. The Council currently oversees and has certified 13 regional academies (four of which are agency academies) to conduct basic law enforcement mandate certification and some specialty certification:

- GPSTC Regional Police Academy Athens
- GPSTC Regional Police Academy Augusta
- GPSTC Regional Police Academy Columbus
- GPSTC Regional Police Academy Dalton
- GPSTC Regional Police Academy Garden City
- GPSTC Regional Police Academy Tifton
- Clayton Regional Law Enforcement Academy (Jonesboro)
- Fulton County Public Safety Training Center (College Park)
- North Central Georgia Law Enforcement Academy (Austell)
- Atlanta Police Academy
- Cobb County Police Department Training Academy (Marietta)
- DeKalb County Police Academy (Lithonia)
- Gwinnett County Public Safety Training Center (Lawrenceville)

In addition, basic law enforcement mandate certification can be obtained at seven certified college/university police academies:

- Augusta Technical College Police Academy
- Georgia Northwestern Technical College Police Academy (Calhoun)
- DeKalb Technical College Police Academy (Covington)
- Ogeeche Technical College Police Academy (Claxton)
- Savannah Technical College Police Academy

- South Georgia Technical College Police Academy (Americus)
- Reinhardt College Public Safety Institute (Alpharetta)

Miscellaneous training units also certified by the Council are coordinated through the Georgia Sheriff's Association and the Georgia Association of Chiefs of Police, and include basic mandate training as well as intermediate and advanced certifications (P.O.S.T. Council, 2011).

Basic Mandate Certification — Local

At the local level, there are currently four basic mandate courses provided by P.O.S.T.: basic law enforcement officer certification, basic jail officer certification, basic communications officer certification, and basic municipal probation officer certification.

Law Enforcement Certification

For basic law enforcement mandate certification, the Georgia P.O.S.T. Council set the training at 408 hours. The purpose of the course is to "provide training which results in peace officer certification through the Georgia Peace Officer Standards and Training Council in compliance with O.C.G.A. §35-8 and the applicable P.O.S.T. Council Rules" (Basic Law Enforcement Training Course, 2006).

The basic law enforcement mandate certification course consists of the following blocks of instruction (Basic Law Enforcement Training Course, 2006):

• **Introduction to Law Enforcement**	**(6 hours)**
- The Criminal Justice System	3 hours
- Ethics and Professionalism	2 hours
- Peace Officer Standards and Training	1 hour
• **Basic Law**	**(58 hours)**
- Georgia Criminal Law	16 hours
- Criminal Procedure	34 hours
- Rules of Evidence	4 hours
- Peace Officer Liability	4 hours
• **Community Relations**	**(31 hours)**
- Interpersonal Communication	8 hours
- Officer and the Public	2 hours
- Mental Health, Mental Retardation, and Substance Abuse	6 hours
- Media Relations	1 hour

- Crisis Intervention	4 hours
- Family Violence, Domestic Disputes, and Disturbances	4 hours
- Community Policing Crime Prevention Techniques	2 hours
- Cultural Diversity	2 hours
- Crime Victims Compensation	2 hours

- **Law Enforcement Procedures**   **(73 hours)**
  - Patrol and Observation   6 hours
  - Crimes in Progress   8 hours
  - Communications and GCIC Procedures   3 hours
  - Vehicle Pullovers   12 hours
  - Interviews and Interrogations   8 hours
  - Hazardous Materials   6 hours
  - Officer Survival   8 hours
  - Arrest Booking Procedures   2 hours
  - Report Writing   8 hours
  - Courtroom Demeanor and Testimony   4 hours
  - Terrorism   4 hours
  - NIMS: Incident Command System   4 hours
- **Investigative Services**   **(59 hours)**
  - Fundamentals of Investigation   4 hours
  - Crime Scene Processing   16 hours
  - Sex Crimes Investigation   4 hours
  - Arson Investigation   2 hours
  - Burglary Investigation   2 hours
  - Robbery Investigation   2 hours
  - Crimes Against Children   6 hours
  - Juvenile Offender   6 hours
  - Surveillance   2 hours
  - Bombs and Explosives   2 hours
  - Motor Vehicle Theft Investigation   2 hours
  - Organized Crime and Gangs Investigation   4 hours
  - Controlled Substances Investigation   4 hours
  - Death Investigation   2 hours
  - Environmental Crimes   1 hour
- **Traffic Services**   **(36 hours)**
  - Motor Vehicle Law   8 hours
  - Traffic Enforcement   4 hours
  - Accident Reporting   12 hours
  - Impaired Driving   8 hours
  - Traffic Direction and Control   2 hours

- Vehicle Occupant Protection	2 hours
• **Law Enforcement Skills**	**(123 hours)**
- Fingerprinting	4 hours
- Firearms	32 hours
- Defensive Tactics	32 hours
- First Aid and CPR	9 hours
- Emergency Vehicle Operations	24 hours
- Stress	3 hours
- Universal Precautions	3 hours
- Judgmental Simulation in the Use of Deadly Force	16 hours
• **Administrative**	**(22 hours)**

Participation in the basic law enforcement mandate course includes a minimum of 14 written examinations, administered at different intervals throughout the course in the following areas: eight periodic examinations; Hazardous Materials; Georgia Crime Information (GCIC)/Communications; First Aid; Cardio Pulmonary Resuscitation (CPR); Judgmental Pistol Simulation (JPS); and Emergency Vehicle Operations Course (EVOC).

To pass all basic law enforcement mandate certification written testing, a minimum score of 70 percent is required. In addition, to pass GCIC/Communications requires a minimum score of 90 percent and to pass EVOC requires a minimum score of 80 percent. All students must achieve two qualifying scores of 80 percent to pass firearms qualification. Students are afforded one retake per periodic written examination; however, failure on the third period written examination will result in dismissal from the course (Basic Law Enforcement Training Course, 2006).

Jail Officer Certification

For basic jail officer mandate certification, the Council set the training at 80 hours. The purpose of the course is to "prepare the jail officers to conduct themselves in a manner consistent with legislative and case law decisions" (Basic Jail Officer, 2010).

The basic jail officer mandate certification course consists of the following blocks of instruction (Basic Jail Officer, 2010):

• **Basic Issues**	**(22 hours)**
- Introduction	1 hour
- The American Jail: Its Origins and Development	1 hour
- Ethics and Professionalism	2 hours
- Health and Wellness	2 hours

- Basic Report Writing	4 hours
- Inmate Rights	6 hours
- Use of Force	2 hours
- Courtroom Testimony and Demeanor	3 hours
- Sexual Harassment	1 hour
• **Jail Operations**	**(29 hours)**
- Admissions and Release	4 hours
- Basic Jail Security Procedures	3 hours
- Searches and Security inspections	5 hours
- Supervision of Inmates	8 hours
- Emergency Procedures	3 hours
- Abnormal Behavior and Suicide Prevention	3 hours
- Inmate Medical	1 hour
- Fingerprinting	2 hours
• **Jail Skills**	**(24 hours)**
- Emergency Medical	8 hours
- Universal Precautions for the Detention Officer	2 hours
- Defensive Tactics	14 hours
• **Administration and Testing**	**(5 hours)**

All basic jail officer mandate certification testing requires a minimum passing score of 70 percent on all written examinations. In addition, students must complete the Emergency Medical CPR/First Aid performance examination with a minimum score of 80 percent to pass. Students are afforded one retake per written and performance examination (Basic Jail Officer, 2010).

Communications Officer Certification

For basic communications officer mandate certification, the Council set the training at 40 hours. The course is "intended for new communications officers of local governmental agencies who receive, process, or transmit public safety information and who dispatch law enforcement, firefighters, medical or emergency management personnel" (Basic Communications Officer Training Course, 2005).

The basic communications officer certification course consists of the following blocks of instruction (Basic Communications Officer Training Course, 2005):

• Registration and Written Exam	1 hour
• Role of the Communications Officer	1 hour
• Communications Officer Liability	2 hours

- Telephone Techniques   4 hours
- Communications Impaired Callers   4 hours
- Telephone Crisis Intervention   4 hours
- Radio Broadcast Techniques   4 hours
- Law Enforcement Dispatch   4 hours
- Fire and Hazardous Materials Dispatch   3 hours
- Medical Dispatch   2 hours
- Terrorism and WMD   3 hours
- Written Examination   1 hour
- Performance Examination   7 hours
- Stress Management and Emergency
  Management   (Independent Study)

All basic communications officer mandate certification students must achieve a minimum score of 70 percent on a 50-question examination in order to pass. Students must also achieve a minimum score of 80 percent on a series of four simulated scenarios, based on the Standardized Evaluation Guidelines, for successful completion of the course. In addition, under O.C.G.A. §35-8-23, attendance is mandatory for the Communications Impaired Callers block of instruction (Basic Communications Officer Training Course, 2005).

Municipal Probation Officer Certification

The Georgia Corrections Academy is responsible for providing basic municipal probation officer mandate certification. The Council set the training at 120 hours, comprised of six blocks of instruction, plus administrative hours (Basic Municipal Probation Officer Course, 1999):

- **Introduction**   **(5 hours)**
  - History of Probation/U.S. Constitution   3 hours
  - Ethics and Professionalism   2 hours
- **Legal Issues**   **(11 hours)**
  - Peace Officer Liability   4 hours
  - Courtroom Testimony and Revocation Hearings   4 hours
  - Delinquent Reports and Warrants   2 hours
  - Interstate Compact   1 hour
- **Interpersonal Relations**   **(18 hours)**
  - Interpersonal Communications   6 hours
  - Cultural Diversity   2 hours
  - Supervision Techniques: Mental Health, HIV,
    Alcohol and Substance Abuse Probationers   6 hours

- Crisis Intervention	4 hours
• **Probation Procedures**	**(31 hours)**
- Report Writing	8 hours
- Continuum of Intermediate Sanctions	4 hours
- Communications and Georgia Crime Information Center Procedures	3 hours
- Interviews and Interrogations	6 hours
- Financial Compliance	2 hours
- Officer Survival	6 hours
- Probation Sentencing and Termination	2 hours
• **Investigative Skills**	**(7 hours)**
- Pre-Sentence Investigation	4 hours
- Surveillance	2 hour
- Data Collections	1 hour
• **Skills**	**(42 hours)**
- Firearms	24 hours
- Mechanics of Arrest	16 hours
- Recognizing and Managing Stress	2 hours
• **Administrative**	**(6 hours)**
- Course Introduction	1 hour
- Periodic Testing	3 hours
- Course Evaluation	1 hour
- Graduation	1 hour

Basic Mandate Certification — State

Georgia Bureau of Investigation

The Georgia Bureau of Investigation (GBI) certification training includes the 408 hours of P.O.S.T. basic law enforcement mandate, but adds an additional 258 hours for its agents. The following additional hours are added throughout the six blocks of instruction in basic law enforcement mandate, plus additional administrative hours. Additional hours in the Traffic Services block of instruction are not included (Georgia Bureau of Investigation [GBI] Basic Agent Course, 2011):

• **Introduction to Law Enforcement**	**(additional 16 hours)**
- Ethics and Professionalism	2 hours
- GBI Orientation/GBI History	13 hours
- GBI Accreditation	1 hour

- **Basic Law**   (**additional 6 hours**)
  - Criminal Procedure   6 hours
- **Community Relations**   (**additional 3 hours**)
  - Media Relations   1 hour
  - Sexual Harassment and Biased Based Profiling   2 hours
- **Law Enforcement Procedures**   (**additional 56 hours**)
  - Crimes in Progress   4 hours
  - Interviews and Interrogations   32 hours
  - Hazardous Materials   2 hours
  - Report Writing   8 hours
  - NIMS: Incident Command System 700 and 100   4 hours
  - Criminal Intelligence   2 hours
  - JIMNET   2 hours
  - Internal Affairs Investigations   1 hour
  - Flying Armed   1 hour
- **Investigative Services**   (**additional 66 hours**)
  - Crime Scene Processing   2 hours
  - Bombs and Explosives   6 hours
  - Death Investigations   22 hours
  - Photography and Digital Photography   4 hours
  - Polygraph Investigations   2 hours
  - Questioned Documents   1 hour
  - Financial Investigations   2 hours
  - GBI Background Investigations   2 hours
  - Use of Force Investigations   8 hours
  - Casting/Imprinting   2 hours
  - Field Training Agent   1 hour
  - Computer Crimes   2 hours
  - Medical and Forensic Aspects of Death (GBI Crime Lab)   6 hours
  - Drug Interdiction   2 hours
  - Healthcare Investigation   2 hours
  - Theft Investigations   2 hours
- **Law Enforcement Skills**   (**additional 143 hours**)
  - Fingerprinting   2 hours
  - Firearms   48 hours
  - Defensive Tactic   16 hours
  - Preparation for Duty   2 hours
  - Physical Fitness   67 hours
  - OC Spray   4 hours
  - Taser   4 hours

- Administrative Issues Tests   (additional 4 hours)

Georgia Department of Corrections

The Georgia Corrections Academy is responsible for providing basic correctional officer mandate certification for the Georgia Department of Corrections (GDC). The purpose of the certification course is to provide "basic training for Correctional Officers so that they will be better prepared to accomplish the Departmental mission of protecting the public, victims of crime, and agency staff" (Georgia Department of Corrections [GDC] Basic Correctional Officer Training, 2011).

For basic correctional officer mandate certification, the Council set the training at 180 hours. The course consists of the following blocks of instruction (GDC Basic Correctional Officer Training, 2011):

• Orientation	8 hours
• Introduction to the Criminal Justice System	1 hour
• Introduction to Corrections	1 hour
• Ethics and Professionalism	2 hours
• Human Diversity	2 hours
• Legal Issues	2 hours
• Drug User Identification	2 hours
• Interpersonal Communications	4 hours
• Emergency Response	8 hours
• Criminal Thinking	2 hours
• What Works	2 hours
• Disciplinary Procedures	1 hour
• Report Writing	6 hours
• Inmate Supervision	8 hours
• Patrols, Inspections, and Counts	8 hours
• Health Care	4 hours
• Mental Health and Mental Retardation	4 hours
• Grievance Procedures	1 hour
• Contraband	16 hours
• Critical Materials	2 hours
• Firearms	28 hours
• Use of Deadly Force	4 hours
• CPR/First Aid/AED	8 hours
• Health and Wellness	2 hours
• Fire Safety	8 hours

• Defensive Tactics	30 hours
• Introduction to Hispanic Culture	4 hours
• Introduction to Security Threat Groups	4 hours
• GDC SOP Review	4 hours
• Basic Shotgun Qualification	4 hours

In order to pass all basic correctional officer mandate certification testing, a minimum score of 70 percent on all written examinations is required. In addition, students must complete the following performance examinations with corresponding minimum percent scores to be considered passing:

- Firearms—75 percent on the Georgia Semi-Automatic Pistol Qualification Course (GSAC) with service weapon
- CPR/First Aid/AED—100 percent accuracy in rescue breathing, CPR, and correct use of an AED, and 80 percent accuracy in identifying basic principles of CPR and First Aid
- Fire Safety—70 percent in proper procedure for donning, wearing, and removing self-contained breathing apparatus (SCBA) and extinguishing a fire
- Defensive Tactics—100 percent in demonstrating proper procedure techniques for retaining a weapon from front and rear holstered defense
- Basic Shotgun Qualification—100 percent accuracy in ability to fire a qualifying score with the Remington Model 870 pump shotgun

The Georgia Corrections Academy is also responsible for providing basic probation officer mandate certification. The Council set the training at 160 hours, comprised of five blocks of instruction, plus administrative hours (Basic Probation Officer Training, 2002):

• **Basic Issues**	**(17 hours)**
- Introduction to Basic Training	1 hour
- Alternatives/Programs	4 hours
- Interstate Compact	2.5 hours
- Data Collections	1.5 hours
- Probation Sentencing	2 hours
- Equipment Issue	1 hour
- SCRIBE and Introduction to Word	5 hours
• **Legal/Investigative Procedures**	**(15 hours)**
- Probation Officer Liabilities and Responsibilities	2 hours
- U.S. Constitution and Georgia Law	4 hours
- Violations: DR's and Warrants	1.5 hours
- Report Writing	1.5 hours

- Courtroom Testimony and Revocations	4 hours
- Pre-Sentence Investigations	2 hours
• **Health and Human Services**	**(13 hours)**
- Health and Wellness	2 hours
- Stress Management	1 hour
- Cultural Diversity	4 hours
- Victim's Issues	4 hours
- Workplace Violence and Community Assistance	2 hours
• **Caseload Supervision**	**(50 hours)**
- Risk Based Supervision	16 hours
- Interviewing Skills	6 hours
- Supervision Techniques	8 hours
- Supervising Specialized Populations	4 hours
- Financial Compliance	2 hours
- Search and Seizure	2 hours
- Gang Identification and Trends	3 hours
- Surveillance Techniques	2 hours
- Defusing Hostile Situations	3 hours
- Drug Testing	4 hours
• **Use of Force**	**(54 hours)**
- Semi-Auto Transition Course	16 hours
- Firearms Skills	12 hours
- Night Firing Skills	4 hours
- Defensive Tactics	14 hours
- Use of Force	3.5 hours
- Mechanics of Arrest	2.5 hours
- OC Spray	2 hours
• **Administrative**	**(11 hours)**
- Risk Based Supervision Exam	1 hour
- Report Writing Exam	1 hour
- Exam I	1.5 hours
- Exam II	1.5 hours
- Exam III	1.5 hours
- Exam IV	1.5 hours
- Class Wrap-up and Graduation	3 hours

Georgia Department of Natural Resources

The Georgia Department of Natural Resources (DNR) certification training includes the 408 hours of P.O.S.T. basic law enforcement mandate, along

with the following additional 280 hours (Georgia Department of Natural Resources [DNR] Extended Basic Class, 2011):

• ATV Training	8 hours
• Boat EVOC/Boating Safety	40 hours
• Boating and Hunting Incident Investigation	4 hours
• Boating Safety Exercises	12 hours
• Courtroom Demeanor and Testimony	8 hours
• Customer Service	2 hours
• Environmental Law	8 hours
• Federal Game and Fish Laws	4 hours
• Archeological Laws, Regulations, and Violations	4 hours
• Game and Fish Laws (saltwater)	4 hours
• Game and Fish Laws	12 hours
• Helicopter Training	2 hours
• HGN	24 hours
• Hunter Education	16 hours
• Intox 5000	16 hours
• Port Security and Marine Anti-Terrorism	4 hours
• Ranger and the Public	4 hours
• Swiftwater Training	8 hours
• Wilderness Training	20 hours
• Wildlife Training (including Trapping)	80 hours

Georgia State Patrol

The Georgia State Patrol (GSP) provides the 408 hours of P.O.S.T. basic law enforcement mandate training, but incorporates an additional 1,271 training hours for its troopers. The additional hours are distributed throughout eight blocks of instruction as follows (Georgia State Patrol [GSP] Cadet-Trooper Training, 2011):

• **Introduction to Law Enforcement**	**(additional 10 hours)**
- GSP Organization/Tapes	2 hours
- Georgia State Patrol History	2 hours
- Courtesy and Personal Appearance	2 hours
- Georgia Highways	1 hour
- Promotion System	1 hour
- Open Records	2 hours
• **Basic Law**	**(additional 3 hours)**
- Civil Rights	3 hours

- **Community Relations**   (additional 26 hours)
  - Interpersonal Communication   2 hours
  - Spanish   24 hours
- **Law Enforcement Procedures**   (additional 55 hours)
  - Vehicle Pullovers   28 hours
  - Report Writing   4 hours
  - Courtroom Demeanor and Testimony   7 hours
  - Hot Wires   2 hours
  - Unlawful Harassment   1 hour
  - VIP Protection   1 hour
  - Security and Integrity   2 hours
  - Use of Force   10 hours
- **Investigative Services**   (additional 4 hours)
  - Bombs and Explosives   2 hours
  - Firearms Trafficking   2 hours
- **Traffic Services**   (additional 130 hours)
  - Motor Vehicle Law (Driver License Laws/
    GA Traffic Code/ALS)   1 hour
  - Traffic Enforcement   2 hours
  - Accident Reporting/Crash Investigation   108 hours
  - Impaired Driving/SFST   16 hours
  - Racial Profiling   1 hour
  - Operation Lifesaver   2 hours
- **Law Enforcement Skills**   (additional 488 hours)
  - Firearms   134 hours
  - First Aid and CPR   2 hours
  - EVOC/Driver Training   158 hours
  - Physical Training/Assessments/Drill   122 hours
  - Mobile Field Force Basic   11 hours
  - RADAR   16 hours
  - Intoximeter   16 hours
  - LASER   8 hours
  - CS Gas Exposure and Mask Familiarization   4 hours
  - Verbal Judo   4 hours
  - Active Shooter   13 hours
- **Administrative**   (additional 555 hours)
  - Opening/Graduation   3 hours
  - Periodic Testing and Review   6 hours
  - Logistics/Administrative   65 hours
  - Core Values   1 hour

- Field Training   480 hours

In-Service Training

O.C.G.A. §35-8-21 provides the annual training requirements for peace officers. During each calendar year, "any person employed or appointed as a peace officer shall complete 20 hours of training" and the training "shall be completed in sessions approved or recognized by the Georgia Peace Officer Standards and Training Council" (O.C.G.A. §35-8-21, 2011). According to the code, any peace officer who does not complete the required 20 hours will lose his or her powers of arrest.

As part of the 20 hours of annual training, under Chapter 464-5.03.1 of the Rules of Georgia Peace Officer Standards and Training Council, the Council also requires that every individual employed or appointed as a peace officer complete annual firearms training, consisting of, at a minimum, two hours of training provided by a P.O.S.T. certified firearms instructor (P.O.S.T. Council, 2011). The training will include the use of deadly force, agency policies and procedures regarding the use of deadly force, and a demonstration of proficiency in the use of the primary handgun carried and/or used that meets or exceeds the minimum standards used in the basic mandate course of instruction.

Career Development Certification

In addition to the basic mandate certifications, the Council has established six areas of supplemental training to assist those criminal justice personnel who are seeking advancement within their field and/or agency. Each level of training leads to certification as distinguished by the courses of instruction in each area.

Intermediate Certification

For the intermediate certification, the officer must meet the following minimum qualifications (P.O.S.T. Council, 2011):

- be a certified, registered, or exempt peace officer currently employed by a Georgia law enforcement agency;
- have at least two years of experience as a full-time peace officer;
- have successfully completed the five required core courses at a Georgia P.O.S.T. Council certified training facility; and

- have a minimum of ten quarter or six semester hours from an accredited college or university.

Although the qualifications list five required courses, students have choices for three of the five courses (P.O.S.T. Council, 2011):

• Criminal Procedures	40 hours
• Health and Wellness Awareness	22 hours
OR Health and Wellness Instructor	40 hours
• Interpersonal Relations/Crisis Intervention	8 hours
OR Verbal Judo	minimum 16 hours
• First Responder	40 hours
OR Emergency Medical Technician Training	
OR Paramedic Training	
• Officer Survival	40 hours

Advanced Certification

For the advanced certification, the officer must meet the following minimum qualifications (P.O.S.T. Council, 2011):

- possess the intermediate certification;
- be a certified, registered, or exempt peace officer currently employed by a Georgia law enforcement agency;
- have at least four years of experience as a full-time peace officer;
- have successfully completed the seven required core courses at a Georgia P.O.S.T. Council certified training facility; and
- have a minimum of 20 quarter or 12 semester hours from an accredited college or university.

Although the qualifications list seven required courses, students have choices for six of the seven courses (P.O.S.T. Council, 2011):

• Advanced Traffic Law	24 hours
OR United Laboratories National Boating Accident	
Investigation and Analysis (Intermediate)	36 hours
• Crime Scene Processing	24 hours
OR Crime Scene Technician	40 hours
OR National Hunting Incident Investigation Academy	44 hours
OR United Laboratories National Boating Accident	
Investigation and Analysis (Advanced)	36 hours

• Specialized Patrol Techniques	14 hours
OR Advanced Patrol Techniques	24 hours
OR Marine Patrol Officers Course	76 hours
• Interviews and Interrogations	24 hours
OR Any Interviews and Interrogations Course	≥ 24 hours
• Search Warrants and Affidavits	16 hours
OR Search and Seizure for Drug Cases	40 hours
OR Advanced Search Warrants and Affidavits	24 hours
• Advanced Firearms	32 hours
OR Semi-Auto Pistol 2	32 hours
OR Firearms Instructor Course	80 hours
• Advanced Report Writing	16 hours

Senior Deputy Sheriff Certification

The Council established a senior deputy sheriff course of study. For senior deputy sheriff certification, the officer must meet the following minimum requirements (Senior Deputy Sheriff Certification, 2003):

• be a certified, registered, or exempt peace officer currently employed by a Georgia law enforcement agency;
• complete the 14 required courses conducted by a P.O.S.T. certified training facility; and
• complete a minimum of 200 hours of P.O.S.T. certified training, other than a) the required courses for the certification; b) in-service training; or c) basic mandate training required for certification issued by the P.O.S.T. Council.

The Council set the training at 117 hours, comprised of two modules (Senior Deputy Sheriff Certification, 2003):

Module I (37 hours)

• Office of the Sheriff	1 hour
• Bonding Procedures	2 hours
• Court Orders	3 hours
• Civil Process	4 hours
• Court Services	16 hours
• Mental Commitments and	
Transportation of the Mentally Ill	3 hours
• One-Man Car Patrol Tactics	4 hours

- Prisoner Transport   4 hours

Module II (80 hours)

- Search Procedures for Wanted and Missing Persons   3 hours
- Water Accidents and Drowning   3 hours
- Advanced Report Writing   16 hours
- Basic Jail Officer Course   47 hours
- Public Relations   3 hours
- Interpersonal Relations/Crisis Intervention   8 hours

There are no cognitive or performance examinations for Module I. However, for Module II, written examinations are included in the Basic Jail Officer Course, as well as the Interpersonal Relations/Crisis Intervention and Report Writing blocks of instruction, on which a minimum score of 70 percent is required to pass. In addition, a performance examination is included in the Report Writing block of instruction, with a minimum passing score of 70 percent required. Students must achieve a minimum score of 80 percent to pass the Emergency Medical CPR/First Aid performance examination in the Basic Jail Officer course. In both modules, students must attend at least 90 percent of the total course for successful completion and certification (Senior Deputy Sheriff Certification, 2003).

Supervisory Certification

The Council established a supervisory development course of study, "to provide current, new and potential managers with a basic foundation of the prerequisite knowledge, skills and abilities necessary to effectively function in a management position" (Supervisory Certification, 2010).

The officer must meet the following minimum requirements for supervisory development certification (Supervisory Certification, 2010):

- currently hold a supervisory position, for at least one year, defined as "the direct supervision of personnel occupying basic operational line positions—patrol, investigation, or support";
- possess 45 quarter or 30 semester hours from an accredited college or university; and
- complete the P.O.S.T. Supervisory Development course or equivalent.

The Council set the training at 120 hours, comprised of three modules, with successful completion of module I being required to attend module II, and successful completion of module II being required to attend module III (Supervisory Certification, 2010):

Module I (40 hours)

• Registration/Introduction	1 hour
• Roles and Responsibilities of a Supervisor	7 hours
• Organizing an Effective Work Unit	5 hours
• Supervising in a Changing Environment	3 hours
• Ethics and Professionalism	8 hours
• Managing Civil Liability	8 hours
• Planning and Goal Setting	6 hours
• Managing Information	1 hour
• Testing and Evaluation	1 hour

Module II (40 hours)

• Registration	2 hours
• Performance Appraisals	6 hours
• Leadership	8 hours
• Training and the Adult Learner	4 hours
• Employment Law	4 hours
• Performance Management	8 hours
• Employee Counseling	4 hours
• Staffing	2 hours
• Administration and Testing	2 hours

Module III (40 hours)

• Registration	1 hour
• Communication	7 hours
• Motivation and Productivity	8 hours
• Stress Management	8 hours
• Supervisor's Role in Internal Affairs	8 hours
• Time Management	6 hours
• Media Relations	1 hour
• Examination and Evaluations	1 hour

Testing for each module includes a final written examination, on which a minimum passing score of 70 percent is required (no retest is allowed). Also, students must attend at least 90 percent of the total course for successful completion and certification (Supervisory Certification, 2010).

Management Certification

The Council established a management development course of study "to provide current, new and potential managers with a basic foundation of the prerequisite knowledge, skills and abilities necessary to effectively function in a management position" (Management Certification, 2010).

For management development certification, the officer must meet the following minimum requirements (Management Certification, 2010):

- currently hold a management position, for at least one year, defined as a position within a law enforcement agency that falls between the supervisor and the executive;
- possess 90 quarter or 60 semester hours from an accredited college or university;
- complete Supervision Level I, II, and III; and
- complete the P.O.S.T. Management Development course or equivalent.

The Council set the training at 120 hours, comprised of three modules, with successful completion of module I being required to attend module II, and successful completion of module II being required to attend module III (Management Certification, 2010):

Module I (40 hours)

• Registration	1 hour
• Overview of Managers and Management	3 hours
• Fundamentals of Organizing	4 hours
• Fundamentals of Directing	8 hours
• Fundamentals of Controlling	8 hours
• Stress Management	8 hours
• Fundamentals of Planning	6 hours
• Examination and Evaluation	2 hours

Module II (40 hours)

• Welcome and Registration	1 hour
• Management Accountability	7 hours
• Budgeting	8 hours
• Communication	8 hours
• Problem Solving/Decision Making	8 hours
• Staffing and Scheduling	7 hours
• Written Examination	1 hour

Module III (40 hours)

• Welcome and Registration	1 hour
• Comprehensive Public Safety Project	31 hours
• Project Presentation	7 hours
• Final Examination, End of Course Critiques, Graduation	1 hour

Testing for each module includes a final written examination, on which a minimum passing score of 70 percent is required (no retesting allowed). In addition, for module III, a final student presentation is required, on which a minimum score of 80 percent is required to pass. Also, students must attend at least 90 percent of the total course for successful completion and certification (Management Certification, 2010).

Executive Certification

The Council established an executive development course of study, "designed for directors, chiefs, sheriffs, wardens, and other heads of public safety agencies," with the purpose of providing "public safety executives with basic skills and knowledge necessary to successfully lead public safety organizations toward accomplishment of their missions" (Executive Certification, 2009).

The officer must meet the following minimum requirements for executive development certification (Executive Certification, 2009):

- currently hold an executive position, for at least one year, defined as "the highest level official with direct operational responsibility for a law enforcement agency";
- possess 90 quarter or 60 semester hours from an accredited college or university; and
- complete the P.O.S.T. Executive Development course or equivalent.

The Council set the training at 120 hours, comprised of five blocks of instruction, plus administrative hours:

• Registration and Introduction	1 hour
• Leadership and Team Building	38 hours
• Legal Issues	38 hours
• Strategic Planning	16 hours
• Fiscal Management and Control of Agency-Owned Property	16 hours
• News Media Relations	6 hours
• Administration and Testing	5 hours

Testing is based on three written examinations, and students must attain a minimum score of 70 percent on all written examinations in order to pass. In addition, students must attend at least 90 percent of the total course for successful completion and certification (Executive Certification, 2009).

Instructor Certification

The Council has established instructor training courses to afford local and state officers the opportunity to achieve a level of competence in particular instructional areas. Once certified, these instructors are able to provide P.O.S.T. certified instruction to officers at the agency level. Each instructor training course has specific blocks of instruction, examination requirements, and hours of content. Individuals may choose to obtain a variety of instructor certifications or may choose to establish an expertise in one area of training.

General Instructor Training

The Council established the general instructor training course as the entry-level course, which is used as the pre-requisite for further specialized and advanced instructor training. Qualifications for attendance include a detailed letter from the applicant explaining the desire to attend the course, what material he/she intends to teach, and why he or she would make a good instructor. Also required is a detailed letter of recommendation from the academy director, training officer, or agency head explaining the impact the individual will have on the training capabilities of the agency (Instructor Training, 2009).

The Council set the training at 80 hours, comprised of the following blocks of instruction (Instructor Training, 2009):

• Welcome and Orientation	1.5 hours
• Instructor Liability	2.5 hours
• Adult Learning	4 hours
• Communication Skills	3 hours
• Effective Presentation Skills	2 hours
• Classroom Management	2 hours
• Instructional Systems Design	2 hours
• Constructing Effective Performance Objectives	6 hours
• Lesson Planning (Structure and Purpose)	6 hours
• Testing and Evaluation	2 hours
• Practical Exercise Construction	2 hours
• Teaching Methods	2 hours

- Written Examination   2 hours
- Managing Training Aids   3 hours
- Lesson Plan Workshop and Review   8 hours
- 50 Minute Practice Presentations   16 hours
- Lesson Plan Grading (Performance Exam)   8 hours*
  (*concurrent hours with 50 Minute Practice Presentation)
- 50 Minute Final Presentations (Performance Exam)   14 hours
- Conclusion/Wrap-up/Course Evaluation   2 hours

Testing includes a written examination, on which a minimum score of 80 percent is required to pass (no retest is allowed). In addition, two performance examinations are provided, both of which require a minimum passing score of 80 percent. Also, students must attend at least 90 percent of the total course for successful completion and certification (Instructor Training, 2009).

Additional levels of instructor training may be obtained for instructors who wish to train others in the general instructor training course. The *Senior Instructor Trainer* is identified as having taught in a general instructor training course. The *Master Instructor Trainer* is identified as having taught at least ten general instructor training courses and having evaluated at least ten other instructors (Instructor Training, 2009).

Department Training Officer

The Department Training Officer training course is designed "to provide the training necessary to effectively manage a departmental training function for law enforcement, fire service, jail or communication disciplines" (Department Training Officer, 2010). For certification, the officer must meet the following minimum requirements (Department Training Officer, 2010):

- possess P.O.S.T. certified general instructor status;
- possess P.O.S.T. certified Field Training Officer status or three years of experience in law enforcement; and
- complete the P.O.S.T. Department Training Officer training course.

The Council set the training at 52 hours, comprised of both independent study and classroom hours, in the following blocks of instruction (Department Training Officer, 2010):

- Registration and Course Introduction   1 hour
- Course Design   16 hours

- Training Needs Analysis   8 hours
- Training Records System (independent study)   2 hours
- Liability in Training   2 hours
- Training Budgeting   2 hours
- Equipment, Specifications, Acquisition, and Management   1 hour
- Presenting Your Findings: Developing a Position Paper   4 hours
- Training Systems Overview (independent study)   2 hours
- Instructor Selection and Performance (independent study)   1 hour
- Standard Operating Procedures and Policies for Training
  Program Support (independent study)   1 hour
- Comprehensive Curriculum Project   12 hours

Testing consists of the development of a Comprehensive Curriculum Project, on which a minimum passing score of 80 percent is required. In addition, students must attend at least 90 percent of the total course for successful completion and certification (Department Training Officer, 2010).

Field Training Officer

The Field Training Officer (FTO) training course serves as a pre-requisite to obtain certification as a Field Training Officer. The Council set the training at 40 hours, comprised of the following blocks of instruction (Field Training Officer, 2010):

- Registration   1 hour
- Role of the Field Training Officer   3 hours
- Professionalism and Ethics for the Field Training Officer   4 hours
- Adult Learning   4 hours
- Effective Communication Strategies   4 hours
- Stress Management   4 hours
- Cultural Diversity   2 hours
- Liability for the Field Training Officer   4 hours
- Evaluations and the Daily Observation Report   8 hours
- Counseling the Field Training Officer Recruit   4 hours
- Examination and Evaluation   2 hours

Testing consists of a written examination, on which a minimum score of 70 percent is required to pass. In addition, a scenario-based performance examination is required, on which a minimum passing score of 70 percent is required (no retest is allowed). Also, students must attend at least 90 percent of the total course for successful completion and certification (Field Training Officer, 2010).

Communications Training Officer

The Communications Training Officer training course provides certified and registered communications officers with the knowledge and skills to effectively train other communications officers. The Council set the training at 40 hours, comprised of both independent study and classroom hours, in the following blocks of instruction (Communications Training Officer, 2005):

- Ethics in Communications Training (independent study)   2 hours
- Principles of Effective Writing (independent study)   8 hours
- Console Training Delivery (independent study)   3 hours
- Stress Management in Communications Training (independent study)   3 hours
- Registration and Entry Testing   1 hour
- The Role of the Communications Training Officer   2 hours
- Training Officer Liability   2 hours
- Adult Learning Principles   3 hours
- Implementing Effective Training   3 hours
- Principles of Training Evaluation   2 hours
- Supervision for the Communications Training Officer   3 hours
- Performance Examinations   8 hours

Testing consists of an entrance examination, on which a minimum score of 80 percent is required to continue in the course, and a final examination, on which a minimum score of 80 percent is required to pass the course (no retest is allowed). In addition, a performance examination will be administered as part of the final evaluation, on which a minimum passing score of 80 percent is required. Also, students must attend at least 90 percent of the total course for successful completion and certification (Communications Training Officer, 2005).

Specialized Instructor Certification

Individuals who have successfully completed the general instructor training course may receive additional instructor training in a variety of specialized areas, meeting specific educational and training requirements.

Defensive Tactics Instructor

The Defensive Tactics Instructor training course is designed to "teach certified P.O.S.T. instructors the concepts involved in coordinating and teaching a basic defensive tactics class" (Defensive Tactics Instructor Training, 2009). To be accepted into the course, the student must be a member of a local, state, or federal law enforcement agency, be currently certified as a general instructor by P.O.S.T., and have attended a basic defensive tactics course in the past 12 months (Defensive Tactics Instructor Training, 2009).

The Council set the training at 80 hours, comprised of the following blocks of instruction (Defensive Tactics Instructor Training, 2009):

- Orientation/Registration   1 hour
- Legal Issues and Use of Force   4 hours
- In-Custody Death Awareness   1.5 hours
- Handcuffing Techniques   5.5 hours
- Control and Restraint   6 hours
- Active Countermeasures   6 hours
- Expandable Metal Baton Instructor Training   12 hours
- Oleoresin Capsicum (OC) Spray Instructor Training   8 hours
- Edged Weapons Defense   4 hours
- Defensive Tactics—related medical issues   3 hours
- Grappling/Weapon Retention   4 hours
- Student Teaching Research/Preparation   5 hours
- Student Presentations   18.5 hours
- Written Test/Evaluations/Graduation   1.5 hours

Testing consists of a written examination, on which a minimum score of 80 percent is required to pass (no retest is allowed). In addition, an initial performance examination is administered, on which a minimum passing score of 100 percent is required. A student presentation/teach-back is also administered, on which a minimum score of 80 percent is required to pass. Students must attend at least 90 percent of the total course for successful completion and certification (Defensive Tactics Instructor Training, 2009).

Driver Instructor

The Driver Instructor training course is designed to "teach a select group of P.O.S.T. certified general instructors the basic driving techniques applicable to emergency vehicle operation (EVO)" (Driver Instructor Training Program, 2010). To be accepted into the course, the student must be certified as a general instructor and have attended the 24-hour Basic Emergency Vehicle Operations course in the past 12 months. To remain in the course, all students must qualify in the Precision Cone Course, and in the Braking and Skid Recovery exercises by the end of the first day of the course (Driver Instructor Training Program, 2010).

The Council set the training at 42 hours, comprised of the following blocks of instruction (Driver Instructor Training Program, 2010):

- Orientation/Registration   1 hour
- Fundamentals of Basic Emergency Vehicle Operations   1 hour
- Practical Driving Exercises: Precision Driving, Braking,
  and Skid Control   2 hours
- Performance Evaluation: Precision Driving, Braking,
  and Skid Control   4 hours
- Coaching as an Instructional Strategy Lecture   2 hours
- Coaching Activity and Rotations Through a Basic
  EVO Course   8 hours
- Emergency Response Driving Techniques (includes
  performance examination of Evasive Maneuvers and
  Threshold Braking)   8 hours
- Night Driving Lecture and Practical Exercise   4 hours
- Practical Driving Exercises and Performance
  Evaluations: Rural and Urban Ranges   10 hours
- Final Exam (Written) and Graduation   2 hours

Testing consists of a written examination, on which a minimum score of 80 percent is required to pass (no retest is allowed). In addition, students must attain a passing score on five performance examinations (including requalification on the precision cone course, braking and skid recovery courses, and high speed response on the rural and urban courses). Students must also attend at least 90 percent of the total course for successful completion and certification (Driver Instructor Training Program, 2010).

Firearms Instructor

The Firearms Instructor training course is designed to "develop firearms instructors who can manage and conduct firearms training programs for their agency" (Firearms Instructor, 2009). To be accepted into the course, the student must be a P.O.S.T. certified general instructor. In order to remain in the course, students will be required to score a 90 percent or higher on the Georgia Semi-Automatic Pistol Course on the first day of the course (Firearms Instructor, 2009).

The Council set the training at 80 hours, comprised of the following blocks of instruction (Firearms Instructor, 2009):

• Registration/Course Requirements	1.5 hours
• Qualification Pre-Requisite	2.5 hours
• Firearms Safety	1 hour
• Marksmanship Fundamentals	2 hours
• On-Line Instructional Techniques and Problem Shooters	1.5 hours
• Use of Deadly Force	1 hour
• Weapons Maintenance	2.5 hours
• Target Analysis	0.5 hour
• Equipment Selection	1 hour
• Demonstration Technique	1 hour
• Dim Light Firing	1 hour
• Firearms Instructor Liability	1 hour
• Tactical Shooting/Course Design	1 hour
• Range Organization and Administration	1 hour
• Body Armor	1 hour
• Ballistics	2.5 hours
• Semiautomatic Pistol	1.5 hours
• Shotgun Nomenclature	1 hour
• Shotgun Fundamentals and Shooting Positions	1 hour
• Range Exercises	28 hours
• Student Presentations and Administration and Testing	26.5 hours

Testing consists of a written examination, on which a minimum passing score of 80 percent is required (no retest is allowed). In addition, students must attain a minimum score of 80 percent on the performance examination on a general course of fire. Students must also attend at least 90 percent of the total course for successful completion and certification (Firearms Instructor, 2009).

Hazardous Materials Instructor

The Hazardous Materials Instructor certification requires the individual to be a P.O.S.T. certified general instructor and successfully complete the Hazardous Materials Technician certification course. The Hazardous Materials Technician course is designed to address "minimum training requirements for emergency responders to incidents involving hazardous materials who are expected to perform technically advanced operations to mitigate the emergency" (Hazardous Materials Technician Certification, 2002). To be accepted into the course, the student must be fire service personnel trained to the level of basic firefighter and completed hazardous materials: first responder operations NPQ.

The Council set the training at 48 hours, comprised of the following blocks of instruction (Hazardous Materials Technician Certification, 2002):

• Welcome, Registration, and Distribution of Equipment/Materials	1 hour
• Introduction and Emergency Response to Hazardous Materials	0.5 hour
• Incident Response Operations: Safety Plans and SOPs	1 hour
• Incident Command (ICS) System	1.5 hours
• Characteristics of Hazardous Materials	1 hour
• Principles of Toxicology	1 hour
• Information Resources	1.5 hours
• Exercise: Information Resources	1.5 hours
• Identifying Hazardous Materials	1.33 hours
• Response Operations: Size-up/Strategy and Tactics	1.5 hours
• Levels of Protection	0.75 hour
• Chemical Protective Clothing	1.5 hours
• Scene Control, Reconnaissance and Entry	1.25 hours
• Incident Control: Confinement and Containment	1.16 hours
• Exercise: Level "B" Dressout, SCBA Checkout	2.25 hours
• Regulatory Overview	1.5 hours
• Air Monitoring Instruments	1.5 hours
• Radiation Survey Instruments	0.33 hour
• Response Organization/Warehouse and Transportation	0.75 hour
• Exercise: Use of Direct-Reading Instruments	2 hours
• Exercise: Level "A" Dressout, Plug and Patch	1 hour
• Decontamination	1.5 hours
• Exercise: Decontamination Set-up	1.5 hours
• Exercise: Field and Radiation Survey Instruments	1.5 hours
• Exercise: Abandoned Chemical Factory Incident	4 hours
• Exercise: Transportation Incident	4 hours
• Course Examination	8 hours

Testing consists of a written examination, on which a minimum passing score of 70 percent is required (no retest is allowed). In addition, performance examinations will be administered throughout the course, on each of which a minimum score of 100 percent is required to pass. Students must also attend at least 90 percent of the total course for successful completion and certification (Hazardous Materials Technician Certification, 2002).

Speed Detection Instructor

The Speed Detection Instructor certification consists of two training courses: RADAR Instructor training and LIDAR Instructor training. Individuals may obtain certification in one or both areas. Both training courses require the student to be a P.O.S.T. certified general instructor. The LIDAR training course also requires the student to be a P.O.S.T. certified RADAR/LIDAR Operator. In addition, both courses are designed to meet the academic training requirements for the Specialized Instructor Certification in Speed Detection (P.O.S.T. Council, 2011).

The Council set the training for the RADAR Instructor certification at 24 hours, comprised of the following blocks of instruction (RADAR Instructor Training, 2006):

• Overview and Introduction	1 hour
• Speed Offenses and Enforcement	2 hours
• Basic Principles of RADAR	5 hours
• Same Direction Tracking	2 hours
• Legal and Operational Considerations	3 hours
• Operation of Specific RADAR Devises (Classroom)	1 hour
• Performance Exam (Set-up and Verification of Calibration)	1 hour
• Practical Exercise #1 (Tracking History)	3 hours
• Practical Exercise #2 (Student Presentation)	4 hours
• Witten Exam, Review, Evaluation	2 hours

Testing consists of a written examination, on which a minimum passing score of 70 percent is required (no retest is allowed). In addition, a performance examination consisting of conducting a four-part check for accuracy on the RADAR device requires a minimum score of 100 percent to pass. Students must also attend at least 90 percent of the total course for successful completion and certification (RADAR Instructor Training, 2006).

The Council set the training for the LIDAR Instructor certification at 16 hours, comprised of the following blocks of instruction (LIDAR Instructor Training, 2008):

• Overview and Introduction	1 hour
• Basic Principles of LIDAR	3 hours
• Legal and Operational Considerations	2 hours

- Operation of Specific LIDAR Devises (Classroom)   1 hour
- Performance Exam (Set-up and Verification of Calibration) 1 hour
- Practical Exercise #1 (Tracking History)   2 hours
- Practical Exercise #2 (Student Instructor Presentation)   4 hours
- Witten Exam, Review, Evaluation   2 hours

Testing consists of a written examination, on which a minimum passing score of 70 percent is required (no retest is allowed). Also administered is a performance examination consisting of conducting a four-part check for accuracy on the LIDAR device, on which a minimum score of 100 percent is required to pass. Students must attend at least 90 percent of the total course for successful completion and certification (LIDAR Instructor Training, 2008).

Criminal Justice Education

Criminal justice education in the State of Georgia consists of various programs with numerous formats and options to suit a range of students, from those just entering the field to those with years of practical experience who want to obtain higher education.

University System of Georgia

The mission of the University System of Georgia (USG) is to "contribute to the educational, cultural, economic, and social advancement of Georgia by providing excellent undergraduate general education and first-rate programs leading to associate, baccalaureate, masters, professional, and doctorate degrees; by pursuing leading-edge basic and applied research, scholarly inquiry, and creative endeavors; and by bringing these intellectual resources, and those of the public libraries, to bear on the economic development of the State and the continuing education of its citizens" (University System of Georgia [USG], 2011).

The USG is comprised of 35 junior and senior colleges/universities, as well as one research unit and the Georgia Public Library Service. Thirteen junior colleges, or two-year institutions, offer the Associate of Arts in Criminal Justice and Associate of Science in Criminal Justice degrees, while 17 four-year institutions offer the Associate degrees as well as Bachelor of Arts in Criminal Justice, Bachelor of Science in Criminal Justice, and Master of Science in Criminal Justice degrees. One institution offers the Doctor of Philosophy in Criminal Justice and Criminology degree (USG, 2011).

Specializations and course offerings are as varied as the criminal justice field, ranging from core lower-division courses in law enforcement, courts, and corrections, to advanced courses in forensics, terrorism, homeland security, ethics, crime prevention, juvenile justice, and more.

Technical College System of Georgia

There are 26 technical colleges located throughout the State of Georgia. These schools are part of the Technical College System of Georgia (TCSG), whose mission is to provide "technical, academic, and adult education and training focused on building a well-educated, globally competitive workforce for Georgia" (Technical College System of Georgia [TCSG], 2011).

Of the technical colleges in the TCSG, 22 have criminal justice programs, within which three distinct academic programs are available (TCSG, 2011):

- Degree programs require eight quarters to complete (two years) and result in obtaining an Associate of Applied Science degree in:
  - Criminal Justice Technology
  - Crime Scene Investigation Technology
- Diploma programs require four quarters to complete (one year) and result in obtaining the Criminal Justice Technology Diploma
- Technical Credits of Completion (TCC) programs require two quarters to complete and result in obtaining a Certificate in:
  - Basic Law Enforcement
  - Crime Scene Investigations
  - Crime Scene Technician
  - Criminal Justice Investigative Specialist
  - Criminal Justice Specialist
  - Criminal Justice Supervisor
  - Criminal Justice Technician
  - Law Enforcement Investigations Assistant
  - Law Enforcement Management
  - Law Enforcement Specialist
  - Law Enforcement Technician
  - Law Enforcement Technician Level I
  - Private Security Specialist
  - Public Safety Technician

In addition, the technical colleges offer dual credit programs that "provide exceptional opportunities for Georgia high school juniors and seniors to take college level courses at TCSG colleges and earn credit toward a high school diploma and a college degree at the same time" (TCSG, 2011). Within the dual credit program, eligible high school students can participate in several ways (TCSG, 2011):

- dual enrollment—students receive simultaneous course credits counting toward the high school diploma and future postsecondary education.
- career academies—the curriculum integrates academics and career-based learning, linking high school to business, civic community, and higher education
- joint enrollment—students take courses at TCSG colleges but earn only postsecondary credits
- ACCEL—students take postsecondary courses in core courses only (English, foreign language, mathematics, social studies)
- articulated credit—specific high school courses are identified as equivalent to postsecondary credits, so students do not need to repeat courses mastered in high school
- youth apprenticeship program—students can earn 2,000 hours of on-the-job training while completing 144 hours of classroom instruction in their career field

Private Higher Education Institutions

In addition to the various public state institutions that provide criminal justice degrees, there are both junior and senior level private institutions that offer a wide array of criminal justice courses and programs. These programs offer numerous variations of the criminal justice degree, focusing on major issues such as public safety, forensics, and legal studies. "The Georgia Independent College Association (GICA) is an association of Georgia's 25 private (independent) colleges and universities. Through partnerships with institutions, businesses, and community leaders, GICA supports private higher education in Georgia in the areas of public policy, fundraising for student financial aid, and collaborative programs" (Georgia Independent College Association [GICA], 2011). All of the private institutions are fully accredited, non-profit liberal arts colleges and universities, and currently serve more than 60,000 students (GICA, 2011).

Other institutions are gaining ground in the criminal justice degree arena with the establishment of online degree programs. The online experience is unique in that students are able to complete a college degree from the comfort and convenience of home. These programs are also varied in course requirements and focus in terms of the types of required and elective courses available. In addition, with the ease of Internet delivery, students may take courses from schools located anywhere in the world, and with professors also located anywhere in the world. Online education, although a growing phenomenon in higher education, is typically available at significant cost, and lacks the personal one-on-one experience available at traditional colleges and universities. These facts, however, have not slowed the rate of new online programs developing across the country and, indeed, across the globe.

Accreditation

One aspect of higher education that is of significance to any student of higher education is accreditation. "Accreditation is a process of external quality review used by higher education to scrutinize colleges, universities and educational programs for quality assurance and quality improvement. In the United States, accreditation is carried out by private, non-profit organizations designed for this specific purpose. Institutions and educational programs seek accredited status as a means of demonstrating their academic quality to students and the public and to become eligible for federal funds" (Council for Higher Education Accreditation, 2011).

The Council for Higher Education Accreditation, a national agency, and the U.S. Department of Education, a federal agency, create standards by which accrediting commissions are evaluated, thus providing national standards for the evaluation of higher education institutions and individual degree programs. The accrediting commissions are established on several levels: regional accrediting organizations, national faith-related accrediting organizations, national career-related accrediting organizations, and programmatic accrediting organizations. The accreditation process varies, but is typically completed every five to seven years for higher education institutions, and more frequently for some individual degree programs.

Many employers as well as graduate programs require that a prospective employee or student obtain a college degree from an accredited college or university, or complete a degree program that is itself accredited. It is important for both institutions and students to understand the accreditation process and the significant impact that attending a non-accredited institution or obtaining a degree that is viewed as non-accredited will have on future employment and schooling.

Professional Academic Organizations

There are numerous professional academic organizations on the international, national, and local levels that focus specifically on criminology and criminal justice. These organizations have members residing and working in the State of Georgia, most of whom are academics, practitioners, students, and others interested in the criminal justice field.

American Society of Criminology (ASC)

Founded in 1941 as the National Association of College Police Training Officials, the organization grew and membership diversified to include academics, practitioners, and policy makers, eventually leading to the renaming of the organization in 1946 as the Society for the Advancement of Criminology. With membership growing to include international academics and government officials, the organization again changed its name in 1957 to the current American Society of Criminology. The organization publishes *Criminology*, an interdisciplinary journal, and has an annual conference in November (ASC, 2011; Sorensen, Widmayer, and Scarpitti, 1994).

Academy of Criminal Justice Sciences (ACJS)

Founded in 1963 as a split from the American Society of Criminology, members initially named the organization the International Association of Police Professors. With increased membership of academics, practitioners, and state and local government officials, the organization became the Academy of Criminal Justice Sciences in 1970. The organization publishes two journals, *Justice Quarterly* and *Journal of Criminal Justice Education*, and holds an annual conference each March (ACJS, 2011; Sorensen, Widmayer, and Scarpitti, 1994).

American Criminal Justice Association-Lambda Alpha Epsilon (ACJA-LAE)

Originating in 1937 at San Jose State College as the California Technical Institute for Peace Officer Training for in-service law enforcement personnel, the American Criminal Justice Association has expanded to become a national professional organization for officers and criminal justice students. Holding its first police competition in 1964, today ACJA-LAE has 150 chapters, 12 located in Georgia, which compete in regional and national competitions of skill and knowledge. In addition to competition opportunities, ACJA-LAE also offers scholastic honor awards and competitive scholarships to undergraduate and graduate students in criminal justice degree programs (ACJA-LAE, 2011).

Southern Criminal Justice Association (SCJA)

Established in 1972 as a regional affiliate of the Academy of Criminal Justice Sciences, SCJA's membership is composed of academics, practitioners, and criminal justice students, and promotes education, training, and research in the criminal justice field. The organization publishes the *American Journal of Criminal Justice* and holds an annual meeting in September, in one of its 11 member states (SCJA, 2011).

Criminal Justice Association of Georgia (CJAG)

The Criminal Justice Association of Georgia was established in 2000 as a state organization for criminal justice academics, practitioners, and students. The organization was incorporated in 2003 and holds an annual meeting in November, in conjunction with the Georgia Political Science Association. CJAG also encourages student participation at the annual conference by recognizing student achievement with an Outstanding Paper Award (CJAG, 2011).

Conclusion

Criminal justice training and education abounds throughout the state of Georgia. Those interested in a career within the field of criminal justice and those already employed are able to increase their level of expertise through numerous venues and in all areas of criminal justice. Traditional education can be found in both public and private institutions, and online education is becoming a popular choice for both the traditional and non-traditional student. The Georgia P.O.S.T. Council maintains up-to-date training and is constantly working to produce the most qualified and effective criminal justice practitioners in the nation.

Chapter Review Questions

1. Explain the purpose of the Georgia Peace Officer Standards and Training (P.O.S.T.) Council.

2. Why do you think it is important for all peace officers to be certified by the state?

3. Explain why it is important for the state to require all peace officers to obtain a certain number of training hours per year. Is there additional training not currently required that you believe should be included? What is that training and why is it needed?

4. Explain why the mandatory two hours of firearms training a year is required for all peace officers. Is two hours of this training enough? Explain why or why not.

5. What is accreditation? Why is it important in higher education?

References

Academy of Criminal Justice Sciences. (2011). Retrieved from: http://www.acjs.org.

American Criminal Justice Association—Lambda Alpha Epsilon. (2011). Retrieved from: http://www.acjalae.org.

American Society of Criminology. (2011). Retrieved from: http://www.asc41.com.

Basic Communications Officer Training Course. (2005). *Georgia Peace Officer Standards and Training (P.O.S.T.) Council.*

Basic Jail Officer. (2010). *Georgia Peace Officer Standards and Training (P.O.S.T.) Council.*

Basic Law Enforcement Training Course. (2006). *Georgia Peace Officer Standards and Training (P.O.S.T.) Council.*

Basic Municipal Probation Officer Course. (1999). *Georgia Peace Officer Standards and Training (P.O.S.T.) Council.*

Basic Probation Officer Training. (2002). *Georgia Peace Officer Standards and Training (P.O.S.T.) Council.*

Chapter 464-5.03.1 Training. (2011). *Georgia Peace Officer Standards and Training (P.O.S.T.) Council.*

Communications Training Officer. (2005). *Georgia Peace Officer Standards and Training (P.O.S.T.) Council.*

Council for Higher Education Accreditation. (2011). Retrieved from: http://www.chea.org.

Criminal Justice Association of Georgia. (2011). Retrieved from: http://organization.northgeorgia.edu/cjag.

Defensive Tactics Instructor Training. (2009). *Georgia Peace Officer Standards and Training (P.O.S.T.) Council.*

Department Training Officer. (2010). *Georgia Peace Officer Standards and Training (P.O.S.T.) Council.*

Driver Instructor Training Program. (2010). *Georgia Peace Officer Standards and Training (P.O.S.T.) Council.*

Executive Certification. (2009). *Georgia Peace Officer Standards and Training (P.O.S.T.) Council.*

Field Training Officer. (2010). *Georgia Peace Officer Standards and Training (P.O.S.T.) Council.*

Firearms Instructor. (2009). *Georgia Peace Officer Standards and Training (P.O.S.T.) Council.*

Georgia Bureau of Investigation (GBI) Basic Agent Course. (2011). *Georgia Public Safety Training Center.*

Georgia Department of Corrections (GDC). 2011. Retrieved from: http://www.dcor.state.ga.us.

Georgia Department of Corrections Basic Correctional Officer Training. (2007). *Georgia Peace Officer Standards and Training (P.O.S.T.) Council.*

Georgia Department of Natural Resources Extended Basic Class. (2011). *Georgia Public Safety Training Center*

Georgia Independent College Association (GICA). (2011). Retrieved from: http://www.georgiacolleges.org.

Georgia Peace Officer Standards and Training (P.O.S.T.) Council. (2011). Retrieved from: http://www.gapost.org.

Georgia Public Safety Training Center (GPSTC). (2011). Retrieved from: http://www.gpstc.org.

Georgia State Patrol Cadet-Trooper Training. (2011). *Georgia Public Safety Training Center.*

Hazardous Materials Technician Certification. (2002). *Georgia Peace Officer Standards and Training (P.O.S.T.) Council.*

Instructor Training. (2009). *Georgia Peace Officer Standards and Training (P.O.S.T.) Council.*

Management Certification. (2010). *Georgia Peace Officer Standards and Training (P.O.S.T.) Council.*

O.C.G.A. §35-8. (2011). Official Code of Georgia Annotated.

O.C.G.A. §35-8-3. (2011). Official Code of Georgia Annotated.

O.C.G.A. §35-8-7.1. (2011). Official Code of Georgia Annotated.

O.C.G.A. §35-8-8. (2011). Official Code of Georgia Annotated.

O.C.G.A. §35-8-21. (2011). Official Code of Georgia Annotated.

O.C.G.A. §35-8-23. (2011). Official Code of Georgia Annotated.

Senior Deputy Sheriff Certification. (2003). *Georgia Peace Officer Standards and Training (P.O.S.T.) Council.*

Sorensen, J.R., Widmayer, A.G., and Scarpitti, F.R. (1994). Examining the Criminal Justice and Criminological Paradigms: An Analysis of ACJS (Academy of Criminal Justice Sciences) and ASC (American Society of Criminology) Members. *Journal of Criminal Justice Education, 5*(2), 149–166.

Southern Criminal Justice Association. (2011). Retrieved from: http://www.scja.net.

Supervisory Certification. (2010). *Georgia Peace Officer Standards and Training (P.O.S.T.) Council.*

Technical College System of Georgia (TCSG). (2011). Retrieved from: http://www.tcsg.edu.

University System of Georgia. (2011). Retrieved from: http://www.usg.edu.

About the Author

Deborah Mitchell Robinson, Ph.D., is a Professor of Criminal Justice at Valdosta State University, having joined the faculty in 1996, and is currently the Undergraduate Coordinator for Criminal Justice. She teaches in a wide range of areas across the criminal justice field. Her research and publications have focused on sexual deviance and crime prevention, and she has developed courses in both of these areas. She is an author and editor of *Policing and Crime Prevention*. She is actively conducting Crime Prevention Though Environmental Design (CPTED) crime prevention and security assessments for several school systems, including local K–12 and technical college systems, and at Valdosta State.

INDEX

A

Accreditation, 115, 118, 126, 128–130, 172, 190, 220, 246, 249
Accusation, 25, 41, 82, 93–95, 154
Adjudicatory Hearing, 198–199
Administrative Office of the Courts of Georgia, 140–141, 182
Affidavit, 66, 88–89, 183, 229
Aftercare, 200–201
Alibi, 45–46
Arraignment, 82, 95–97
Arrest, 6, 8, 10, 11, 13, 15, 27, 41, 43, 60, 63, 82, 84, 85, 87, 88, 90–92, 102, 103, 111, 113, 114, 120, 174, 183, 198, 204, 205, 216, 220, 224, 227
Arrest Warrant, 87–90, 92, 127, 148, 149, 183
Attorney General of Georgia, 21, 23, 30, 31, 58, 64, 152, 153, 156, 212

B

Basic Mandate Certification, 214–227
Bill of Rights, 28, 30, 33, 60–62, 64, 68, 69, 79, 138
Booking, 82, 92, 216
Boot Camp, 164, 167–169, 177, 190

C

Campus Police, 77, 124, 125
Capital Felony, 96, 101, 102, 146, 153
Career Development Certification, 227–234
Chain Gang, 162, 183
Chief of Police, 92, 123, 125, 212
Classification, 74, 162, 164–166, 183, 189, 199
Clerk, 21, 36–38, 77, 95, 98, 143, 202
Close Security, 164
Coercion, 43, 45, 46, 54
Commitment, 93, 190, 192, 199, 200, 204–207
Community Oriented Policing, 128, 133
Concurrent Jurisdiction, 150, 151, 193
Conspiracy (Title 16, Chapter 4), 40, 46, 54
Constitution, 20–33, 36, 38, 39, 54, 86, 100, 138, 141, 142, 145–150, 152–154, 166, 172, 219, 223
Controlled Substances (Title 16, Chapter 13), 40, 53, 115, 116, 216
Conviction, 22, 27, 29, 40, 47–52, 64, 66, 76, 89, 100–102, 119, 138, 145, 168, 175, 190
Correctional Emergency Response Team, 179
Corrections, 6, 8, 70, 82, 83, 102, 103, 120, 121, 127, 148, 160, 161, 180–184
County Marshal, 120, 124, 130

County Police, 123
County Prison, 169
Crime Victims' Bill of Rights, 60–62,
    64, 68–69, 79
Crime Victims Compensation Pro-
    gram, 58
Crimes Against the Person (Title 16,
    Chapter 5), 40, 46–48
Criminal Attempt (Title 16, Chapter
    4), 40, 46
Criminal Justice Coordinating Coun-
    cil, 58, 69, 114
Criminal Justice System, 4–8, 10, 11,
    16, 24, 33, 59, 70, 78, 82, 84, 114,
    155, 179, 183, 193, 212, 215, 222
Criminal Liability (Title 16, Chapter
    2), 40, 41, 42

D
Damage to and Intrusion Upon Prop-
    erty (Title 16, Chapter 7), 40, 48,
    49
Day Reporting Center, 5, 177
Death Penalty, 8, 51, 98, 100, 102,
    147, 155, 156, 165, 166
Declaration of Fundamental Princi-
    ples, 24, 26, 28, 33
Defenses to Criminal Prosecution
    (Title 16, Chapter 3), 40, 42–46
Delinquent Act, 66, 193, 194, 207
Delinquent Child, 66, 67, 150, 194,
    207
Department of Corrections, 4, 6, 7, 64,
    67, 68, 70, 102, 108, 161, 164, 165,
    173, 189, 200, 214, 222
Department of Juvenile Justice (DJJ),
    7, 8, 64, 188–193, 196–201, 204,
    206, 212, 214
Department of Natural Resources, 31,
    109–110, 214, 224, 225

Environmental Protection Divi-
    sion, 109, 110
Wildlife Resources Division, 110
Department of Public Safety, 7,
    110–114, 212, 214
Capital Police, 111
Executive Security Division, 113
Georgia State Patrol, 111–113
Legal Services and Special Investi-
    gations, 110–111
Motor Carrier Compliance Divi-
    sion, 113
Designated Felony, 189, 195–197,
    200, 207
Detention Hearing, 198
Disposition Hearing, 67
District Attorney, 69, 94, 95, 102, 115,
    153, 154, 156, 196, 197, 201
Diversion, 66, 177, 206, 207

E
E911, 123, 127, 128
Entrapment, 43, 45
Equal Protection Clause, 30, 33
Exclusive Jurisdiction, 83, 146–148,
    193, 196
Exclusive Original Jurisdiction, 149,
    150, 192
Executive Branch, 20, 22, 23, 31, 108,
    113, 114, 155, 172

F
Family Violence Statistics, 12, 13, 16
Federal Bureau of Prisons, 160, 161
Federal Law Enforcement Training
    Center (FLETC), 108, 109, 133
Felony, 23, 27, 40, 44–53, 55, 66, 76,
    88, 93, 96, 98, 100–102, 114, 119,
    121, 146, 147, 152, 153, 168, 169,
    183, 189, 195, 197, 200, 201, 207

Forcible Felony, 40, 44, 45, 47

Forcible Misdemeanor, 40

Forgery and Fraudulent Practices (Title 16, Chapter 9), 40, 49, 50

G

General Assembly, 5, 6, 12, 16, 22–33, 36, 38, 53, 54, 58, 60, 111, 131, 132, 138, 140–142, 146–148, 161, 162, 166, 172, 183, 188, 189, 190, 212

General Provisions (Title 16, Chapter 1), 40, 41

Georgia Accountability Court, 151

Georgia Association of Chiefs of Police, 118, 130, 131, 212, 215

Georgia Bureau of Investigation, 11, 58, 76, 112, 113, 130, 175, 212–214, 220

    Division of Forensic Sciences, 115

    Georgia Crime Information Center (GCIC), 11, 97, 114, 116, 133, 220

    Investigative Division, 114

    Medical Examiner's Office, 116

Georgia Court of Appeals, 7, 146

Georgia Emergency Management Agency/Homeland Security, 117

Georgia Sheriff's Association, 212

Governor, 4, 5, 16, 22, 23, 25, 27, 29, 30, 31, 36, 37, 38, 58, 113, 114, 117, 118, 132, 145, 152, 153, 161, 162, 170, 172, 182, 190–192, 212

Governor's Office of Highway Safety, 117, 118

Grand Jury Indictment, 82, 93, 94

H

Habeas Corpus, 22, 23, 25, 64, 142, 143, 147, 149

I

Initial Appearance, 92, 93

Inmates Under Death Sentence, 165–167

In-Service Training, 119, 123, 227, 229

Instructor Certification, 234, 237, 240, 242

Intake, 189, 196, 197, 206

Investigations, 85, 109, 110, 112, 114, 115, 118, 121–124, 126, 144, 153, 173, 191, 203, 212, 213, 221, 224, 244

Involuntary or Voluntary Intoxication, 43

J

Jail, 6, 22, 38, 91, 93, 95, 100, 102, 121–123, 127, 154, 160, 180–182, 184, 215, 217, 218, 230, 235

Judicial Branch, 30, 31, 108, 149, 153

Judicial Council of Georgia, 144

Jurisdiction, 6, 9, 11, 22–24, 29, 31, 2, 38, 39, 51, 58, 70, 77, 82–84, 86, 88, 92, 97, 114, 118, 120, 138–140, 142, 146–152, 182, 192, 193, 196–198, 202–204

Jury, 22, 23, 25, 29, 30, 31, 42, 95–97, 99, 103, 138, 140, 141, 148–150, 166

Jury Deliberations, 100, 102

Jury Selection, 98

Justice Defined, 6–9

Justified Conduct, 43

Juvenile Court, 66, 67, 122, 140, 141, 147, 150–153, 188–190, 192, 193, 195–203

Juvenile Justice, 6–8, 64, 66, 79, 131, 188–193, 196, 198–200, 204, 206–208, 212, 214, 244

Juvenile Justice System, 66, 79, 131, 189–192, 206–208

L

Law Enforcement, 4, 5, 6, 8–12, 20, 39, 50, 52, 62, 63, 69–75, 77, 82–89, 90–92, 108, 128, 131, 133, 151, 164, 179, 180, 183, 196, 198, 201, 212, 214, 215–222, 224–229, 232, 233, 235, 238, 243, 244, 247
Campus Police, 124, 125
County, 119–124
Federal, 108, 109
Municipal, 125–128
State, 109–119
Legislative Branch, 23, 108
Limitations on Prosecution, 84
Local Ordinance, 38, 39, 54, 55, 84, 194

M

Magistrate Court, 32, 88, 92, 93, 124, 140, 141, 145, 149, 150
Medium Security, 160, 164
Mental Capacity, 43
Metropolitan Atlanta Rapid Transit Authority (MARTA), 118
Minimum Age, 42
Minimum Security, 160, 161, 164, 165, 177
Miranda v Arizona, 91
Misdemeanor, 31, 40, 46–53, 55, 66, 84, 93, 98–103, 121, 138, 140, 148, 149, 154, 182, 183, 201, 213
Municipal Court, 151

N

National Crime Victimization Survey (NCVS), 10, 16

National Incident-Based Reporting System (NIBRS), 9, 16
Non-Secure Residential Treatment, 206

O

Offenses Against Public Administration (Title 16, Chapter 10), 40, 50, 51
Offenses Against Public Health and Morals (Title 16, Chapter 12), 40, 53
Offenses Against Public Order and Safety (Title 16, Chapter 11), 40, 51–53
Offenses Involving Theft (Title 16, Chapter 8), 40, 49
Office of Victim Services, 67, 68, 173
Official Code of Georgia Annotated, 5, 36, 60

P

Patrol, 108–113, 118, 120–126, 128, 216, 222, 225, 229, 230
Peace Officer, 40, 50, 74, 87, 91, 102, 108, 111, 113, 114, 118–121, 123, 125, 127, 132, 172, 174, 182, 183, 212, 213, 215, 219, 227–229, 247, 248
Peace Officers' Annuity and Benefit Fund of Georgia, 132
Peace Officers Association of Georgia, 132, 133
Peace Officers Standards and Training (P.O.S.T.) Council, 212–215
Perjury, 51
Plea Bargaining, 96
Preamble, 25
Preliminary Hearing, 82, 93, 148, 149, 151

Pre-Release Center, 169
Presentation of Evidence, 98–100, 103
Pretrial Motions, 97
Private Prison, 167
Probable Cause, 25, 82, 84–91, 93–95, 183, 198, 199, 203, 207
Probable Cause/Detention Hearing, 198, 199
Probate Court, 38, 94, 140, 141, 149
Probation, 5, 6, 68, 74, 75, 95, 103, 140, 160, 164, 167, 168, 174–178, 182–184, 192, 193, 196, 197, 199, 200, 203–207, 213–215, 219, 220, 223
Professional Academic Organizations, 246–248
Prosecuting Attorney, 6, 60, 62–66, 72, 82, 93, 94, 96, 97, 152–154
Prosecuting Attorneys' Council of Georgia, 69, 70
Prosecution, 7, 32, 40–45, 55, 60, 72, 83, 84, 93, 96–100, 124, 153, 155, 198
Public Defender, 154–156
Punishments, 7, 25–28, 47–50, 52–54, 96, 100–103, 154, 165, 166, 183, 193, 213

R

Rape, 9, 10, 12, 13, 48, 54, 62, 71, 72, 84, 99, 101, 102, 114, 122, 127, 147, 163, 165, 169, 190, 193, 204, 205
Reentry Initiatives and Services, 170, 171
Regional Youth Detention Center (RYDC), 188–190, 198, 199, 204–206

Robbery, 9, 10, 12, 13, 31, 40, 49, 62, 84, 101, 102, 114, 127, 147, 163, 169, 190, 193, 195, 204, 205, 216
Rules and Regulations of the Colony of Georgia, 20–22

S

Sealing Records, 201
Search and Seizure, 25, 85, 86, 103, 224, 229
Secure Detention, 198, 204–206
Sex Offender Registry, 71–79
Sexual Offenses (Title 16, Chapter 6), 40, 48
Sheriff, 5, 6, 7, 38, 75–78, 89, 92, 119–123, 129–132
Sheriff's Office, 120
Solicitation (Title 16, Chapter 4), 40, 46, 48, 50, 54, 62
Solicitor General, 69, 94, 102, 154, 156
Specialized Instructor Certification, 237–243
State Bar of Georgia, 144, 145, 154, 203
State Board of Pardons and Paroles, 29, 31, 62, 64, 67–70, 168, 172, 173, 212, 214
State Court, 23, 31, 32, 138, 140, 141, 148, 149, 152, 154, 155
State Prisons, 103, 161, 162, 165–169, 171, 178, 183
Status Offender, 189, 193, 194, 207
Street Gang Terrorism and Prevention (Title 16, Chapter 15), 40, 53, 54
Superior Court, 6, 22, 24, 31, 32, 38, 77, 95, 98, 116, 138, 140–142, 145, 147, 148, 150, 152–155, 177, 188, 193, 196, 199, 201, 202

Supreme Court of Georgia, 5, 22–24, 29, 31, 32, 111, 140–147, 153, 166

T
Technical College System of Georgia, 214, 215, 244
Title 17, 40, 60, 82
Transitional Center, 164, 169–171

U
Uniform Crime Reports (UCR), 9, 11, 16, 204
United States Court of Appeals, 138, 139
United States District Court, 139, 140
University System of Georgia, 243
Unruly Child, 150, 194, 207
Use of Force (Title 16, Chapter 3), 40
   Defense of Habitation, 44
   Defense of Persons, 43, 44
   Defense of Property Other than Habitation, 44, 45
   Immunity Exception, 45
   In Arrest, 91, 92

V
Venue, 83, 88, 97
Victim, 8, 10, 11, 13, 14, 16, 48–50, 52, 58–79, 84, 85, 98, 99, 101–103, 116, 123, 124, 128, 154, 161, 173, 175, 201, 216, 222, 224
Victim Impact Statements, 69
Victim Information Program (V.I.P.), 68, 69, 173
Victim-Witness Advocacy Office, 69, 70
Voluntary Certification, 213

Y
Youth Detention Center, 188
Youth Development Campus (YDC), 189, 190, 199, 200, 205, 206